GREENOVATION

GREENOVATION

URBAN LEADERSHIP ON CLIMATE CHANGE

JOAN FITZGERALD

OXFORD

UNIVERSITY PRESS

OXFORD
UNIVERSITY PRESS

Oxford University Press is a department of the University of Oxford. It furthers
the University's objective of excellence in research, scholarship, and education
by publishing worldwide. Oxford is a registered trade mark of Oxford University
Press in the UK and certain other countries.

Published in the United States of America by Oxford University Press
198 Madison Avenue, New York, NY 10016, United States of America.

Library of Congress Cataloging-in-Publication Data
Names: Fitzgerald, Joan, Ph. D., author.
Title: Greenovation: urban leadership on climate change / Joan Fitzgerald.
Description: New York, NY: Oxford University Press, [2020] |
Includes bibliographical references and index. |
Identifiers: LCCN 2019047209 (print) | LCCN 2019047210 (ebook) |
ISBN 9780190695514 (hardback) | ISBN 9780190695538 (epub) |
ISBN 9780190938345
Subjects: LCSH: City planning—Climatic factors. | Sustainable urban development. |
Local government and environmental policy. | Climate change mitigation.
Classification: LCC TD168.5 .F58 2020 (print) | LCC TD168.5 (ebook) |
DDC 307.1/216—dc23
LC record available at https://lccn.loc.gov/2019047209
LC ebook record available at https://lccn.loc.gov/2019047210

1 3 5 7 9 8 6 4 2

Printed by Sheridan Books, Inc., United States of America

TO SHELLY FITZGERALD—WITH ME ALL THE WAY.

CONTENTS

ACKNOWLEDGMENTS

The book's title, *Greenovation*, was adapted from Greenovate Boston, the city's program for working with Boston residents and communities in implementing the Climate Action Plan. It was easy to turn the verb into a noun to represent the innovation—in planning, policy, and technology needed to address climate change. I thank those engaged in climate action planning in Boston city government. In particular, John Dalzell, Carl Spector, and Bradford Swing have met with me over the years to discuss their latest priorities, successes and barriers to action. Although no longer with the city, I thank Travis Sheehan for numerous meetings to explain the regulatory environment framing different aspects of climate action.

Several students, past and present, have provided research assistance—my thanks to Scarlett Ho, Erin Macri, and Jaclyn Roache. In addition to research assistance, Emily Bryant prepared the bibliography and index.

I am thankful to those who read chapters or parts of chapters and/or have taken the time to do extensive, repeated interviews: Allan Larsson, Ed Mazria, Tim McDonald, Paul Robbins, Rob Thornton.

Having friends who edit is a gift. I thank Henrietta Davis and Cathy Tumber, who read most chapters and provided valuable feedback on style and substance. And my husband, Robert Kuttner, did the same—as always.

I thank my editor at Oxford University Press, Dave McBride, for appreciating the message of this book.

My extended family has been a source of joy, support, and many a climate discussion. I thank them all simply for being there—Shelly Fitzgerald and Vincent, James and Amaryah Lorenzo; Jessica Kuttner and Jack, Owen and Eli Stewart; Gabriel Kuttner and Lori Taylor and Alexander Kuttner and Lula Taylor; and my brother, Gary Hufnagel. As always, it is the love, care, humor, and intellectual camaraderie that my husband, Bob Kuttner, and I share that provides such a sturdy base.

CITIES ON THE FRONT LINES

CITIES COVER ABOUT 3 PERCENT of the land on earth, yet they produce about 72 percent of all global greenhouse gas emissions.[1] Given their enormous environmental footprint, cities must lead in devising solutions to the climate crisis. But can they? Cities are, of course, creatures of state and national governments, and their ability to develop policies for drastic reductions in climate-destroying greenhouse gasses varies widely with constitutional arrangements, national politics, and the ingenuity of local governments, businesses, and citizens. Yet my decade-long exploration of cities and the climate crisis suggests that urban leadership is pivotal to both reducing greenhouse gas (GHG) emissions within municipalities and devising the policy innovations that are necessary at all levels of government to bring about further, more geographically expansive GHG reductions.

In a word, cities are in a singular position to pursue what I call *greenovation*, and to do so at the speed our circumstances require. While larger governmental entities—states and provinces, national governments, and intergovernmental bodies—must broker broad geopolitical differences and economic interests, cities can be fast, nimble, and effective on the ground. They can require more efficient energy usage in buildings. They can structure patterns of development and transportation to minimize energy consumption and maximize deployment of state-of-the art technology. They can link greening of low-income neighborhoods with job creation. They can partner with the private sector to pilot and perfect new green technologies.

Cities are already pursuing some of these measures, but most are not doing nearly enough to meet the challenge, and we are running out of time. The planet is close to a point of no return. Climate experts agree that global GHG emissions must reach net-zero by 2050 to limit global warming to 1.5 degrees Celsius.[2] The

2018 United Nations Environment Programme *Emissions Gap Report* reveals that existing nationally determined contributions cannot bridge the gap by 2030.[3] In view of these alarming findings, we have no choice but to support the most aggressive actions possible. Yet most cities pride themselves on simply plucking the low-hanging fruit—the easy fixes that require little systemic change.[4] The list is long: bike-rental systems, solar waste containers, weak green building requirements, and some recycling efforts. The assumption is that these little measures add up and build public awareness and receptivity to bigger change.

Going after the low-hanging fruit yields benefits, to be sure, but unless such measures are part of a larger, coherent strategy for altering broad patterns of energy consumption and transportation emissions, these efforts are simply *random acts of greenness*. We must be honest about what cities are accomplishing. Evidence suggests that most cities are not reducing emissions any more than their respective nations and that reductions that have occurred may be due more to state and national than city policy.[5] Electricity consumption is rising in most of the cities ranked high for their energy-efficiency programs. Most of the reduction in GHG emissions in the United States is from natural gas substituting for coal, federal vehicle fuel-efficiency standards, and state building energy codes—not municipal action.[6] The reason many of the leading cities on climate action in the United States are in California is because of state mandates. Likewise, European Union and national mandates are responsible for most emission declines in European cities.

This doesn't mean cities can't lead, but that they have to take more aggressive action on energy and transportation. Focusing on small-bore measures fosters the illusion among elected officials and citizens alike that "we're doing a good job" or "we've tackled climate change." Such overconfidence conceals the enormous political will required to take on the climate crisis in a systematic, integrated fashion. Even worse, cities may be taking steps that are both expensive and ineffective. We have to call out random acts of greenness for what they are. Rather than celebrating every action a city takes under the banner of "climate change," we must focus on getting more cities on a path to greenovation.

This book takes readers on a tour of greenovating cities in North America and Europe, exploring their strategies and successes, along with the opportunities and obstacles they have encountered along the way. In general, European cities have lower per capita GHG emissions than US cities due to their higher density, more diverse transit options, historically high gasoline prices, and long-standing climate policy at the EU, national, and municipal levels (Tables 1.1, 1.2).

Table 1.1 Comparison of the GHG Emissions by the Source in Selected North American Cities

	Transportation (%)	Buildings (%)	Energy & other (%)
San Francisco	51	45	4
New York City	23	72	5
Seattle	66	32	3
Boston	24	76	0
Los Angeles	22	72	6
Washington, DC	19	72	2
Chicago	25	72	3
Philadelphia	18	73	9

Source: Compiled by author with most recent available data.

Table 1.2 Comparison of the GHG Emissions by the Source in Selected European Cities

	Transportation (%)	Buildings (%)	Energy & other (%)
Copenhagen	37	62	1
Stockholm	48	52	0
Oslo	58	38	4
Vienna	37	0	63
Amsterdam	16	84	0
Berlin	17	56	27
Paris	13	79	8

Source: Compiled by author with most recent available data.

A broad literature has emerged on urban climate change and sustainability planning, much of it focusing on what constitutes successful practice.[7] The emphasis of much of the literature is on the *what* of climate and sustainability planning—on climate action plans, eco-districts, green roofs, zoning codes, and the like. In contrast, this book focuses on the *how*—the "in-between bits," to use a term coined by Harriett Bulkeley, of how elected officials, planners, and other stakeholders design and implement effective policy and programs.[8] In the course of writing this book and in my years of observing cities' climate action planning, I have attempted to identify the elements that characterize effective practice and to understand how they interact and reinforce each other. No one greenovating city exemplifies all of them, but several come close, and the book will explore how they've done it.

Cities in Nations and Federations

Cities, to be sure, are constituent units of nations. They often operate in federated governmental systems, with multiple jurisdictional tiers of responsibility for policy. The United States, with its federal, state, and local system of government, presents one variation. Though it has a parliamentary government, in Canada the relationship between the federal government and its provinces, and provinces and cities, is similar to the United States. The European Union, with its 28 member states, offers another variant. In general, national governments set broad policy frameworks, giving lower units of government plenty of room to go beyond national minimums.

In some parts of Europe, as this book will recount, there is a tradition of extensive public planning and public ownership of land at the city level, which gives cities more ability to maximize environmental goals. The EU requires its member states to comply with numerous directives related to various aspects of climate change. National governments, in turn, can take these mandates to higher levels of, say, adoption of renewables, building energy-efficiency, or electric vehicle infrastructure. And many European nations and cities have devised policies that exceed national standards. Germany, for example, a leader in renewable conversion among European nations, uses several policy mechanisms to increase the amount of power generated from renewable sources; over and above that, several German cities are on their way to sourcing 100 percent of their energy from renewable sources. In both Denmark and Sweden, national governments made commitments in the late 1970s to wean their economies off fossil fuels, and those national policies created a friendly policy context for cities.

The United States has lagged Europe in setting national policies to address climate change. With the election of Donald Trump, a climate change denier, conservatives in Congress and state governments have become more aggressive at using preemption to limit environmental regulation in jurisdictions governed by liberals. Because of the immense political influence of the fossil fuel industry and its political allies, American national standards for renewables, energy efficiency, and the use of mass transit all tend to be weaker than Europe's. Even so, until Trump, American federalism often—but not always—set a national regulatory floor, while states were free to go beyond it. California has had more stringent fuel-efficiency standards for autos, which predated federal rules, and 12 other states adopted California's standards. Trump proposed to roll back national fuel-efficiency standards and to challenge California in setting its own. In response, California and 17 other states have filed a suit against the administration, calling these actions arbitrary and capricious.

State governments controlled by Republicans also have sought to preempt more assertive regulation by cities. A fracking ban passed by Denton, Texas, was preempted by the Republican-dominated state legislature. Idaho, Arizona, Missouri, and Michigan have passed state laws that prohibit cities from regulating (banning or charging for) plastic bags and other containers. While plastic bags may seem a small point of contention, in the current political environment more state legislatures are attempting to reverse more crucial climate action measures cities have taken. Preemption legislation Arizona passed in 2016 included a bill that forbids cities from requiring property owners and landlords to disclose their energy use.[9] Disclosure, as we'll see in chapter 2, is crucial to cities seeking to move to higher levels of building efficiency.

These examples of environmental preemption are part of a larger initiative to limit the power of progressive cities in "red" states, led by the conservative American Legislative Exchange Council (ALEC), which has been drafting model preemption and other bills for state legislatures since the early 1970s. In part, state legislatures are able to preempt city ordinances because gerrymandering has reduced the legislative power of cities to the point where an important divide in American politics is not just between red states and blue states but between red states and their blue, or in this case green, cities.[10] In Republican-led redistricting, cities are concentrated within a small number of state legislative districts so that their votes are substantially outnumbered by rural and outer-ring suburban districts. Gerrymandering produces state legislatures that are less responsive to cities. So, for example, they can turn down funding for items such as hybrid or electric buses or mass transit improvements in favor of expanding suburban highways, as we'll see in chapter 6.

In 2014 Indiana's Republican-led legislature, with the support of Governor Mike Pence, prohibited a metropolitan Indianapolis referendum that would have funded transit projects unless a light-rail line and a corporate tax were dropped from the proposal, essentially gutting its purpose. An initiative to build a bus rapid transit line in Nashville, Tennessee, was stopped by state legislation endorsed by suburban Republican lawmakers worried about loss of parking spaces. The project eventually was allowed to advance, but the legislature drove through a measure requiring legislative approval on future transit initiatives, even if they do not involve state funding.

Another blow to cities acting on climate change was President Trump's June 2017 decision to leave the Paris Agreement, reneging on America's commitment to reduce greenhouse gas emissions by 26–28 percent from 2005 levels by 2025. But cities are defying Trump—383 members of the organization Climate Mayors, representing 74 million people, committed to the goals of the Paris Agreement without him.[11] And former New York City mayor and United Nations special envoy for climate action Michael Bloomberg started a Cities and Climate Change campaign with 30 mayors, the governors of California, New York, and Washington (who are also coordinating a separate Climate Alliance of states), 82 university presidents, and more than 100 businesses on a "We Are Still In" pledge to meet the Paris Agreement targets. The group now has 2,300 participants and is seeking United Nations approval to be a signatory to the agreement.[12] Bloomberg committed $14 million over two years from his philanthropy to help cities achieve climate goals. These two coalitions are joined by several others.

So we must acknowledge that greenovation in cities is political: even though many of the measures cities are taking improve quality of life and opportunity, there are entrenched interests seeking to halt their progress in the United States. The politics in Canada are mixed and, in Europe, widely supportive.

Where Cities Need to Lead

The two biggest sources of greenhouse gas emissions for most cities are buildings and transportation (Tables 1.3, 1.4). Emissions in both sectors are connected to the type and amount of energy used—district energy for heating and cooling is more efficient than individual systems in each building; renewable energy reduces emissions in both sectors. Thus, this book focuses on these areas of climate action planning and policy: increasing the efficiency of buildings; employing district energy; promoting adoption of renewable energy; electrifying transportation; and deprioritizing cars while developing public transit, biking, and walking. The discussion then turns to integrating initiatives in these five areas with district-scale

Table 1.3 Per Capita GHG Emissions in Selected North American Cities

	Year	Per capita emissions (metric tons CO_2)
San Francisco	2015	5.4
New York	2015	6.1
Seattle	2014	4.5
Boston	2015	9.6
Los Angeles	2014	8.3
Washington, DC	2014	12.4
Chicago	2014	13.3
Philadelphia	2014	12.4
United States	2015	15.5

Source: Compiled by author with most recent available data.

Table 1.4 Per Capita GHG Emissions in Selected European Cities and Countries

Country	City	Year	Per capita emissions (metric tons CO_2)
Denmark		2016	6.66
	Copenhagen	2017	2.50
Sweden		2016	4.54
	Stockholm	2014	2.70
Norway		2016	8.28
	Oslo	2014	2.00
Austria		2016	8.47
	Vienna	2011	3.10
Netherlands		2016	9.61
	Amsterdam	2014	5.50
Switzerland		2014	1.17
	Zurich	2004	3.70
Finland		2016	9.31
	Helsinki	2007	6.01
Germany		2016	9.47
	Berlin	2014	6.20
Belgium		2016	8.31
	Brussels	2005	3.91
France		2016	4.57
	Paris	2014	3.30

Source: Compiled by author with most recent available data.

solutions, economic development, and community revitalization (the equity link). Many of the innovations in these policy areas are inherently local, and thus protected from preemption politics. Others are constrained by what higher levels of government permit or prohibit, the funding streams they make available or withhold, as well as tax policies that incentivize behavior of private players.

A theme present throughout this book is that climate action cannot be undertaken in isolation from other stark realities facing cities, particularly high and widening income inequality. I argue that both climate and inequality can, and indeed must, be addressed together. This view is increasingly well supported in theory, starting with Julian Agyeman defining just sustainability as that which seeks a better quality of life for all, now and into the future, while living within the limits of our ecosystem.[13] But the connection between inequality and climate is not well supported in practice. Social and environmental justice have not been significant components of sustainability and/or climate action plans of many cities, either in the United States or internationally. While many mayors cite poverty and income inequality as troubling issues facing their cities, and many mayors say they are committed to climate action, too few city leaders connect the two goals.[14] An analysis of climate and sustainability plans of 28 US cities found that equity was a relatively low priority.[15] An international survey of more than 100 cities implementing at least 600 climate change experiments found that about one-fourth included environmental justice concerns.[16]

Building on Susan Fainstein's *The Just City*, which examines how principles of equity, diversity, and democracy can underpin urban planning, an emerging climate-just city framework calls for integrating considerations of social, environmental, and ecological justice into urban climate action planning.[17] This framework focuses on the fact that effects of climate change are not evenly distributed internationally and within cities. While the focus is on climate adaptation, a related energy democracy movement on the mitigation side calls for integrative policies that link social justice and economic equity with renewable-energy transitions.[18]

Likewise, climate justice has gained momentum in labor, environmental justice, and environmental organizations that seek a just transition to a more sustainable economy that provides "decent work and social protection for those whose livelihoods, incomes and employment are affected by the need to adapt to climate change and by the need to reduce emissions to levels that avert dangerous climate change."[19] This framing makes a critical link between equity and economic development, specifically to identify pathways for low-income residents to access jobs in the green economy. In each chapter, detailed in what follows, I examine the extent to which the climate agenda links to social equity and economic development.

Energy efficiency: from buildings to districts and neighborhoods (chapter 2). Improving building energy efficiency is the single most important lever cities can use to reduce their levels of GHG emissions. Buildings constitute about 40 percent of the world's energy use and produce about 40 percent of carbon emissions.[20] The next two decades will see about 900 billion square feet of building space built or rebuilt, and every foot of it that isn't up to high energy-efficiency levels locks in at least 30 years of wasted energy.[21] Cities must respond in three ways: making sure the toughest standards on new construction are in place; driving deep retrofitting of existing buildings; and ensuring that all housing, including low-income housing, is green.

I argue that cities that aren't adopting two of the highest standards for building energy efficiency—zero net emissions and passive house—are lagging. Cities that aren't at this level need pathways to get there, which is the focus of this chapter. I examine several aspects of green building—from building codes to benchmarking in New York City to different types of district-scale approaches in Charlotte, Seattle, Freiburg, and Fort Collins. I tell the story of how Cambridge, Massachusetts, is implementing citywide zero-net-energy policy and discuss how institutional sectors, such as hospitals, can lead the green building charge. Finally, we'll examine how an architect in Philadelphia is building low-income housing to the passive-house standard and leading a campaign to make it standard practice. Similarly, New York State has put low-income housing front and center in its approach to building energy efficiency. And we'll see how Malmö, Sweden, links green low-income housing and neighborhood development.

Beyond the building: district heating and cooling (chapter 3). District heating systems with combined heat and power (CHP) start with a central power plant that converts fuel into electricity. The thermal heat from generating electricity is then distributed in underground pipes to buildings connected to the system. There are two types of district cooling—those that use electricity to make and store large volumes of ice at night and then, as the ice melts, distribute cold water to buildings to use as air conditioning. The second type of system uses bodies of water to supply air conditioning to buildings.

In this chapter, I explain the technology behind district heating and cooling, emphasizing its ability to reduce greenhouse gas emissions, and examine how it can be more widely deployed. We will explore how district heating is being built in Copenhagen, Vancouver, and London, and how district cooling works in Austin and Toronto. We see in these cases that funding and ownership of systems differ, as does the type of technology employed.

Renewable cities (chapter 4). About 70 percent of the world's electricity is produced from fossil fuels.[22] The International Energy Agency estimates that we must reduce that amount to 7 percent by 2050 if global warming is to be limited to 2 degrees Celsius. Cities have a role to play in accelerating adoption of renewable energy, but policy at the national and state or provincial level is what will drive a major transformation. Still, cities can be turned into renewable-energy production facilities, aggregating demand and, through their policies, dramatically increasing the amount of renewable energy fed into existing power grids.[23]

Chapter 4 starts by examining where such a commitment makes sense in terms of renewable resources. I then move to a discussion of various cities that have committed to obtaining 100 percent of their electricity from renewable energy, with particular emphasis on solar. Cities that own their own utilities, such as Austin, Texas, can require them to adopt renewables in the same way states can. A pathway some cities are taking, particularly in Europe, is remunicipalizing their utilities. We look at Hamburg, Germany, where a citizen-led campaign to buy back its utility has put the city on a pathway to 100 percent renewable energy. We often think of renewable energy as a liberal endeavor, but we see in San Diego and Lancaster, California (the former is the largest city in the United States to commit to a 100 percent renewable energy), that Republican mayors are on board as well. The takeaway from this chapter is that renewable energy is the future and smart cities are embracing it.

Electrifying transportation (chapter 5). Transportation accounts for 14 percent of emissions worldwide, 26 percent in the United States and 24 percent in the European Union.[24] Key methods for reducing emissions from cars and trucks are to increase fuel efficiency, which is largely done at the national or state level, and to transition to electric vehicles. Since greater gains can be made in electrification of the fleet, this chapter focuses on several cities that are leaders in the transition to electric vehicles.

Several European cities are moving toward emission-free transit. The first case presented is Oslo, considered the world's capital for electric vehicles. Next is Amsterdam, which is electrifying its buses, ferries, and trolleys, which will be powered by locally produced solar energy. We then turn to London, which is one of four UK cities to be awarded £40 million to develop innovative ideas for battery-charging infrastructure.[25] In the United States I focus on Los Angeles and Atlanta—two car-centric cities that are at opposite ends of the spectrum in terms of state support to achieve a rapid transition to electric transportation.

Liberating cities from cars (chapter 6). We have to get more people out of cars. The number of cars worldwide will likely double by 2030, and if we continue on the path we are on, the world will have 2.5 billion cars by 2050. Driving less means using other modes more—public transit, biking, and walking. The obvious solution is to build more public transit, but that is an expensive option, and many cities do not have the density to support it. Some cities are finding that bus rapid transit (BRT) is a lower-cost alternative that can also revitalize the communities it serves.

But what about biking? The US city that has been most successful in increasing biking is Portland, Oregon. But Portland has been building its biking infrastructure since 1973, and yet only about 6 percent of commuting to work is done by bike. Compare this to Copenhagen and Amsterdam, where bike commuting is around 50 percent, or Freiburg at 34 percent.[26] It may be hard for American cities to get to the levels of these compact cities with a tradition of biking.

Both BRT and biking improve quality of life in cities, but to have both, we have to deprioritize cars. So in this chapter we look at how cities are deprioritizing cars to increase mobility options. We start with Oslo, which is creating a car-free area in a large part of its downtown. Here, going car-free is part of an integrated strategy of building out public transportation and biking, but also of deliberate actions to deprioritize cars. Our first case in the United States is Seattle, which is building out light rail, street cars, bus rapid transit, and bike lanes. But with only so much space, conflicts have emerged. We see in this case that deprioritizing cars is disruptive and bound to create conflicts. We then examine Nashville, a city that has looked to Seattle for help in developing bus rapid transit and light rail. The state legislature and right-wing Citizens for Prosperity have successfully blocked Nashville's attempts at public transportation, revealing the challenges green cities face in red states. Finally, we turn to a green city in a red state—Salt Lake City. Hemmed in by mountains and the lake, the city enjoys widespread support for public transit, and projects keep coming in ahead of time and under budget. It's a good government story.

How eco-innovation districts can accelerate urban climate action (chapter 7). Eco-districts are large areas in which cities concentrate sustainability efforts at the neighborhood or district level. They are getting a lot of attention as many practitioners and foundation officers see this approach as the "sweet spot" between the building scale and the city scale in achieving climate action, economic development, and neighborhood revitalization goals. Eco-districts can serve as test beds for experimenting with new technologies and new urban planning strategies. But there is a lot of variation in how eco-districts are defined and in their impact.

After reviewing the general approach, we focus on Stockholm, a city that has embraced eco-innovation. We start with one of the world's first eco-districts, Hammarby Sjöstad, and examine how city planners have learned from it to achieve even more ambitious goals in the Royal Seaport. While there are many eco-districts in Europe, North America, and elsewhere, an intensive case study of Stockholm reveals their potential.

Cities and a Green New Deal (chapter 8). The green economy is booming, and many cities are connecting climate action with economic development. Cities making this link aren't necessarily topping the most sustainable city charts, but the strong economic link can pave the way for more aggressive climate action. We begin by examining how solar and wind technology production has shifted internationally and how China has become the dominant player in solar energy and a leader in wind energy. We then move to three historically industrial cities that are seeking to transition to different green economy sectors. New York State is paying $750 million of the $900 million cost to build the nation's biggest new solar production facility in Buffalo, and we'll examine the long-term potential of the plant succeeding in the highly competitive international solar industry. Cleveland, a city highlighted in my 2010 book, *Emerald Cities*, has continued its efforts to develop offshore wind on Lake Erie. The project is going forward, and efforts to transform existing manufacturers into parts suppliers for the wind industry are promising. I then discuss the potential for manufacturing along the eastern seaboard that could result from offshore wind development. The final case is Los Angeles, which is linking electrification of its buses and development of subways to manufacturing. This chapter reveals that transitioning regional economies in highly competitive industries can enjoy an economic advantage, but it is not a strategy for the faint-hearted.

The elements of greenovation (chapter 9). Several practices and strategies come up repeatedly in the stories of this book. This chapter identifies them and discusses how they can become standard practice in more, if not most, cities. Included in the discussion are a number of factors: leadership—from above and below; better integration of siloed city government departments; experimentation and organizational learning; citizen and private-sector engagement; and supportive state and national policies.

Ultimately, the context for implementation is political. European cities have much higher levels of support at the national level and from the European Union. There are many more contradictions in the North American context, particularly in the United States, where the Trump administration thinks of climate change as a hoax. In many ways, greenovation is about establishing economic leadership on the green technologies of the future—this is a fact that China, several European nations, and many cities in the United States and Canada understand. Just as important, greenovation is about cultivating broad civic will by making it inclusive—both are connected and reinforced by embracing the green economy as an opportunity. Making social equity a priority—whether in the form of energy democracy, environmental justice, or other aspects of social inclusion, is also a political decision. We can only be hopeful that a new round of political activism will move it to the top of the political agenda.

The need for greenovation is urgent. It is my hope that this book provides examples of how cities can greenovate to reduce carbon emissions and in so doing create a thriving and more equitable economy. Climate action is a win-win.

2

ENERGY EFFICIENCY

From Buildings to Districts and Neighborhoods

IMPROVING ENERGY EFFICIENCY IN buildings is the single most important lever cities have for reducing their GHG emissions. Buildings use about 40 percent of the world's energy and produce about 40 percent of carbon emissions.[1] Yet in cities, that number can be far higher: two of the cities discussed in this chapter, New York and Cambridge, Massachusetts, report that building energy accounts for 70 to 80 percent or more of their carbon emissions. The next two decades will see about 900 billion square feet of building space built or rebuilt, and every foot of it that isn't up to high energy-efficiency levels locks in at least 30 years of wasted energy.[2]

The payoffs are enormous. Aggressive action on building efficiency not only reduces carbon emissions, but also saves consumers money and creates jobs that can't be exported.[3] Every dollar spent on reducing electricity consumption saves twice as much in increasing electricity supply and lowering distribution costs.[4] On the residential side alone, the untapped market for energy-efficiency investment in the United States is estimated at $182 billion and, if fully utilized, could reduce national GHG emissions by more than 5 percent.[5] Moreover, leadership and innovation related to building efficiency in both Europe and the United States will have powerful transfer effects, helping rapidly urbanizing developing countries transform themselves with more efficient building. If energy-efficiency measures are implemented globally, the building sector's emissions could be reduced by 83 percent, eliminating 5.8 billion tons of carbon.[6]

An added benefit, greening the workforce, would enhance equity and social justice. Retrofitting 40 percent of US building stock would create more than

600,000 jobs. A 27 percent increase in energy efficiency in Europe by 2030 (compared with 2005 levels) would create two million new jobs.[7]

In this chapter I present a continuum of building-level actions cities are taking in light of the political and economic constraints they face. I begin by explaining the continuum of building-efficiency standards cities are using as well as a continuum of action that runs from individual buildings to all buildings in a defined district. We examine two categories of standards: those for constructing new buildings and those for retrofitting existing buildings, which can be very challenging. Further, I explore how cities are engaging the private sector. In the United States, where most of a city's building stock is privately owned, property owners usually have to be on board to meet ambitious city efficiency goals. I also discuss the social justice issues greenovators must address in all sustainability efforts. The design, building, and operation of buildings is no exception. Toward the end of this chapter we turn to the question of who gets to occupy green buildings—with the reduced energy costs they make possible—highlighting how some cities are building green low-income housing using methods that are then taken statewide. Finally, we examine how cities, in collaboration with the private and nonprofit sectors—and in Europe, though EU mandates—are serving as test beds for technical, financing, and equity greenovations that can be scaled for policy in larger political geographies and for private-market participation.

A Continuum of Action on Building Efficiency

Many US cities started action on green building in the 1990s by imposing standards for new buildings that required some level of Leadership in Energy and Environmental Design (LEED) certification developed by the US Green Building Council (USGBC), a nonprofit organization, in 1993. LEED is based on earning points in five areas of sustainable construction: siting, water efficiency, energy and atmosphere, materials and resources, and indoor environmental quality. The more points, the higher the LEED rating, which runs from platinum (highest) through silver, gold, and certified. More than a thousand American cities now require some level of LEED certification on some construction, and many of these offer expedited permitting, subsidies, or technical assistance to those using the standard.

While LEED put green building on the map, it is a weak standard for energy efficiency, even at the highest level of certification. Its impact on a city's overall building efficiency is minimal, because most cities require the standard only for a small subset of new construction, such as buildings larger than a certain square footage or those receiving subsidies. And because energy use contributes only about one-third of all possible LEED points, the system isn't designed to get cities to the deep efficiency needed to reach the goal of reducing GHG emissions 80 percent by 2050 (80 × 50) or more.

The equivalent of LEED in Europe is BREEAM (Building Research Establishment's Environmental Assessment Method), which also is used in some US cities. Like LEED, BREEAM criteria go beyond energy efficiency to include sustainability and toxicity of construction materials, water management, waste handling, health and well-being, and energy consumption. BREEAM has about 80 percent of the market in certified sustainable buildings in Europe, with about 540,000 buildings certified worldwide. A key difference between LEED and BREEAM is that BREEAM, in compliance with the European Union's 2003 Energy Performance of Buildings Directive, calculates a building's carbon emissions.

Green building systems around the world offer variations of LEED and BREEAM, but these two prevail because, as the oldest, they have gained credibility as a standard and include design, indoor air quality, and related features that buyers and tenants want. For most cities, however, these certifications apply only to a small percentage of construction because cities cannot mandate that all new construction meet these requirements.

Greenovating cities and the developers working in them are building to more rigorous standards—passive house and zero net emissions (ZNE). A passive-house building consumes about 90 percent less energy than a typical building and does not require active heating and cooling systems because the buildings are extremely well insulated and have air exchangers that use the heat produced from lighting, cooking, and other sources to warm incoming cold air.

The ZNE standard (sometimes called zero net energy) also requires high levels of efficiency and, in addition, demands that all energy be renewable—either produced on site or purchased from carbon-free sources. In both cases, these buildings can be initiated by the owner or developer, or the fruit of incentives created by the city or national government. Dozens of European cities require the passive-house standard for some construction—particularly in Germany, where it was developed.[8] Several European cities, including Hamburg and Copenhagen, require ZNE for some buildings. In the United States, Fort Collins and Boulder, Colorado; Cambridge, Massachusetts; and several California cities have ZNE policies or ordinances.[9]

Getting to the highest levels of energy efficiency in new buildings requires applying stringent municipal building codes to all buildings. It also requires building energy-use transparency in both new and existing buildings to motivate owners to invest in efficiency. These two measures are steps on the path to passive house and ZNE.

Building Codes: Targeting New Buildings and Retrofits

The surest path to dramatically improving buildings' energy efficiency is through adoption of strict mandatory building and energy codes. Establishing a national code requirement is improbable in the United States, where federalism and the tradition of municipal home rule generate a maze of city and state codes. Most states use the International Energy Conservation Code (IECC), established in 2000 by the International Code Council, as the minimum standard for new residential construction, and either IECC or the roughly equivalent American Society of Heating, Refrigerating and Air Conditioning Engineers (ASHRAE) 90.1 for commercial construction. The standards establish criteria for building design and construction, but not all states have adopted them.[10]

While some states encourage cities to adopt stricter energy codes that are higher than the base code, referred to as stretch codes, others prohibit cities from adopting codes stricter than their state's. In home-rule states, a city can adopt its own code rather than using that of the state.[11] But even that practice is not consistent. For instance, Massachusetts, a home-rule state, requires local jurisdictions to use the state code. Massachusetts cities cannot exceed the base code unless they adopt a specified stretch code. Nevertheless, as evidenced in Charlotte, North Carolina and elsewhere, cities can still find creative ways to promote efficiency beyond state requirements.

The situation in Europe is different. The EU Energy Efficiency Directive, established in 2012, requires member countries to set minimum energy performance requirements for new buildings and major renovations toward the goal of reaching nearly zero energy by 2020.[12] Most European countries and cities use an outcome-based standard, measured as the kilowatt-hours per square meter per year ($kWh/m^2/year$), a measure of a building's energy use intensity that is monitored after construction. Countries and cities vary on whether this standard includes all energy consumed in the building or only electricity. Builders are typically given considerable discretion in how they meet the standard.

Turning to Existing Buildings: Benchmarking and Transparency in Building

Energy Performance

Only a small proportion of any city's building stock is new construction, so most of a city's actions relative to the building sector must be directed at dramatically improving efficiency in existing buildings. This is a greater challenge than that posed by new buildings, as governmental levers requiring efficiency in existing building energy performance are less available.

That situation will shift as more and more cities require owners to disclose how much energy and water a building uses. The operative strategy is that, as buyers and renters become aware of their choices, the market will act as a force in promoting efficiency. By analogy, most people are accustomed to the ubiquitous MPG charts on automobiles, and they depend on that information when purchasing a car. The same is not true of buildings. Whether in the market for commercial or residential properties, renters and buyers don't have much to go on when evaluating their operating costs. With transparent reporting, consumers faced with the choice between a building that is an energy guzzler and one that sips its energy will be equipped with valuable, budget-useful information.

Benchmarking is a first step in evaluating a city's existing building stock: that is, measuring a building's energy use and comparing it to similar building types. On a policy level, this information allows cities to target the most inefficient buildings for intervention. For example, Hilary Firestone, former senior project manager for energy efficiency at the Los Angeles Mayor's Office of Sustainability, noted that merely 4 percent of LA's commercial buildings (buildings larger than 10,000 square feet) account for half of the city's total energy usage. Almost 70 percent of the city's buildings are single-family homes, yet they use only about 25 percent of total energy. Having this information in hand allows a city to focus incentives on achieving the biggest impact.

As of June 2019, 31 US cities required some level of benchmarking and transparent reporting of energy use information, with California being the only state that requires it for public, commercial, and multifamily buildings.[13] Cities vary in the size and type of building required to report and whether the information is available publicly and to whom—to buyers, or to city government. Most building owners use the US Environmental Protection Agency's free Energy Star Portfolio Manager tool, which can track energy use in a single building or a group of buildings. The tool measures a building's energy use intensity, which, like kWh/m²/year, is a building's total annual energy consumption divided by its size in square meters.[14] The calculations take into account weather, building type, age, size, and characteristics of occupants, such as the number of computers, to compute energy use intensity.

New York City Leads on Disclosing Building Energy Use

New York City is a leader in transparent reporting of energy use. In 2007, when buildings accounted for about 71 percent of the city's GHG emissions and

94 percent of its electricity consumption, former mayor Michael Bloomberg focused on energy efficiency as a central part of the city's climate agenda. New York City pioneered in developing building-disclosure ordinances with the 2009 Greener, Greater Buildings Plan, consisting of four laws that apply to buildings of 50,000 or more square feet.[15] These laws cover 15,000 large commercial buildings that comprise only 2 percent of the city's buildings yet account for almost 48 percent of the city's energy use.

The first law, Local Law 84, requires building owners to submit energy and water use data annually, using Portfolio Manager, or face a fine of $500.[16] A US Department of Energy–sponsored evaluation of the law estimated that over the program's first four years, participating buildings realized a cumulative energy savings of 5.7 percent.[17] Not surprising, the biggest gains were in older buildings that replaced aging heating and cooling systems.

Local Law 85 makes it mandatory for building owners doing renovations to upgrade systems to meet the city's current code. Previously, the city granted exemptions if less than half of a building was being renovated, covering the majority of renovations. Local Law 87 requires building owners to conduct energy audits and examine major building systems every 10 years to ensure equipment is running properly and to make operational and maintenance improvements.[18] The city provides online tools for both reports and levies a fine of $3,000 for the first year of nonreporting and $5,000 for every subsequent year of noncompliance.

Finally, Local Law 88 requires nonresidential building owners to install high-efficiency lighting and to submeter large tenant spaces so that each tenant receives individual bills based on use.[19] The city expanded Local Law 88 to capture smaller buildings (25,000 to 50,000 square feet), which would cover an additional 5,000 buildings and, with their inclusion, eliminate 60,000 metric tons of GHG emissions and save $35 million in energy costs annually.[20]

The Institute for Market Transformation, a Washington, DC-based nonprofit that provides technical assistance to cities and states on developing building-efficiency policies, provided extensive support to the Bloomberg administration in developing a building energy-use transparency and disclosure ordinance that identifies 27 architectural types and lays out pathways for achieving deep energy savings in each type.

In 2014, Mayor Bill de Blasio accelerated New York City's climate goal by committing the city to reducing GHG emissions 80 percent by 2050 (80 × 50), which requires even more aggressive action on building efficiency. In September 2015, the administration announced a road map for achieving the new goal and launched the NYC Retrofit Accelerator to provide free technical assistance to building owners in installing and financing energy and water efficiency upgrades and incorporating renewable energy.[21] By supporting retrofits in up to 1,000 properties per year, the program is projected to reduce another million metric tons of GHG emissions by 2025. In addition to its own financial incentives, the city draws on the state's energy-efficiency financing programs, which allocate nearly $250 million per year.

New York City is now implementing its own green new deal—the Climate Mobilization Act—released in April 2019. It establishes emissions caps for different building types larger than 25,000 square feet and fines for landlords who don't comply. Beginning in 2024, landlords will be required to retrofit buildings to reduce their emissions by 40 percent by 2030 and 80 percent by 2050. Mark Chambers, Director of the Mayor's Office of Sustainability, says affordability is front and center in implementing the requirements. There is a different compliance path for affordable housing and mechanisms are in place to ensure that building owners don't pass costs off onto tenants. And to transition away from burning fossil fuels for space heating and hot water, New York is one of four cities participating in a pilot called the Building Electrification Initiative (BEI), which started in October 2017 (Washington, D.C., Boulder, and Burlington are the other cities).

Beyond the Building: District-Scale and Sectoral Approaches to Efficiency

Several cities have created pilot districts to demonstrate that higher levels of efficiency are possible by motivating building owners and developers in a defined area to voluntarily retrofit buildings to high standards. When owners and developers in a district take action, mutual learning can accelerate adoption of effective techniques. This section examines four very different types of district-scale efforts: Envision Charlotte and Seattle's 2030 District in the United States, and eco-districts in Malmö, Sweden, and Freiburg, Germany. A related approach, taken in Fort Collins, Colorado, and in Cambridge and Boston, Massachusetts, is to motivate key sectors with campus-style properties, such as healthcare centers and institutions of higher education, to take the lead. These approaches illustrate different paths to achieving higher levels of building energy efficiency.

Envision Charlotte: A Voluntary District Model to Change Behavior

North Carolina is among 15 states using older, less stringent ASHRAE codes. Because North Carolina is not a home-rule state where cities can independently set code, the city of Charlotte had to use a voluntary strategy to promote building energy efficiency. Its energy-efficiency initiative, Envision Charlotte, is a non-profit public-private partnership organized in 2011 to accelerate building energy efficiency and sustainability in the downtown district—home to several major banks—with 61 (of 64) buildings participating in the project. Smart Energy Now, its first project, sought to reduce building energy consumption over a five-year period by focusing on the behaviors of building occupants. Electric power company Duke Energy is measuring and verifying the results by placing meters in the 61 participating buildings that collect energy-use data on a more frequent basis than the usual periodic meter reading. In addition, Cisco donated interactive energy-monitoring kiosks placed prominently in the lobbies of the commercial buildings to build awareness of the initiative.

The participating buildings achieved the 2017 goal of a 20 percent energy use reduction. The group is examining how to obtain deeper reductions in the district. This district-level success motivated Duke Energy to expand the program to offices throughout the city.

Crucial to reaching Envision Charlotte goals, according to Amy Aussieker,[22] its executive director, were three bank headquarters that are among the downtown's largest buildings. "Their influence," she noted, "allowed us to get as much square footage as we did." She also credited the role of "champions," tenants who educate and encourage other tenants to make changes, such as turning down thermostats, powering down computers, and other actions. She estimated that the district's 61 participating buildings have 300 tenants and 20,000 people working in them. Having a champion in each building spurred almost total participation by occupants.

2030 Districts and the Case of Seattle

In 2011, Ed Mazria built on the Architecture 2030 Challenge, which supports cities seeking to make all new and renovated buildings carbon neutral by 2030, by creating a new program, 2030 Districts. The goal is for a group of building owners in a defined 2030 District to commit to progressive and ambitious reductions in building energy use, water consumption, and transportation GHG emissions (figure 2.1). For these targeted reductions, a building's energy and water use is compared to the national median for similar buildings. To date, at least 17 cities have established 2030 Districts.[23] Together they form the 2030 Districts Network, which enables cities to learn from one another's experiences.

Seattle launched the first 2030 District. Planning had started two years earlier in 2009 when architect Brian Geller (who became the founding executive director of the district) and a handful of architects, engineers, property managers, and city planners decided that the approach was ideal for motivating private-sector leadership on building efficiency. In its first phase, December 2009

ACHIEVING DISTRICT-WIDE GOALS
2030 Districts commit to reducing:

BUILDING ENERGY USE + WATER CONSUMPTION + TRANSPORTATION GHG EMISSIONS

50% BY 2030

Figure 2.1 Architecture 2030 Goals
Source: Architecture 2030.

through 2011, the group reached out to property owners in the eight-square-mile downtown area to encourage them to commit to district goals. In 2014, after three years of fiscal sponsorship by Architecture 2030, the Seattle 2030 District became a 501(c)(3) nonprofit organization with 60 founding members.[24] As of October 2016, members have committed 242 buildings (covering 48 million square feet) to meeting the goals of the district, with funding from various federal grants.

The district uses the Energy Star Portfolio Manager for collecting building performance data and measuring progress. It is experimenting with various approaches to determine which technologies save building owners the most money on energy. In addition to measuring energy use in individual buildings, the district aggregates the data to track overall progress.

Brett Phillips, founding member and board chairman of Seattle's 2030 District, comments that a certain level of efficiency can be achieved with everyone acting independently, but getting to higher levels requires working together. Phillips, who is director of sustainability at Unico Properties, found that the collective nature of the 2030 District's decision-making helped to counteract market barriers to higher building efficiency. For example, collectively members have helped create demand for energy-saving products and now purchase products and services at discount prices through the 2030 Marketplace, an online platform. Another success he cites is that members frequently advocate collectively for municipal policies, such as zoning incentives. Phillips notes that members were instrumental in promoting the Seattle Living Building Pilot Program, which allows variances from the city's land-use code and offers height and floor-area incentives for buildings meeting the Living Building Challenge, the world's most rigorous building performance standard. [25]

Another illustration of district-scale thinking in Seattle is the heating system developed by McKinstry Engineering for Amazon's four-building campus. McKinstry is a Seattle-based company that designs, builds, and operates high-performance, energy-efficient buildings. Its Amazon initiative pipes heated water from a data center, based in the 34-story Westin Exchange Building, to Amazon's nearby high-rise building. Serving that building is a 400,000-gallon water reservoir and a heat-reclaiming chiller plant that circulates data center hot water to the other Amazon buildings—serving a total of four million square feet. The system loops warm water through the building and returns cool water back to Westin, where the cycle repeats (figure 2.2).

Prior to the McKinstry design, waste heat from the data center was released outside, as it still is in the summer when heat isn't needed. The system is four times more efficient than a traditional electric heating system.[26] Building owners realize further cost savings because the data center does not need cooling towers.

There is even more potential in the Amazon complex, as it will only use 5 of the daily 11 megawatts of energy produced by the Westin Exchange Building.[27] Unlike European cities, Seattle cannot require building owners to hook into the system. Seattle 2030 executive director Susan Wickwire points out that information

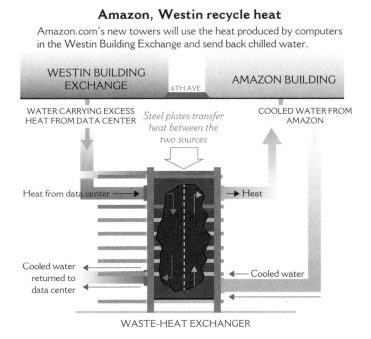

Figure 2.2 Amazon-Westin Heat Exchange
Source: McKinstry.

dissemination plays a crucial role in expanding the district plan: in 2016, Seattle had more construction than New York City and San Francisco combined, yet many developers weren't aware that capturing waste heat was an option in building their energy systems.

In February 2017, Wickwire said that other sources of waste heat (including that generated from other data centers and a sewer line running through South Lake Union) could be added to the steam system operated by the utility Enwave. Recently, the 17-story Cyrene Building tapped into Enwave Seattle's steam plant system next door and will contribute its building's excess heat, lightening the load for Enwave's boilers. The city of Seattle rewarded Cyrene for its participation: in exchange for hooking up to the system and realizing substantial efficiencies, the city allowed Cyrene to build with larger windows than permitted by the municipal energy code. Furthermore, because its building did not need a heating and cooling system, Cyrene was able to create amenity space on the roof and to build more units.

Reflecting on the value of the district approach to building energy efficiency, Ash Awad, chief market officer at McKinstry, noted that when building owners act independently to retrofit for efficiency, and in the process raise rents to cover the expense, they potentially put themselves at a disadvantage in the market-place.[28] However, when a group of building owners acts collectively to do the same retrofits, the ones who don't participate are at a disadvantage and will find themselves left behind. Second, the 2030 District has challenged building owners to transform their practices and model innovative thinking for the entire city. In one case, district members provided leadership in producing a uniform approach to what are called green leases. The Seattle model green lease aligns the financial incentives of owners and tenants so they can cooperate on and mutually benefit from reducing building energy consumption.

Malmö's Building/Living Dialogue Yields High Building Efficiency in Its Western Harbour Eco-district

The city of Malmö, at the southern tip of Sweden, has transformed a 160-hectare (395-acre) abandoned shipbuilding area, known as Western Harbour, into a mixed-use eco-neighborhood that integrates all of the city's sustainability goals—building efficiency, renewable energy adoption, green stormwater management, plenty of green space, bike paths, and biogas-fueled buses—and is completely powered by renewable energy. It has also set construction standards that have put the city and region on track to construct more buildings meeting passive-house criteria than any other metro in the world.[29]

Built out in phases, the project allowed city planners to learn from successes and failures in each phase. Disappointed that building-efficiency targets weren't met in the first phase of building, city planners created a mandatory, ongoing educational forum, the Building/Living Dialogue, which brings together property developers, architects, and construction firms in a series of lectures and workshops on energy efficiency, renewable energy, green space planning, safety, and affordability to ensure that rigorous standards are met.[30] City planners also take dialogue participants to the region's best-performing buildings to learn how to achieve highly efficient construction.

Starting in 2006, during its second phase (Flagghusen), the city-sponsored dialogue created better understanding of which new technologies were most effective, leading to more efficient buildings in the third phase and the construction of buildings that met passive-house standards. During the third-phase dialogue (Fullriggaren), participants agreed to further raise standards and to set a goal that one-third of area buildings would meet passive-house standards established by the Environmental Building Programme for Southern Sweden. (In that program, Grade A uses 55 kilowatt hours per square meter per year [considered passive]; Grade B uses 65; and Grade C uses 85.)

The Western Harbour district is now completed and the results are impressive. The first phase of the development is powered 100 percent by locally produced renewable energy; most Flagghusen buildings meet Grade B standards; and Fullriggaren's office properties perform to the Green Building Standard (25 percent more energy efficient than mandatory requirements) and have several passive-house buildings. Both photovoltaic (PV) systems and wind turbines link to a district heating system.

Malmö, like many northern European cities, owns most of the land in its boundaries and thus can require developers to build to high energy standards as a condition of development.[31] Even when these cities sell properties to developers, leasehold agreements retain the city's landownership, giving it power to negotiate and plan with potential lessees.[32] Planners, architects, and developers alike agree that the Building/Living Dialogue is why Malmö's construction companies can build to passive-house standards. It has also spurred builders to learn to build to high standards cost-effectively. As an experiment, one property-development company, ByggVesta, built two full-size apartment buildings—one with low-energy technology, the other to a passive-house standard—to compare short- and long-term costs based on actual heating and cooling costs when occupied. When the passive-house approach proved more cost-effective, ByggVesta continued building to a passive-house standard in other parts of Sweden.

Freiburg's Vauban: An Eco-district and a Testing Ground for Multifamily Passive-House Construction

Freiburg, a picturesque university city of 220,000 in southwest Germany that has been a stronghold of the Green Party since the 1970s, is recognized for comprehensive planning to achieve sustainability goals.[33] To ease a housing shortage in the early 1990s, the city purchased Vauban, a 100-hectare abandoned military base, and transformed it into a new eco-neighborhood that houses 5,500 people and attracts thousands of visitors every year who are interested in applying its principles in their own cities. When it began to develop Vauban, Freiburg had already launched an ambitious strategy for promoting solar energy, expanding transit and biking options, and developing green stormwater management.[34] But Vauban also served as a pilot for integrating green practices, particularly in construction, and is now one of the most widely celebrated eco-districts in the world.

Aiming for ambitious energy-efficiency goals, the city used its existing energy standard at the time—65 kilowatt hours per square meter per year, which was lower than the national standard of 75 kilowatt hours. Some buildings surpassed this standard. In fact, about 200 housing units have achieved passive-house standard, and 60 units produce more energy than they use; they are net positive, selling surplus power back to the grid.[35]

An illustration of the role of experimentation in achieving high standards is the completion of the first multifamily passive-house building in Vauban in 1999 (and at the time one of the first in the world), which also boasts passive-house standards in sanitation. The multifamily passive-house concept was the brainchild of an architect, Michael Gies, who was intent on achieving multifamily passive housing, and a biologist, Jörg Lange, who wanted to build wastewater-free housing. The two convinced a group of builders to attempt the construction, which in turn won the support of the Fraunhofer Institute for Solar Energy Systems in Freiburg. Advice from the Passivhaus Institut in Darmstadt, whose research has been instrumental in advancing the concept throughout Germany and internationally, resulted in a building that has demonstrated that a multifamily dwelling can meet the passive-house standard.

Unlike ZNE, the passive-house standard does not have requirements for the energy source. Nevertheless, Vauban aimed for and achieved renewable energy goals as well as goals for efficiency. The district's signature feature is Solarsiedlung am Schlierberg, a housing development where each building's roof is covered with a PV module. Nearly all of the district's energy is renewable and produced on-site—a woodchip-powered combined heat-and-power facility serves the district heating network and supplements rooftop solar electricity.

The Vauban development demonstrates that cities can reach high energy-efficiency standards on a district-wide scale. Further, it allowed the construction sector to gain expertise in how to achieve and replicate these standards. In 2011, Freiburg set its building code to 40 kilowatt hours per square meter per year—not quite at passive-house level, but a standard few cities have achieved to date.

Achieving Zero Net Energy and Zero Net Emissions: Fort Collins, Colorado, and Cambridge, Massachusetts

The terminology of "net zero" or "zero net" can be confusing: sometimes the idea is referred to using one of these terms and sometimes the other. And the *E* in *ZNE* can stand for "energy" or "emissions," meaning different things. A zero-net-energy (ZNE) building generates all the energy it uses on-site, usually from renewable sources. Because a rooftop PV system on top of a high-rise cannot produce enough energy to supply the building, ZNE is almost impossible to achieve in a dense urban setting, where the concept of zero net emissions (or carbon) is a more practical standard in many cities. In these buildings, all energy is sourced or procured from renewable energy, though not necessarily produced on-site (figure 2.3).[36] Some, if not most, ZNE buildings source energy or energy certificates from off-site sources.

In Europe, the 2009 EU Energy Performance of Buildings Directive requires that all new buildings achieve "nearly" zero-energy use by the end of 2020 and offers guidance and a standard format for nations to report progress. In the

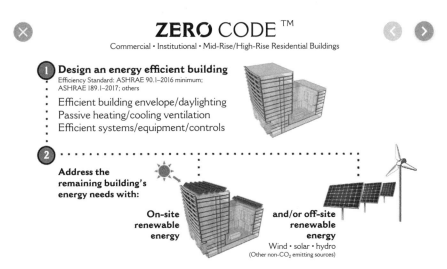

Figure 2.3 Achieving Zero Net Emissions
Source: Architecture 2030.

United States, ZNE cities include Salt Lake City, Utah; Cambridge, Massachusetts; and Palo Alto, Santa Monica, and Santa Clara, California. By 2020, the state of California will require all new residential or single-family homes to be net-zero. The next sections examine two approaches to achieving ZNE: one in Fort Collins, which began by addressing energy use at the district scale and expanded to the rest of the city, the other in Cambridge, which established ZNE as a citywide standard, beginning with new buildings and ultimately encompassing all buildings in the city.

FortZED: District-Level Action on Energy

In 2007, Fort Collins began an experiment that attempted to transform much of its downtown and the Colorado State University campus (a two-square-mile area that comprises 15 percent of the city's electric load) into a "zero energy" district by using smart-grid technology to improve building efficiency and by incorporating multiple sources of renewable energy. Although the experiment was abandoned in late 2017, much was learned and relationships were formed that allowed the city to continue with ZNE standards.

The idea for FortZED (zero-energy district) emerged when the Community Foundation of Northern Colorado conceived and funded UniverCity Connections, an initiative to unite what are considered the three gems of Fort Collins: the university, the river corridor, and downtown. Through a yearlong planning process, various subcommittees focused on envisioning a common future for these areas. One subcommittee concluded that experimenting with ZNE at the district scale could result in substantial energy savings and offer economic development opportunities, and its idea moved forward.

This link between economic development and energy efficiency made FortZED a natural project for the Colorado Clean Energy Cluster (CCEC). Formed in 2006, the CCEC is a nonprofit group focused on attracting, incubating, and expanding the area's clean-energy sector. Judy Dorsey, the CCEC's first executive director and founding director of Brendle Group, a sustainability-focused engineering and planning consultancy, explained that CCEC members knew there were two aspects to district-scale ZNE: figuring out the enabling grid technologies needed to increase energy efficiency "behind the meter" (making energy production and distribution more efficient), and "front of the meter" measures to reduce a building's energy consumption.

The CCEC had six technology partners in the first FortZED demonstration, called the Renewable and Distributed Systems Integration (RDSI) project, which ran from 2009 to 2011. Funded by a $6.3 million grant from the DOE and

$5 million in local matching funds from various local companies and individuals, RDSI tested a number of technologies to reduce peak energy use and integrate renewables into the grid.[37] It sought to balance and reduce electricity loads, referred to as "peak shaving," to reduce the cost of power and create more efficient energy use. Through this demonstration, Fort Collins Utilities (FCU) projected that peak electricity demand could be reduced by 20 to 30 percent.[38]

On the energy conservation side, the FortZED Energy Challenge, launched in 2011, engaged the district's 15,000 residential customers to reduce their energy use. The program divided the district into 31 territories, each with an animal mascot. Trained leaders in each territory encouraged residents to pledge to conserve energy in order to earn rebates. An online tool allowed residents to compare how the territories were doing. Another voluntary program Fort Collins developed, ClimateWise, has businesses committing to energy, water use, and waste reductions to lower their GHG emissions. Businesses achieve partnership levels ranging from bronze to platinum to recognize their efforts.

Successful experiments in FortZED allowed Fort Collins in 2015 to commit to reducing carbon emissions 80 percent by 2030 (relative to 2005), which prompted a number of actions. The building code was revised to reflect stricter standards. The city-owned utility FCU collaborated with the Rocky Mountain Institute, a Colorado-based organization that advances market-based solutions to energy efficiency and renewable-energy systems, to implement several measures to decrease energy and water use that include advanced metering, performance-based incentives for new construction and deep retrofits, and subsidies for purchasing efficient appliances. FCU had already begun its Solar Power Purchase Program in 2013, which offers a fixed-price 20-year power purchase agreement to commercial customers. And in January 2017, Colorado State University committed to becoming a 100 percent renewable campus by 2030.

Yet in the face of these advances, the steering committee announced in September 2017 that FortZED would be dissolved. Mayor Wade Troxell commented that it was no longer essential, now that FortZED's various partners were moving on its agenda.[39] Katy McLaren, senior environmental planner for Fort Collins, who formerly coordinated FortZED, explained to me that once the goals were extended beyond the original geographic boundaries, the focus of the work became more about leveraging relationships between the public sector, the university, and the business community (such as the ClimateWise agreement). McLaren commented that FortZED ended not because it failed, but because it had served its purpose: "Because of what we learned from the FortZED project, we are delivering on one of the most ambitious climate action plans in the world. We have achieved our milestones toward the city's 80 X 50 goal—we were at

12 percent at the end of 2016 (below 2005 emissions), and if a large-scale wind project goes online by 2020, we'll be at the 20 percent milestone."[40] It's hard to argue with success.

Cambridge, Massachusetts: Citywide Zero Net Emissions

It is not surprising that a progressive city known as the "People's Republic of Cambridge" was one of the first US municipalities to commit to citywide zero-net-emissions policies. ZNE is an extension of a series of Cambridge policies that started with the 2002 Climate Protection Plan, which sought to reduce emissions 20 percent below 1990 levels. It wasn't the most aggressive plan, but it represented an approach that would become Cambridge's standard on climate action—setting achievable rather than aspirational goals.

Cambridge had been taking steps to improve building energy efficiency, such as adopting the state's stretch energy code, which is about 20 percent more energy efficient than the state's building base code and has separate requirements for new construction and renovation of residential and commercial properties. Another step was the passage of the Building Energy Use Disclosure Ordinance in July 2014, which requires owners of larger buildings to report annual energy use.

While resistance to disclosure requirements is common in some cities, Cambridge has seen a different response: a 95 percent reporting compliance rate in 2015, the program's first year of operation. Susanne Rasmussen, director of environmental and transportation planning, attributes the city's high compliance rate to the prevalence of sophisticated builders who want to be seen as leaders and understand the market value of green buildings. Further, she notes, the city provided information and ongoing support to building owners as they collected data.[41]

In the first year of data collection the city requested data only on nonresidential parcels with one or more buildings totaling 50,000 square feet or more, and on parcels with residential units of 50 or more units and municipal buildings larger than 10,000 square feet. Owners enter energy-use data by type of fuel into the Portfolio Manager on a monthly basis to calculate a building's energy-use intensity. The Cambridge website has an interactive map that reveals the energy performance of individual buildings.[42]

City council members and planners realized that the city's fast pace of growth would make it difficult to reach the climate plan's targets, as even efficient buildings add GHG emissions. When the Massachusetts Institute of Technology (MIT) announced an ambitious plan for adding about one million square feet of new development to the rapidly expanding Kendall Square area in 2013, local environmental groups, led by activist Michael Connolly, began investigating ZNE, as did then-mayor Henrietta Davis. Connolly's group began circulating a net-zero zoning petition to require that all new buildings be built to that standard, and they quickly got more than 500 signatures in support.

Earlier, Davis had attended a conference showcasing a ZNE school in Bowling Green, Kentucky, and soon secured agreement from the city council to attempt to meet ZNE standards in constructing a new public school. The Dr. Martin Luther King, Jr. School was completed in April 2016. Although it did not meet ZNE standards, it will achieve LEED platinum certification and consumes 60 percent less energy than other school buildings of comparable size in New England.[43] The school's planning and design laid the groundwork for viewing ZNE as feasible when the Connolly proposal for a ZNE ordinance was presented to the city council. Nonetheless, some groups adamantly opposed the proposal, arguing that imposing untested standards could drive new commercial development to the suburbs.[44]

The proposal was referred to a committee, usually the kiss of death for an initiative. But a Getting to Net Zero Task Force was staffed, with Rasmussen at the head, and charged with determining whether ZNE was attainable citywide. The composition of the 15-person task force ensured a thorough analysis—it included sustainability directors from Harvard and MIT, two leading developers, the head of the city's planning board, the president of the Boston Society of Architects, and former mayor Davis. The task force sought widespread community engagement, reaching out to leading civic groups such as the Mass Biotech Council, the chamber of commerce, and the Cambridge Compact for a Sustainable Future.

After meeting for 15 months, the task force recommended that the city phase in ZNE, starting with city-owned buildings, which should achieve ZNE by 2020. Next would be new residential buildings, with a 2022 goal; multifamily, commercial, and institutional buildings with a 2025 goal; and labs, which are very energy intensive, with a 2030 goal. The 25-year ZNE timeline would increase the energy efficiency of existing buildings by 70 percent.[45]

In June 2015, the Cambridge Net Zero Action Plan, a 25-year road map to a 70 percent reduction in emissions by 2040, was adopted by city council. Furthermore, city council members realized that if they were serious about implementing a multiyear plan with 60 actions, someone would need to be in charge of carrying it out. To this end, they appropriated funds to cover a net-zero-energy planner and action plan activities for five years.

City planners realized that differentiating by building type would be essential to gaining widespread support for the proposal. Labs are among the highest energy-using type of building, and Cambridge—home to Harvard, MIT, and a thriving high-tech sector—has many. The main concern of owners of lab buildings was that reporting on building energy use had to include the context so that the public wouldn't argue against this type of building. Rasmussen estimated that it would cost about $1 million a year for a lab to offset its emissions and stressed the importance of universities and tech companies with lab facilities to participate in early task force discussions so that they could be assured that the city "wasn't trying to kill their industry."[46] Even beyond this sector, Rasmussen emphasized the need to seek consensus across a broad range of civic actors as key to gaining the city council's full support for the ZNE goals.

Seth Federspiel, the city's net-zero-energy planner, regarded the disclosure ordinance as an essential step to implementing ZNE.[47] Several zoning changes are being considered to harmonize existing regulations with ZNE goals. One potential change would add flexibility to zoning variances for buildings that violate setback requirements by adding insulation. Another is to offer density bonuses for new buildings with exceptional energy performance.

The next step on Cambridge's road to ZNE is adding renewable energy. A project that mapped the city's solar potential determined that only 11 percent of existing buildings were optimal for solar, so most of ZNE's renewable-energy requirements would have to be met by purchasing what is known as renewable-energy credits (RECs)—new amounts of renewable energy that are fed into the grid. Federspiel undertook a study to identify the extent to which the city could move to low-carbon and renewable-energy sources for electricity and heating needs. It estimated the potential new solar capacity, if all new buildings and major retrofits were required to be solar-ready, at 3 to 5 megawatts of additional capacity yearly, with a total potential of 300 megawatts of rooftop solar. As a first step in achieving this goal, the city is pursuing a 100 percent renewable-energy supply for all municipal buildings.

Boston's Healthcare Sector: Leading on Building Efficiency with the Boston Green Ribbon Commission

In the United States, the healthcare sector accounts for about 8 percent of total GHG emissions. Hospitals consume about 2.5 times the energy of the average building, so reducing their impact yields big payoffs in reducing a city's GHG emissions. For Boston, where healthcare facilities occupy more than 30 million square feet of real estate, reducing their energy consumption is essential to achieving the city's goal of lowering emissions by 25 percent by 2020 and being carbon neutral by 2050.

Fortunately, Boston is one of a growing number of cities that has a group of corporate and institutional leaders committed to advancing climate action. The

35-member Green Ribbon Commission (GRC) was conceived in 2010 by then-mayor Tom Menino and Amos Hostetter, a trustee of the Barr Foundation, a generous local funder. They realized that to achieve Boston's climate goals, business community leaders had to be on board and bring along their own sectors, so working groups were established in healthcare, real estate, higher education, and finance. The GRC's Health Care Working Group has shown how this sector can dramatically reduce its carbon footprint and, in the process, create co-benefits for the community. Although many hospitals were already working on energy efficiency, the GRC accelerated their action and expanded their focus from energy cost savings to climate and resilience measures.

The Health Care Working Group is coordinated by Health Care Without Harm, an organization created in 1987 to work with hospitals on reducing their output of toxic substances, such as mercury, and eliminating incineration. While there was a lot of change in these areas, Bill Ravanesi, senior director of Health Care Without Harm's Health Care Green Building and Energy Program, notes that hospitals were not as eager to incorporate energy efficiency and other aspects of environmental design into all hospital expansions, something that local architects had also noticed. In September 2004, Ravanesi organized a two-day summit for 85 Boston-area hospital administrators and 20 more from other parts of the country focused on green building in hospitals. He brought in energy innovator Amory Lovins and others from the Rocky Mountain Institute to make the case for building energy efficiency, as well as trainers on other features of green buildings such as healing gardens and roof gardens. The summit proved to be the tipping point. Ravanesi says that six months later, architects were telling him that whatever he did worked: hospitals were asking them about how to incorporate these features in their buildings. The summit produced a collective action plan and one for individual hospitals to move forward on environmental stewardship and performance.[48]

In 2010, Paul Lipke, a senior energy advisor of Health Care Without Harm, convinced 20 Boston hospitals to upload their energy use data to the Energy Star Portfolio Manager so they could see how energy is being used. To comply, the hospitals use building energy management systems to monitor equipment. These systems detect and send a signal when energy demand is outside normal parameters. Lipke notes that the equipment and staffing to monitor and troubleshoot a hospital's systems is a significant investment, but one they are willing to make to save on energy costs and to be leaders in lowering emissions. When Boston passed its Building Energy Reporting and Disclosure Ordinance, which required owners of medium and large buildings to report their annual energy and water usage as of May 2017, the city's hospitals were already collecting the data.[49]

From 2011 to 2015, Boston's hospitals reduced their electricity consumption by 13.1 percent and natural gas consumption by 26.1 percent. That represents $12 million in savings that can be invested in patient care, and translates into a 20 percent reduction in GHG on the way to a goal of 33 percent by 2020.[50] Health Care Without Harm calculated that the reduction in pollution resulting from these energy conservation measures saved an estimated $1.6 million in societal costs and helped prevent hundreds of asthma incidents and other respiratory ailments. These savings are impressive given that the healthcare sector typically sees a 1.5 to 3 percent annual increase in energy use due to expansion and increased use of energy-intensive medical equipment.

Boston's GRC is a model for creating business leadership on climate action. Ravanesi credits the Barr Foundation's funding and policy guidance, concluding "It's hard to overstate the importance, not only of Barr's funding, but the willingness of its program officers to be creative in thinking what will motivate, inspire, and enable action in the private sector." Ravanesi notes that participation in the Health Care Working Group has spawned a friendly rivalry among hospitals.[51] Each has a slightly different emphasis in approach and area of leadership. Partners, a chain of 13 facilities that includes the Massachusetts General Hospital, for example, is a leader in greening its supply chain. Partners has also installed solar panels on most of its facilities and recently committed to purchasing 24 megawatts of wind energy from a wind farm in southern New Hampshire. Boston Medical Center is also a leader in purchasing renewable energy.

I asked Paul Lipke whether Boston's experience—having a foundation willing to invest millions, a committed business community, and a large world-class healthcare sector—can be replicated. Lipke says yes, absolutely, and points to innovative approaches to greening healthcare underway in Cleveland at University Hospitals and the Cleveland Clinic. He notes that the case for going green varies among cities, but that the movement is growing through Health Care Without Harm's Global Green and Healthy Hospitals initiative.[52] And foundations in other cities are on board. The Chicago-based Joyce Foundation, for example, has been an ongoing funder of Chicago's Green Healthcare Initiative.

Boston Medical Center: Building Efficiency and Renewable Generation

One of the leaders of the Health Care Working Group, Boston Medical Center (BMC), is on a path to being carbon neutral by the end of 2020. It claims to be one of the greenest hospitals in America, and that is surely true. While the Green Ribbon Commission helped to accelerate BMC's achievements, its energy agenda is in fact part of its long-standing commitment to protecting community health. The efficiency push started when BMC was on the brink of receivership in 2009–2011. Beginning in 2013, BMC launched a redesign of its campus, reducing its 2.5 million square feet by 400,000 square feet, saving about $25 million in operating expenses annually.[53] BMC has worked with the utility Eversource to complete more than nearly 40 efficiency projects, saving more than 10 million kilowatt hours of energy annually.

In another move to increase energy efficiency and resiliency, BMC extended its combined heat and power (CHP, also called cogeneration) system through which it produces its own electricity from natural gas. Like all CHP systems, it is about 35 percent more efficient than traditional fossil fuel plants because the waste heat is used for heating rather than being released into the atmosphere. The system supplies more than 41 percent of BMC's electricity and 20–25 percent of its heat load in the winter and 100 percent in the summer—a savings of about $1.5 million in electricity and heating costs per year.

BMC had been pursuing the CHP project for well over a decade, Bob Biggio, senior vice president of facilities and support services, relates, but he couldn't get it off the ground financially. So Biggio invited the Boston Public Health Commission to partner on CHP by extending the system across the street to the building where Boston's emergency telecommunications infrastructure is located. If the grid goes down, the natural gas system is unaffected, so neither the hospital nor the city's emergency systems lose electricity in a power outage. The system has the capability of starting if the complex loses power (referred to as a black start) and to operate independent of the grid (referred to as islanding).

By partnering with a city agency, BMC's cogeneration project became eligible for a grant from the Massachusetts Department of Energy Resources Community Clean Energy Resiliency Initiative. The $3.7 million grant BMC received made the project financially feasible. The expanded system went live in spring 2017.

To achieve carbon neutrality, BMC also needed renewable energy. Biggio had been working on placing a small (2–3 megawatts) solar array on a parking garage jointly owned with Boston University, which was struggling to get off the ground. A call from A Better City (ABC), a business membership organization that seeks to shape policy in land use, transportation, and energy and efficiency, put BMC on a much more ambitious solar path. ABC, funded by the Barr Foundation and with a $100,000 renewable-energy leadership prize, was looking for a way to motivate GRC members to aggregate large renewable-energy purchases. In order to accelerate the city's progress on renewable energy, the Barr Foundation funded ABC to work with GRC members to figure out the myriad financial and legal details of aggregated purchases. When ABC reached out to BMC in October 2015, Biggio was ready to move on a project larger than the garage.

BMC and several other partners put out a request for proposals for a joint purchase of 100,000 megawatt hours of renewable energy. Among the criteria were that it be a new project in New England that would be additive—taking brown power off the grid. And it had to be cost neutral. Most respondents offered wind, and the only New England project that worked financially was not new, missing the additive criterion. At this point, MIT, a nearby institution with a firm commitment to sustainability, entered the aggregation partnership and provided scale that allowed considering a solar proposal from North Carolina.

Solar developer SunEnergy 1 submitted a proposal that resulted in a 25-year power purchase agreement (PPA) for BMC, MIT, and the Post Office Square Parking Garage. Through the agreement, signed in October 2016, the partners agreed to purchase all the output (60 megawatts) for 25 years. The electrons produced in North Carolina don't actually travel to Boston. The deal works through a market for renewable-energy credits through which RECs for new renewable energy are granted. Since the energy is from a different grid operator, BMC uses an agent that sells the power back to PJM, the grid operator for that region. The bottom line is that it takes brown power (from coal) off the grid and adds solar.[54] A lot has been learned along the way, and the three partners hope this PPA will serve as a guide to other institutions and organizations for making similar large-scale investments in clean energy.[55]

Is Green Building Only for the Wealthy or the Commercial Sector?

Most of the examples cited so far focus on commercial buildings in downtowns, relatively affluent cities, or high-income urban enclaves. But how does a city ensure that housing—for people of all income strata—is green? Examples of passive-house affordable housing are emerging, for example, at Beach Green Dunes in New York City's Far Rockaway, Queens, and at the Orchards at Orenco in Hillsboro, Oregon. But isolated projects aren't enough. The challenge is to create more new affordable green housing and to retrofit existing affordable housing systematically, passing energy savings on to lower-income residents and further reducing GHG emissions.

In Sweden, Malmö's strategy is to link revitalization of troubled neighborhoods with the city's sustainability agenda. Another approach, adopted in some US cities, uses low-income housing in pilot projects to further the ZNE agenda. An architect in Philadelphia and administrators working for the state of New York are attempting to transform the affordable housing marketplace by leading with affordable passive-house construction and retrofits.

Greening Malmö's Augustenborg and Rosengård Neighborhoods

Like several of Europe's eco-districts, Malmö's Western Harbour has been criticized for leading to environmental gentrification—sustainable development that drives out low-income residents for high-end housing and related uses or develops exclusively middle-class housing in previously undeveloped or postindustrial areas.[56] In the city's defense, the second phase of Western Harbour's development required some units to have rent caps, and the third phase required 50 percent of the units to be affordable rentals. But the city planning team knew that to achieve its ambitious goals, they also had to revitalize lower-income neighborhoods.

According to the former head of the sustainable development unit at Malmö's environmental department, Trevor Graham, "The city has more existing areas in need of renovation than it does clean slates."[57] So as part of its master plan, Malmö has been redeveloping five city districts to meet sustainability standards, together totaling 312 hectares (770 acres).[58] Several of these are predominantly low-income, immigrant neighborhoods.

The city's first effort to green an existing low-income neighborhood occurred in Augustenborg, a predominantly immigrant community of 3,000 residents with unemployment rates as high as 70 percent. Integrating a wave of mostly Muslim immigrants has been a challenge for Malmö, and city planners wanted the redevelopment to contribute to this social goal. Starting in 1999, Malmö's Municipal Housing Company (MKB Housing) and other city staff initiated a participatory planning process to include neighborhood residents in redevelopment discussions.

Built during the early 1950s, Augustenborg's apartments were in need of renovation. In particular, city officials' priorities were to improve building energy efficiency and address seasonal flooding with green stormwater management. Residents proposed several ideas, such as erecting solar panels of the sort they saw elsewhere in Western Harbour. They also wanted community gardens and other types of public space. Although these suggestions were not on the city's initial agenda, all became part of the plan.

All buildings (1,800 apartments) received deep energy retrofits that reduced energy consumption by 20 percent, and one building company constructed a new passive-house apartment building to demonstrate the concept. Commenting on this successful redevelopment, Graham noted, "People notice when someone is listening, and it makes a big difference in participating in democratic society. We [planners and city officials] gained residents' trust when they saw that the redevelopment did not lead to gentrification."[59] The neighborhood's greening and densification efforts are ongoing.

These lessons in participatory planning methods and retrofitting existing neighborhoods have been adapted and applied in other Malmö neighborhoods such as Rosengård, another predominantly (80 percent) immigrant neighborhood where there has been considerable social conflict. Here Malmö sought to demonstrate how to redevelop a troubled neighborhood with a focus on environmental technology, increased social and economic integration, and better connectivity to other parts of the city. Twelve neighborhood investments identified through a participatory planning process have begun. As in Augustenborg, improving social housing was a priority. The Hilda cooperative houses 2,400 residents in a highly efficient building. An education program helps Hilda residents reduce energy use and focuses on sustainable living more generally. The city has plans for a large, high-profile urban densification project managed by a new company formed by several housing companies with property in the district and headed by the municipal housing company MKB (the equivalent of public housing in Sweden). A new railway station will also be built to improve the neighborhood's connectivity with the rest of the city.

It is too early to tell if the community change experienced in Augustenborg will take root in Rosengård, and progress is slow. From an urban development perspective, Rosengård has become a much more attractive area, but Graham noted that "there are many good initiatives in the area and many successes on an individual level, but a major structural change has yet to take place and is largely dependent on issues at a more citywide, national, and international level than the district level."[60] Integration of immigrants and refugees is a policy issue that goes beyond urban planning solutions.

Leveraging Affordable Housing to Move Markets to Passive-House Standards

Philadelphia architect Tim McDonald calls himself passive-aggressive—aggressive about the passive-house standard, that is. He is singlehandedly a major force in promoting the standard nationally for low-income housing and in all construction. In 2009, McDonald's development, design, and build firm Onion Flats, which focuses on multifamily urban housing, built a project called Thin Flats. An eight-unit condominium building in Philadelphia's gentrified Northern Liberties neighborhood, Thin Flats was the first set of LEED Platinum duplexes in the country. At the time, this building-level certification was the highest standard of environmental sustainability possible, but the team became committed to further reducing their projects' energy consumption. In 2011, McDonald and his partners set out to build a ZNE-capable housing project that was affordable and scalable. Since the completion of Thin Flats in 2009, they had been training in passive-house energy-efficiency standards. And in 2012, they completed Belfield Townhomes, the first certified passive-house building in Pennsylvania, designed for very-low-income families. Located in North Philadelphia, Belfield Townhomes was commissioned by Raise of Hope, a nonprofit organization that helps homeless people find affordable, permanent housing. With funding from the federal Department of Housing and Urban Development and the city, Belfield Townhomes won a local American Institute of Architects (AIA) award and received the 2014 International Passive House Award from the Passivhaus Institut in Darmstadt, Germany.

How did they do it? McDonald described the components: an efficient heating system, superinsulation, thermal-bridge-free construction, and superior air tightness.[61] The project was Onion Flats' opportunity to design its first passive-house building; more important was the chance to develop an affordable and scalable building *system* that could be replicated for many building types and sites.

McDonald and his team also developed innovations that lowered construction costs. They chose a modular construction system, which allowed them to construct all three floors of each building in a climate-controlled factory. All fixtures and finishes were installed prior to delivering them to the site, allowing the Onion Flats team to build the project from foundation to certificate of occupancy in three months.

The solar panels on each the three Belfield Townhomes produce five kilowatts of energy, and the buildings are seven to 10 times more airtight than standard construction. Even fitted with energy-efficient appliances, the cost was about the same as that of traditional low-income construction in the Philadelphia area— $129 per square foot.

Taking Success in Philadelphia across Pennsylvania

McDonald's accomplishments in Philadelphia inspired him to pursue a project through Temple University to transform the energy-efficiency standards for affordable housing across Pennsylvania. To do that, he would have to convince the Pennsylvania Housing Finance Agency (PHFA), the agency responsible for all federal Low-Income Housing Tax Credit (LIHTC) funding, to prioritize the passive-house standard in funding projects.

In spring 2014, McDonald gathered a group of affordable housing developers, representatives from Philadelphia's Office of Sustainability, the state's Housing

Authority, the Mayor's Offices in Philadelphia and Pittsburgh, and passive-house architects, designers, and builders from Harrisburg. The group proposed to PHFA that it launch a project demonstrating that passive-house construction, design, and building standards can be net-zero-energy capable by 2030.

PHFA was already looking to raise the bar on energy efficiency; developers had been surpassing their standards for years. It welcomed the challenge, and within four months the agency introduced language into its 2015 Qualified Allocation Plan that offered developers coveted 9 percent LIHTC funding if they agreed to design and construct their projects to meet the passive-house standard. To do this, they created a new passive-house category in the highly competitive point-based LIHTC application system and made it worth 10 points. Because PHFA funds only 25 percent of all project applications each year (based primarily on achieving the most points), developers' interest in earning these points was enormous. PHFA has been funding more passive-house projects since then. To date, 900-plus affordable housing units have been built, the largest concentration of passive-house/net-zero-energy-capable dwelling units in the country.

McDonald found that many other state housing finance agencies (HFAs) used the same competitive LIHTC funding process to further state goals such as energy efficiency. This reality, combined with the success of the first two rounds of funding in Pennsylvania, led McDonald to approach other states to adopt the passive-house model. As of early 2017, New York, New Jersey, Washington, DC, Rhode Island, Connecticut, New Hampshire, Ohio, Illinois, Idaho, and South Dakota HFAs have included passive-house incentives in their funding structures, and 36 additional HFAs are considering adopting it.

New York State Adopts the Dutch Energiesprong Standard for RetrofitNY

New York has applied a similar strategy of starting with low-income multifamily housing to transform the market for retrofitting existing housing to passive-house or other high performance standards. An aggressive state energy plan approved in 2015 calls for achieving a 40 percent reduction in GHG emissions from 1990 levels, a 23 percent reduction in building energy consumption from 2012 levels, and obtaining half the state's energy from renewable sources by 2030. Achieving the building-efficiency goals requires deep retrofits in existing buildings; doing them efficiently in what are mostly occupied structures has proven to be the most challenging aspect of plan implementation.

New York's approach is adapted from Energiesprong (Energy Leap), a Dutch initiative launched in 2010. This government-funded, nonprofit program has stimulated national adoption of ZNE retrofitting of Dutch public housing. The idea is to quickly transform the market to ZNE rather than to pursue the incremental change that results from pushing prevailing processes and procedures to their limit. The process uses a design competition whose energy standard for proposals gets more ambitious each year. Additional criteria include design attractiveness, guaranteed energy performance, limited disruption to tenants, and cost effectiveness.

In the pilot round in 2010, renovations to two-story row houses achieved a 50 percent energy-efficiency improvement at a cost of $145,000 each. As of 2017, builders had achieved ZNE in retrofits at 40 percent of the cost of the pilot with tenants in place—and in less than a week. They do it by prefabricating an efficient building exoskeleton, including a roof with solar panels, off-site. It takes only a week to bolt the new exterior onto the building and make interior modifications. In its first six years, the competition retrofitted 1,000 units, with another 9,000 lined up and soft commitments for 100,000 more. The cost of the retrofits for the property owner is financed from the energy savings. Noting its success, in 2016 the European Commission allocated €5.4 million in grant funding to expand the program in the Netherlands, France, and the United Kingdom. In 2019, Energiesprong won the innovation award given during the European Union Sustainable Energy Week.

The RetrofitNY program is part of New York's Reforming the Energy Vision (REV), a comprehensive strategy to transform the state's energy system. REV is supported by a $5 billion, 10-year Clean Energy Fund, administered by the New York State Energy Research and Development Authority, whose funding comes from a systems benefit charge, a surcharge on utility bills. Like Energiesprong, RetrofitNY uses design competitions to accelerate innovation by industry to develop and test solutions for deep renovations that can then be adopted across the housing market. It also addresses financial, regulatory, and supply-chain barriers to achieving the energy goals. The first round of competition, announced in 2016, focused on affordable multifamily units of four or more floors. The approach is expected to save housing agencies money by integrating the deep retrofits into a building's planned major renovation cycles and by lowering ongoing maintenance costs. By 2017, all of the state's major housing agencies were participating in RetrofitNY because they recognized that it allows them to combine goals of comfort, health, and aesthetics with energy efficiency at a lower cost than that of the traditional fix-as-needed approach. In June 2018, NYSERDA awarded $30 million to build affordable multi-family housing that will seek to achieve near net-zero energy.

The significance of RetrofitNY is that it moved the state away from a subsidy-based approach to one that uses all the levers at government's disposal to coordinate the elements necessary to develop a new large-scale, market-based process. As Greg Hale, a senior adviser in the New York Governor's Office of Energy and Finance, explained:

> Traditionally, the clean-energy industry has been built around subsidies, which isn't sustainable. We anticipate that some subsidies will be needed to cover the incremental cost of RetrofitNY's first few prototype projects. But as industry learns from the initial installations and begins to achieve scale, we expect to see a steep cost-reduction curve, similar to the Dutch experience, after which the state will not have to go back to ratepayers year after year to raise additional funding to subsidize these deep energy retrofits.[62]

California: Moving to ZNE Statewide

Given California's climate leadership, it is no surprise that more than half of the nation's 3,500-plus net-zero buildings are located there. California also leads the nation in the number of schools that are being retrofitted to ZNE standards. Starting with the Global Warming Solutions Act of 2006 under then-governor Arnold Schwarzenegger, the state has increased its climate goals, most recently in January 2015, when Governor Jerry Brown set an ambitious goal to generate 50 percent of the state's electricity from renewable energy by 2050. In July 2014, Governor Brown allocated $75 million in cap-and-trade proceeds for weatherization and renewable energy. A portion of these funds will assist in energy-efficiency and renewable-energy projects in disadvantaged communities' low-income housing units. Related legislation, effective in 2017, required that all new residential construction be ZNE by 2020. The law also addressed retrofitting for existing construction, requiring that all new and half of existing state-owned buildings be ZNE by 2025 and that commercial buildings get there by 2030. The standards reduce building energy use by an average of 28 percent over the preexisting code and eliminate 160,000 tons of GHG emissions annually.[63]

California's Title 24 Building Energy Efficiency Standards, effective in 2014, mandate the use of particular technologies to achieve its ZNE goals. One requirement is automated daylighting in which sensors measure the amount of natural light available and automatically adjust artificial lighting. Another requirement for nonresidential buildings over 10,000 square feet is automated demand-response lighting systems that start preprogrammed reductions of at least 15 percent when they receive signals that the electricity grid is approaching peak demand. Utilities are required to articulate strategies for increasing renewables and for reducing peak demand using energy automation technologies such as those demonstrated in FortZED. As implementation advances, the California Legislative Analyst's Office has raised concerns about ZNE costs for state buildings and has recommended cost-benefit analyses for different building types to compare outcomes, especially to the state's carbon tax.[64] In 2018, the New Buildings Institute published a *ZNE Project Guide for State Buildings* to facilitate decision making. [65]

The Politics of Building-Efficiency Policy: City, State, and National

Cities have been able to do a lot as incubators and test beds of climate action, but supportive policies at the state and national levels could make the difference in quickly transforming building standards to those that achieve high levels of energy efficiency. European cities have this support in two EU-wide measures: the 2010 European Energy Performance of Buildings Directive (updated in 2017) and the 2012 Energy Efficiency Directive. Both directives accelerated progress in European cities toward nearly ZNE on new construction (about 15 kWh per square meter per year).

At the state level, California's ZNE policy is interconnected with climate, energy efficiency, and renewable-energy policies—quickly moving the state to leadership in ZNE construction and in the technologies that make it possible. New York State's policies are transforming the housing construction market toward passive house. In contrast, states such as North Carolina, with a low-bar state code and prohibitions on cities adopting codes stricter than that of the state, limit cities to using voluntary efforts to engage people in conserving energy. But to reach 80 × 50 goals, behavioral approaches need to be linked to stronger regulation and market transformation.

On the federal level, the US government has played a significant role through issuing appliance standards. Although the McKinsey Global Institute estimates that existing technologies could reduce US carbon emissions significantly, even more efficient heating and cooling systems are needed to achieve ZNE or passive-house standards. To that end, the US DOE issued standards for rooftop air conditioners, commercial furnaces, and heat pumps at the end of 2015 that were unprecedented in their ambition. The DOE estimated at the time that the standards could save 1.7 trillion kilowatt hours of energy and as much as $50 billion in energy costs for businesses over 30 years. Steven Nadel, executive director of the American Council for an Energy-Efficient Economy, said at the time, "These standards are a game-changer for the commercial sector. Industry and advocates worked closely together to help produce the biggest energy savings standards in U.S. history."[66] Federal efficiency regulations create demand for the most efficient building systems, quickly transforming the market.

Government entities at all levels are using various carrots and sticks to bring the construction industry on board with ZNE and passive-house construction practices. Malmö's Building/Living Dialogue became a learning network for construction companies to develop expertise in effective technologies and methods to meet high standards in a cost-effective manner. Participation has grown Malmö companies' businesses; some of them have gone on to build throughout Sweden as well as in other countries. Similarly, the government-led Energiesprong has created a competitive environment in the Netherlands that has helped builders learn how to rehab buildings to the passive-house standard and has been expanded to other countries. As a result of architect Tim McDonald's success in getting Pennsylvania's state housing agency to amend its competitive low-income housing development funding applications, at least 15 other states are giving builders financial incentives to use new passive-house construction. And RetrofitNY is doing the same in the rehab market, following the Dutch approach.

Given the multiplicity of actors who have a role in creating enforceable green building standards in cities, it is not surprising that competing interests can collide, slowing down greenovation's progress. In some cities, there is political and business resistance to building disclosure requirements and tough building-efficiency regulations, particularly if noncompliance carries penalties. City programs or voluntary business collaborations that encourage building owners to engage in collective problem-solving can change attitudes. I've noted that Seattle's 2030 District building owners are working together to figure out ways to act in unison on energy and water efficiency and also to work with tenants with green leases. If the private-sector voice that 2030 District members provide is essential in a city known for its commitment to sustainable development, it is even more critical in cities with less commitment to climate action. Brett Phillips, then a project manager for one of the banks involved, speaking about the commitment of Envision Charlotte's participating banks, said, "We compete fiercely for financial services work, but we are devoted to transparent sharing of best practices to achieve energy and water savings in our properties."[67] Across the United States, these voluntary business collaborations are creating support for cities' building energy-efficiency policies.

In some cities, builders' resistance to disclosure about meeting environmental requirements raises the question of how to devise accountability for achieving building-efficiency goals. Who is responsible? Is it the city or the developer? In Malmö, the city sets the performance standard and leaves it up to the builder to figure out how to achieve it. That has not been the norm in US cities. In Seattle, a city known for its climate leadership, builders and building owners are resistant to being held accountable for meeting code requirements. While Seattle's energy code defines an alternative compliance pathway that targets building performance, developers are reluctant to use it because when they do, they have to wait at least a year for third-party verification of the building's performance, and they may not be involved with the building that long. Even so, if the building does not perform to standard, the developer is required to fix the problem. (Developers who will not ultimately own or manage the building are particularly hesitant to use this pathway, given that much of a building's performance depends upon its operation by others.) Zachary Hart, director of policy at the AIA, notes that "this issue of how to apportion compliance correctly is significant, yet there's currently no consensus between government and business about the right way to do it."[68]

Until recently, energy policy in the United States has rarely fallen within the purview of cities. Unless a city ran its own utility, issues related to energy were in the private arena—and energy efficiency and emissions reduction have not been of much interest to private utilities. Times have changed. We see more city governments, including those covered here, experimenting with different approaches. Still, there is no single way that works for all cities. One game-changing effort sponsored by the Bloomberg and Kresge Foundations and operated by the Institute for Market Transformation and the National Resources Defense Council has recognized that US cities are only now learning how they can be most effective in this arena. Called the City Energy Project (CEP), it has engaged 20 cities in developing new models of action on the municipal level. Among those cities are Fort Collins, Los Angeles, and Boston. Through the CEP, cities are learning what works best for them and are now developing new models and approaches to energy efficiency in their localities. This knowledge and the local experiences generated by the project are being shared from city to city.

Even before it was involved with the CEP, Fort Collins reorganized its planning department to combine the environmental, economic, and equity offices in 2012. A sustainability advisory board comprising senior staff from all city departments focuses on embedding sustainability into all departments. Bruce Hendee, former chief sustainability officer for Fort Collins, says that city staff from the city manager on down think of the city as a living lab for innovation.

According to Hilary Firestone, Los Angeles had to consider myriad factors in deciding the most effective way to implement ZNE building standards, such as how to support building owners, which departments should oversee implementation and enforcement, and whether they ought to be reorganized into a new agency. While the Department of Building and Safety traditionally would be in the lead, other relevant government entities now include Water and Power,

General Services (for city-owned buildings), the Mayor's Office, and Los Angeles County. In January 2015, the Mayor's Office held a workshop that began a five-month dialogue among experts from all relevant arenas to share ideas about these and other aspects of the program. The results of the collaborative process became the basis for a ZNE building-efficiency plan that was approved by the city council in fall 2015.

To achieve the goals of the Paris Agreement on climate change and go beyond them, greenovating cities must lead successful efforts to reduce energy use and emissions from buildings. As we have seen, such leadership involves helping to change the behavior of building occupants and managers, getting consensus on regulation among builders, and, ultimately, transforming markets. Above all, greenovation leadership must balance many competing interests and bring all the players to the table. Only then can cities execute effective building- and district-scale innovations, along with other climate action policies that will be explored in the next chapters.

BEYOND THE BUILDING

District Heating and Cooling

District energy is to heating and cooling buildings what public transit is to moving people.

—Climate Toronto

IMAGINE PRODUCING ENERGY IN a way that practically doubles its efficiency. That is exactly what can be achieved by district heating and cooling systems with combined heat and power (CHP). District heating systems typically use a central plant that converts fuel (usually natural gas) into electricity. The thermal energy from the electricity generation (steam or hot water) is then delivered to nearby buildings through an underground piping network that delivers heat and domestic hot water.

Now imagine a building that occupies half a city block and is essentially a giant ice cube. There's one in Austin, Texas. It uses off-peak electricity to make and store large volumes of ice at night and pumps ultrachilled water through a district cooling network to downtown buildings during the day, reducing peak afternoon electricity demand for air conditioning. Those are the basics of ice-storage district cooling. Many systems also produce and store chilled water during off-peak hours to avoid high-cost electricity in the afternoon. Some district cooling systems use rivers, lakes, or the ocean to provide a renewable source of cooling to their buildings. In addition to the cost and space savings, district cooling systems displace building chillers that use refrigerants and cooling towers, reducing operating and maintenance costs.

The community scale of a district energy network creates opportunities to deploy clean, local energy resources that can reduce greenhouse gas emissions and increase energy security.[1] District energy systems can be designed for fuel flexibility, using a variety of fuels, depending on supply, price, and availability. Systems can use geothermal heat, incinerated waste, waste heat from industrial processes, recovered heat from sewers, landfill gas, or biomass for heating, and geothermal pipe, lakes, or the ocean for cooling.

In this chapter I explain the technology behind district heating and cooling, which has the potential to be used throughout the world, and examine how it can be more widely deployed in North America. I explore the different approaches to district energy employed in Copenhagen, London, and Vancouver. We then examine Austin's ice-cooled system and Toronto's deep-lake cooling. The cases illustrate different regulatory barriers, funding and ownership models (municipal vs. private utilities), and technologies. We see that district energy, at its best, is integrated with land use, transportation, community development, and energy planning. We end with a discussion of the policy needed at the regional, national, and local levels for broader implementation of both technologies.

Greenovation with an Old Technology

Traditional electricity power plants are between 30 and 40 percent efficient, meaning that about two-thirds of the energy produced is wasted because the surplus heat is simply dumped into the local environment. Employing CHP with district energy, by contrast, converts up to 90 percent of the fuel into useful energy by distributing steam or water through insulated underground pipes (figure 3.1).[2] The district energy heating or cooling network typically includes separate supply and return loops to optimize and manage the distribution of thermal energy. The water returns to the plant and recirculates in a closed-loop system.[3] In essence, one fuel produces two useful forms of energy—power and heat.

Across North America, hundreds of district heating systems in cities and campuses already distribute steam. Sometimes referred to as first-generation district heating, these systems continue to supply major city networks in New York City, Philadelphia, Boston, Denver, and hundreds of large institutional areas. Robert Thornton, CEO of the International District Energy Association, estimates that almost 80 percent of the 840-plus district heating systems in the United States are located on college campuses, in large airports, and in healthcare institutions—where a reliable energy supply is needed for critical uses in patient care and research. For example, in Boston the Medical Area Total Energy Plant provides

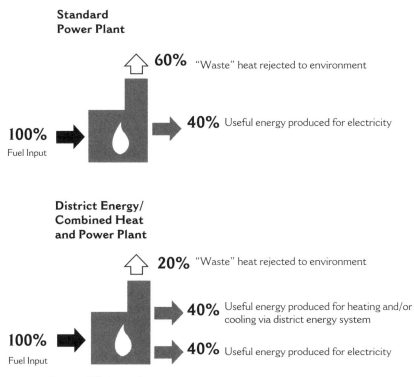

Standard Power Plant

60% "Waste" heat rejected to environment

40% Useful energy produced for electricity

100%
Fuel Input

District Energy/ Combined Heat and Power Plant

20% "Waste" heat rejected to environment

40% Useful energy produced for heating and/or cooling via district energy system

100%
Fuel Input

40% Useful energy produced for electricity

Figure 3.1 Energy-Efficiency Comparisons
Source: Adapted from International District Energy Association illustrations with permission.

steam, chilled water, and electricity to more than nine million square feet of space in the Longwood Medical and Academic Area.

Second-generation systems, built predominantly from the 1930s to the 1970s, often use pressurized, higher-temperature hot water. Third-generation systems, which have been widely deployed across Scandinavia since the 1970s, use pressurized water, but under lower temperatures, and use prefabricated piping.[4] There is an ongoing shift to "fourth generation" district energy that integrates with smart thermal grids, including those powered by renewable energy, that can use heat from different sources and store heat during times of low demand.[5]

One of the key advantages of community-scale CHP district energy is that connected customers avoid the capital, maintenance, and operating costs of installing individual boilers and furnaces, while also preserving space.[6] Additionally, locating generating sources closer to users can enhance the resiliency and reliability of the power supply, reducing the risk of interruption during severe-weather events, a problem that commonly afflicts utility-scale grid-based systems.

Efficiencies can also be derived from combining CHP with thermal storage during off-peak times, preserving heat for peak demand use. In Helsinki, the heat energy produced in the Vuosaari CHP plant is used to heat water that is stored overnight in a large tank at 100 degrees centigrade (212 Fahrenheit). When demand peaks in the morning as people prepare for the day and in the late afternoon when they return home, the tank ensures an adequate supply of hot water.[7]

District cooling delivers chilled water to buildings through a system of pipes in a closed loop (figure 3.2). Chilled water enters buildings at 36–40 degrees and is returned at 55–60 degrees, which is chilled again and sent back out to the body of water. Some systems rely on bodies of water as a natural cooling resource. A chiller is not needed if the water source is 42 degrees or less, so these simple systems require less energy.

Systems without a source of cool water use electricity to make ice or chilled water. These thermal storage systems work in two ways—by cooling water at night when electricity demand and prices are low and dispatching the water during the day or by making ice at night and dispatching a daytime ice slurry. Ice systems have higher initial upfront capital and operating costs but are 16–18 times denser than water systems, so they are a better choice than chilled-water systems where land is at a premium.

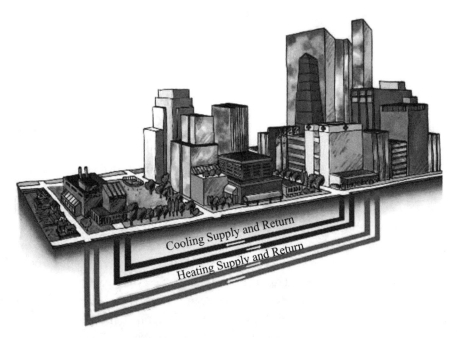

Figure 3.2 District Heating and Cooling
Source: Adapted from International District Energy Association illustrations with permission.

District cooling is becoming more widespread. Stockholm's district cooling system was developed in 1992 and now cools about seven million square meters of space. There are now at least 30 plants in Sweden. Using seawater and geothermal sources, Helsinki expanded into district cooling in 1998, and now has the third largest system in Europe. With the system reducing electricity demand for cooling by almost 90 percent, the city aims to make the district system its primary form of cooling.

In the United States, district cooling systems began popping up in the 1990s with the phaseout of ozone-layer-harming chlorofluorocarbons, mandated under the 1990 amendments to the Clean Air Act. During this period, systems were developed in Atlantic City, Denver, Houston, Portland, and Phoenix; today, the largest district cooling system in North America is in Chicago. In place since 1999, it relies on ice storage to cool 110 buildings in the Loop. Although I primarily address Europe and North America, the most rapid expansion of district cooling has taken place in the United Arab Emirates, where district cooling companies are assessing the growth potential of providing district cooling in Indian cities. China's market is expanding rapidly as well. In its twelfth five-year plan (2011–2015) China developed 1,000 distributed energy projects—heating and cooling—and 10 demonstration districts.[8]

A shift toward fourth-generation systems is now underway, particularly in Europe. Based on existing systems, these "smart" systems use digital technology to combine and coordinate electricity, thermal, and gas grids to identify synergies among them to achieve high levels of system efficiency.[9] Heat Roadmap Europe, a collaborative of 14 EU nations and a host of research universities, municipalities, and businesses, calls for installing fourth-generation district energy systems that can integrate with future renewable-energy systems.[10] They estimate that doing so can expand district energy from 13 percent of Europe's energy supply now to 50 percent by 2050. Further, they project that deploying industrial and other waste heat in district heating networks could replace all the natural gas currently used in the EU. Finally, they recommend connecting renewable energy to thermal storage, which is a thousand times less expensive than battery storage. By combining old technologies such as recycled steam with new ones such as renewable energy and the smart grid, district energy systems are contributing to impressive reductions in GHG emissions.

If It's So Great, Why Isn't It Everywhere?

Because district energy systems are capital-intensive investments, speculative real estate developers seeking short-term returns are typically not inclined to build these networks. It is also hard to make the case for investment when building operators are often unable to estimate the total cost of producing a unit of cooling or heating under varying load conditions.[11] For these reasons, institutions with longer-term investment horizons, patient capital, and comprehensive ownership models have been the customary owners and operators of district energy systems.

Not surprisingly, there has been little interest in developing a regulatory or policy framework to facilitate deployment of district energy systems in the United States. Senators Bernie Sanders (IN-VT) and Jeff Merkley (D-OR) introduced the Thermal Energy Efficiency Act of 2009, which set a national goal of meeting at least 20 percent of total US electrical power capacity with CHP/district energy by 2030, but the legislation never made it out of committee. A year later, Minnesota congresswoman Betty McCollum, Senator Al Franken (D-MN), and Senator Roy Blount (R-MO) sponsored House and Senate versions of the Thermal Renewable Energy and Efficiency Act (TREEA) to provide funding to support public-sector development of district energy and CHP systems. President Obama's stimulus package, the American Recovery and Reinvestment Act, initially included $1.6 billion in funding for the TREEA district energy package, but the provision was eliminated during conference committee negotiations. Ultimately, the US Department of Energy established a CHP/district energy grant program of $156 million. The program attracted more than $3.9 billion in project proposals and was oversubscribed by 25 to 1, but was not expanded beyond the initial recovery act funding.

In the current political environment under President Trump, federal support for district energy is highly unlikely. A few states and cities specify CHP/district energy (DE) in their renewable portfolio standards or climate action plans. US cities are only just now beginning to do energy planning; as more cities establish goals for renewable energy, CHP/DE should become an attractive goal for reducing energy consumption. But for the most part, policy is controlled at the state level and includes establishing standards for CHP networks and connecting them to the grid, and offering incentives and other supportive policies. Using these criteria, only four states stand out in an assessment by the American Council for an Energy Efficient Economy: California, Maryland, Massachusetts, and Rhode Island.[12]

For example, the Massachusetts Alternative Energy Portfolio Standard, established in 2008, counts recovered waste heat from CHP as an energy-efficiency measure eligible for funding by utilities, which has stimulated CHP/district energy deployment across the Commonwealth. A qualifying CHP unit can receive credits that can be sold to the utilities to meet alternative portfolio standard compliance obligations. Credits are based on a formula that calculates the energy (and hence GHG) savings associated with CHP versus meeting the electric demand from the grid and thermal demand with a boiler. This performance-based incentive provides additional revenue throughout the years of operation.

In Canada, energy policy is mostly left to the provinces. British Columbia's Energy Plan: A Vision for Clean Energy Leadership, along with its 2016 Climate Leadership Plan, sets goals for renewable-energy adoption and GHG emissions reductions (80 percent below 2007 levels by 2050) that support expansion of district energy. The province provides funding for cities and towns to conduct feasibility studies on developing or expanding district energy systems and capital incentives for implementation of the system. The most advanced provinces, British Columbia and Ontario, have established regulatory frameworks to encourage district energy. But as we'll see later in the chapter, city efforts to expand district energy systems can get complicated.

Compared with North America, there is greater market share for district heating in Europe due to higher energy costs and government policy such as fuel tariffs, carbon trading, feed-in tariffs, subsidy programs, and EU mandates. A 2012 EU directive on energy efficiency requires member states to assess the potential of CHP/district heating and cooling and to use the assessments to drive expansion.[13] This commitment was furthered by the 2016 EU Strategy on Heating and Cooling, which promotes CHP/DE to reduce building energy use and GHG emissions.[14] Today, CHP accounts for about 12 percent of electricity produced and 15.2 percent of heat supplied in the European Union. Individual countries vary widely. Germany leads, with 70 percent of heating and 28 percent of electricity produced by CHP.[15] In Denmark, 65 percent of the population is served by district heating, with Finland and Sweden serving 50 and 55 percent, respectively.[16]

In both Europe and North America, older systems have relied on fossil fuels. As we will see, they often use several sources of energy, some of which are renewable. The goal is to greenovate—to expand CHP/district energy, transition existing systems away from fossil fuels, and lay the groundwork for fourth-generation systems that use smart technology.

The Role of Cities in District Heating and Cooling

The 2015 United Nations Environmental Program report *District Energy in Cities* identifies four roles for local governments in promoting district energy/CHP: setting targets for development and expansion; energy planning and mapping; policies to encourage or require building owners to connect to district systems; and waste-to-energy mandates.[17] As we will see, cities have different levers for enacting these and other regulations, depending on their home countries' policies.[18]

In this section, we will look at three cities that have made great progress in developing district energy systems. Copenhagen, which has connected close to 100 percent of its buildings to CHP/district heating, is the city others look to replicate. It is also well on the way to converting entirely to renewable fuels for its systems. Both London and Vancouver adapted Copenhagen's energy mapping and urban planning strategies to build their own more comprehensive systems. London's King's Cross redevelopment further illustrates how district energy can facilitate neighborhood revitalization.

To understand how Copenhagen became the district energy system gold standard, we must first dive into Denmark's energy policy development, which made its capital city's success possible. The oil crisis of the 1970s led Denmark and its sister Nordic countries—Finland, Iceland, and Sweden—to reduce reliance on imported fossil fuels and to drive for more energy efficiency and renewables in district heating. Denmark, which at the time relied on imported oil for 90 percent of its energy, established the Danish Energy Agency in 1976 and over the next few years planned to reduce consumption. The 1979 Heat Supply Act required Danish municipalities to develop energy maps and district heating development plans and made it mandatory for households to connect to district heating networks. The Danish government provided investment subsidies and tax exemptions to support the development of CHP/district heating networks through the 1990s. Finally, the fuel tax for CHP systems was made lower than that for other electricity plants.[19]

These policies have made Denmark a world leader in CHP/DH.[20] District systems cover two-thirds of heating and cooling in Denmark. Almost half (48 percent) of the heating and cooling systems are powered by renewable energy (mostly imported biomass).[21] Over time, Denmark has continued to develop more renewable systems using waste-to-energy, biomass, offshore wind, and even large-scale solar thermal projects. District heating is essential to Denmark's goal, established in 2012, to obtain all its energy from renewable sources by 2050.

To increase adoption of district heating, the Danish Energy Agency divided the country into heat districts and identified the most efficient options for providing heat in each. Municipalities were given considerable latitude in developing their systems and the fuels they use. They were required, however, to coordinate plans with nearby municipalities.[22] Municipalities also mapped their heat demand and projected future need and options for meeting it in binding heat plans.[23] After this planning exercise, municipalities used the regional and local maps to create zones for district heating development and to complete cost assessments of development over 20 years. An important aspect of the Danish approach is that decisions about development and expansion of district heating systems must be based on their full socioeconomic benefit—and not only on the profitability of a particular company.[24]

National support has spawned innovation in finding sources of waste heat to fuel district heating/CHP systems. Waste heat is extracted from factories, incinerators, transport systems, solar thermal energy plants, and wind turbines. Coal plants are being replaced with natural gas, and natural gas will be replaced with renewables over time. As noted by Lars Christian Lilleholt, Danish minister of energy, utilities, and climate, CHP/DH has made it possible for Denmark to increase energy efficiency, decouple energy consumption from economic growth, and reduce carbon emissions.[25]

Copenhagen Leads the Way

With this level of long-standing national policy support, Copenhagen's district energy system is the model system many cities are following. Copenhagen's original district heating system, started in 1903, was a steam system powered by a waste incinerator. A more modern regional district heating/CHP system was established in 1984 by five mayors in the region. The speed of expansion and improvement of the network has been impressive. The metropolitan network, which now serves 25 municipalities, is owned and operated by Metropolitan Copenhagen Heating Transmission and an affiliated company. It comprises four CHP plants, three waste incinerators, and more than 50 boiler plants used for peak loads, which together provide heat to 98 percent of the district heating zones (figure 3.3). The network can switch plants and fuels to provide energy at the lowest cost at any given time. It has replaced all first-generation steam and almost completely switched from coal to natural gas, waste heat from incineration plants, and biofuels. By eliminating the use of 203,000 tons of oil, it reduces carbon emissions by 665,000 tons annually.[26]

The next step in Copenhagen's process was to decarbonize the system. Copenhagen's 2013 Climate Plan set a goal of making all district heating and cooling carbon neutral by 2025. As of 2016, Copenhagen prohibited oil-fired furnaces (existing or new) in areas served by district heating networks. But even before this transition is complete, district heating and cooling are cheaper than individual gas boilers or heat pumps, which is why there is little objection to the requirement to connect to the system. Smart urban planning has paved the way for expansion of Copenhagen's system, and it is on course to continue with dense urban development planned around district heating networks.

Following the lead of Copenhagen, cities throughout Denmark have expanded district heating. A notable conversion of a CHP plant from coal to solar with

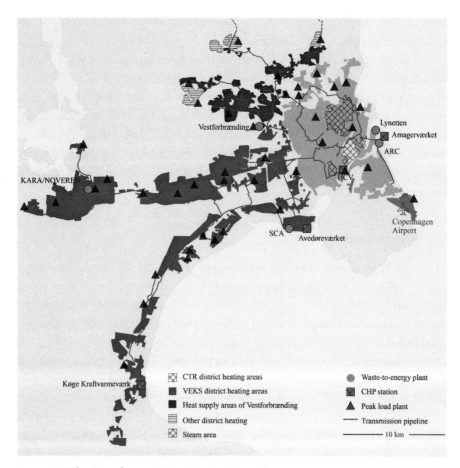

Figure 3.3 The Copenhagen District Heating Network
Source: Ramboll 2015.

thermal storage occurred in the small town of Dronninglund. When the plant's boiler gave out, it was replaced with solar, supplemented by natural gas in winter months. Almost 3,000 solar panels power the system, which stores power as heat in what is literally a thermos—a lined and lidded water basin, which is used to store heat produced during summer months. The system provides about half of total heat from May to October, which is supplemented with natural gas and bio oil (oil produced from plant matter) the rest of the year.[27]

The approach developed for the Dronninglund plant emerged from the research, development, and innovation projects that are ongoing among a consortium of district heating companies, the Danish District Heating Association, universities, and other research centers. Other innovations using thermal storage and even turning moisture into district heating have recently been developed.[28]

By expanding district heating throughout the country, Denmark has created a support system of world-class suppliers and engineering firms that allow for efficient planning, installation, and maintenance of networks. The Danish District Heating Association promotes cooperation and knowledge exchange that keeps all stakeholders on the cutting edge of practice.[29]

Copenhagen has also invested in district cooling, which is 40 percent cheaper than conventional systems in individual buildings and produces 70 percent fewer CO_2 emissions.[30] The Danish District Cooling Act of 2008 enables municipalities with ownership interest in district heating companies to add district cooling. Copenhagen Energy, anticipating the legislation, built the country's first district cooling plant in a former power station in the central city. This flexible and energy-efficient plant uses water from the city's harbor when it is sufficiently cold and otherwise relies on surplus heat from power plants to generate cooling.

The case of Copenhagen illuminates the potential scale of worldwide reduction in GHG emissions that could be achieved from district cooling. The buildings around the city's central square, Kongens Nytorv, reduced emissions by 66 percent, and annual sulfur dioxide and nitrous oxide by 62 and 69 percent, respectively, compared with their former emissions when equipped with air conditioners.[31]

A long-term national policy framework, smart urban planning (land use, energy mapping, and integrating CHP into planned dense development), tax incentives, and research collaboratives have allowed CHP with district heating and cooling to proliferate in Copenhagen and throughout Denmark. All elements are replicable if the political will exists, although a key aspect of Copenhagen's network is that 13 of the 24 DH companies are municipally owned. Over time, the energy industry in Denmark has become democratized with municipal and cooperative ownership of utility systems. This means that profit is not a driver. Rather, the emphasis is on reducing costs and CO_2 emissions and improving service quality, whereas in North America, systems must be justified on market principles.

Vancouver

Blessed with carbon-free hydropower for electricity and a mild climate, Vancouver's per capita GHG emissions are the third lowest globally. Since 2011, the city has been acting on an aggressive Greenest City Action Plan that seeks to reduce GHG emissions 80 percent below 2007 levels by 2050. Given that buildings contribute 56 percent of the city's emissions and 45 percent of its total energy demand, reducing the energy required to heat them is a major focus.

District energy fueled by renewable sources is a cornerstone of the plan, and it is further articulated in a 2012 Neighborhood Energy Strategy. The city has the advantage of an extensive district energy system built out in the 1960s to serve 210 buildings in its downtown, totaling more than 40 million square feet. Part of the city's strategy is to expand this system and convert it to low-carbon fuels. Vancouver's approach integrates land-use, transportation, and energy planning.

Another asset upon which the city is building is the city-owned Neighborhood Energy Utility system, opened in 2010 to serve the Southeast False Creek Olympic Village. Here Vancouver pioneered an innovation using wastewater heat for a district heating network. It works by capturing heat from municipal liquid waste using a heat pump to increase the temperature to the level needed for space and hot-water heating. The energy center is nestled inconspicuously under a bridge in the neighborhood, but its smokestack "fingers" are quite visible, topped with LED lights that indicate how much power is being used (figure 3.4). This unique feature keeps awareness of energy consumption in the public eye. Although it took five years and $32 million to plan and build, Southeast False Creek's highly replicable system has lower upfront costs than most other types of renewable energy.[32]

After the 2010 Winter Olympics, Southeast False Creek was built out as an "eco-neighborhood" (sometimes referred to as an eco-district) of about 16,000 people. It

Figure 3.4 Vancouver's Neighborhood Energy Utility System
Source: City of Vancouver

integrates several aspects of Vancouver's sustainability plan—high-density, mixed-use, mixed-income development, and energy-efficient construction. (Canada's first ZNE multifamily building is here.) The Neighborhood Energy Utility provides the entire area's annual heat and hot-water energy requirements, which reduces GHG emissions from connected buildings by more than 60 percent.[33] The system has expanded by 300 percent since 2010, and now serves about five million square feet of buildings, projected to grow to more than eight million square feet by 2022. The buildout cost of $31 million (US dollars), funded by city-raised debt, and all future capital and operating costs are recovered through utility customer rates.

The success of the publicly owned Neighborhood Energy Utility demonstrated that district heating was economically viable and led Vancouver planners to develop the Neighborhood Energy Strategy for expanding the downtown system and switching from natural gas to wood waste. To promote citywide expansion of district energy, city staff first put supporting policy into place. In particular, city policy requires real estate developments of two acres or more to evaluate the feasibility of utilizing a low-carbon-energy system in their rezoning applications. Also, all rezoning projects must be district-energy compatible. And there are other city enabling tools to support the establishment of low-carbon-energy systems. The approach follows Copenhagen's strategy of decarbonizing the system's energy source and slowly transitioning from steam to hot water while expanding the system.

Not So Fast . . . . . .

The regulatory framework established by the provincial government of British Columbia, however, is slowing Vancouver's progress. Consider the experience of Ian Gillespie, a prominent Vancouver developer who is eager to lead on district energy expansion. Several of his downtown residential buildings were hooked up to the Central Heat (the downtown system serving 210 buildings) steam plant. But it was his company's Telus Gardens building—a 22-story LEED platinum office building with its own district energy system that uses waste heat from a data center in a nearby building—that got him interested in expanding the city's district heating capacity. He was so motivated that he purchased Central Heat in 2014 and renamed it Creative Energy, with a plan to convert it from natural gas to waste wood and to expand the system over time. The former Central Heat, fueled by natural gas, is the largest source of GHG emissions in Vancouver, so Gillespie's plan would be very helpful in achieving the city's 2050 GHG reduction goal.

Gillespie's current project, Creative Fuel Switch, calls for building a new low-carbon steam plant, retiring the existing gas-fired plant except for use during peak demand, and creating interconnections between the two. The plant, which will be named the "Green House," would also have a rooftop farm capable of producing 400 tons of produce annually. It would be located on city-owned land in False Creek Flat (near the Neighborhood Energy Utility). At full capacity, the Green House would eliminate 81,000 tons of GHG emissions annually.

According to Gillespie, the main barrier to developing Creative Fuel Switch is ensuring a sufficiently large customer base to make the project profitable, as building the new plant and its interconnections will require significant investment. If he is to make an upfront investment of tens of millions of dollars, he wants assurance from the city that a certain critical mass of users will make the expansion economically viable. Creative wants to add entire new neighborhoods to cover the costs of building the system. And Vancouver's pending requirement that all new buildings tap into a district heating system would make the economics of Gillespie's project work.

Sounds right, but here's where the project ran into trouble. At another level of government, the British Columbia Utility Commission (BCUC), whose mandate at the provincial level is to ensure that utility customers pay the lowest rate, will not approve Vancouver's requirement that all new buildings tap into the system, arguing that the provision would create a monopoly and could lead to higher rates. Chris Baber, Vancouver's neighborhood energy manager, reacts to BCUC's judgment: "Their decision makes it very risky for a utility, which operates on a low risk/dollar returns basis, to invest in the up-front low carbon infrastructure." He adds, "It was the City's position that the BCUC should not interfere with the monopoly aspects since as a BCUC regulated utility, it would need to operate on an open-books basis and the BCUC would provide the same consumer protection as for other monopoly utilities such as gas." City officials also hold that it is fully within the city's mandate as regulator of land use and development to specify requirements for use of energy systems by developments.[34]

Attempting to switch to renewable-energy sources for district systems pits early adopters such as Gillespie against long-established utilities and, for the time being, British Columbia's public utility commission. The commission supports the status quo, arguing that natural gas is the cheapest source of energy for heating. Trent Barry, a consultant who worked with the city on the Neighborhood Energy Utility and now is working with Creative Energy on the technical and regulatory aspects of the system, explained a further problem. He says the BCUC is applying principles from the building of power plants by large utilities to the building of brand-new thermal networks. But if the BCUC's view prevails and building owners can choose whether to connect, Creative won't be assured of getting the long-term contracts necessary to justify building the new plant. Instead, the system will have to be extended incrementally. "That's not the end of the world," Barry notes, "but it makes expansion more difficult and expensive."[35] It's the classic chicken-and-egg problem—the system developer needs new development to commit to the system, but commercial developers can't commit until the system is in place. Already Creative Fuel Switch has identified several large commercial customers willing to sign on to meet their own corporate sustainability goals. And the market demand for green buildings and noncarbon energy is strong and may yet move the project forward.

Additionally, there are barriers to switching existing district heating systems from fossil fuels to renewables. Current customers are used to paying the price of natural gas, which is at a record low in British Columbia, even with a provincial carbon tax of $30 per ton produced. A financial barrier also exists when connecting a low-carbon district energy system to an existing building if that building has been operating with natural gas boilers. Still, energy manager Baber and city engineer Jerry Dobrovolny are committed to expanding the city's system to other areas, which will require new heat sources.[36] The options are to use heat from the sewer or other waste heat sources (e.g., waste heat from data centers), as in Creative Energy's proposed system, or to add additional wood-waste burning capacity.

New developments are supporting the expansion of the district heating system since they are required to achieve low carbon emissions (with or without a district energy system) under the city's July 2016 Zero-Emissions Building Plan. For new buildings, the plan establishes both GHG and thermal energy limits. It also details a pathway to reduce emissions by 90 percent from 2007 levels by 2025 and to achieve zero emissions by 2030. All in all, for new construction, tapping into renewable district energy networks is an attractive option.

In the absence of provincial support for required building hookup to district energy systems, the city is working on other policies to facilitate district heating expansion. A Metropolitan Vancouver ordinance passed in 2015 bans sending clean waste wood to landfills or incinerators. A mandatory green building policy approved by the city council in July 2016 provides credits for developers who connect to district heating. The city had previously required LEED gold, but moved to its own standard to better align rezoning policy and building bylaw requirements with GHG reduction goals. And as the leader of the C40 Cities Clean Energy Network, Vancouver is learning from and helping other cities.

London: Linking District Energy to Urban Revitalization

Great Britain's North Sea oil and gas reserves are declining, and gas imports now supply more than 40 percent of the United Kingdom's energy. In response, in 2013 the British government put policies in place to increase the number of households connected to district heating networks to 20 percent by 2030, and 40 percent by 2050—both to reduce imports and to achieve its goal of reducing GHG emissions 80 percent by 2050.[37] Given that building heating and hot water comprise 40 percent of energy consumption and 20 percent of UK GHG emissions, district heating can have a significant impact. A national Heat Networks Delivery Unit was established in 2013 as part of the UK's Low-Carbon Heating Strategy to provide funding and technical assistance to local authorities in England and Wales for developing district heating networks.[38] As of 2017, the unit had made seven rounds of funding available to 131 local authorities to develop 200 networks, totaling $14 million.[39]

In response to the national mandate, the Greater London Authority intends to obtain 25 percent of its heat and electricity from local, decentralized energy systems, including district energy, by 2025. Like Copenhagen, planners started by creating a heat map that identifies heat density, power plants, waste energy sources, CHP plants, and CO_2 emissions.[40] Between 2008 and 2010, the authority's Decentralized Energy Master Planning program used mapping and energy master planning to identify opportunities for expansion, resulting in the London Heat Map. The map is an interactive GIS tool that allows planners from the London boroughs, developers, and utilities to figure out how to most effectively build and expand networks.

District heating and cooling serve at least 10 large, mixed-use development projects in London. Among the most impressive is a major redevelopment that links district heating to the revitalization of the King's Cross district, which integrates several aspects of sustainable development.

King's Cross claims to be the most sustainable redevelopment project in the UK. This 67-acre (27-hectare) former rail and industrial area is now a thriving mixed-use district served by six London Underground lines—a true transit-oriented development. The initial target was to reduce GHG emissions to 25 percent below existing national and local regulations through a combination of building energy efficiency, renewable energy, and increased supply efficiency through district heating and cooling. Because the development will be built over a period of 15–20 years, the emissions targets will evolve as technology improves. A mechanism for auditing building emissions, along with requirements that all buildings be submetered for energy use, will make it possible to monitor carbon emissions on both the building and unit levels.[41]

Construction on the King's Cross redevelopment project started in 2007. When completed, the area will have 2,000 new housing units connected to district heating, 25 new office buildings, 20 new streets, 10 new public buildings, and 20 renovated historic buildings situated around 20 hectares (49.5 acres) of green space that includes two parks.[42] All new buildings are constructed to high efficiency standards that call for dense materials that can absorb and release heat to reduce seasonal temperature extremes. Green roofs provide further insulation to support energy efficiency. As in Vancouver, the developer, Argent, expanded requirements from BREEAM, which isn't strict enough to meet the emissions performance sought for the project. Water efficiency is a priority as well, with harvested rainwater and recycled gray water used for toilets, irrigation, and a fountain. Rainwater harvesting is part of a green stormwater management strategy that reduces surface water runoff.[43]

The Energy Centre, a CHP plant, provides electricity, hot water, and district heating and cooling to 99 percent of King's Cross. The rest of the district's energy will be supplied by rooftop solar, ground-source heat pumps, and solar thermal systems. Two buildings, One and Two Pancras Square, produce 40,000 kilowatt hours of electricity. As a result, the district's CO_2 emissions will be 50 percent lower than those in other London boroughs.[44]

Redevelopment planning focuses on people as well as place, and it provides for public spaces teeming with life. As I toured the King's Cross neighborhood, children were splashing in the fountain at the large Granary Square park, and a mix of people were scattered throughout the clusters of benches and other seating throughout the square. Global Generation, a local community organization, engages young people, families, and businesses in gardening and other activities with the goal of building skills and encouraging civic engagement. Another program of Global Generation is Skip Gardens—so called because the gardens move as the development expands: they are part of 26 acres of open space in the area. A social program develops job opportunities for young people in the area through the Construction Skills Centre. It offers apprenticeships and other training programs to provide young people with the skills needed to work in the construction industry. The development's recruitment agency, KX Recruit, reports that it has placed 445 people since opening in January 2014, 69 percent of whom are young people living in the area.[45]

Not everything is working according to plan, however. One controversy facing the project involves affordable housing. Area residents and a Camden district councilor have objected to the developer's attempts to reduce the amount of affordable housing. Argent asked the council to approve a drop from 40 percent of all new units to about 33 percent because of cuts in government grants for social housing. Argent and the King's Cross Central Limited Partnership claim they have spent more on affordable housing than called for in the original plan, which promised 750 affordable units. Critics argue that Argent is profiting handsomely and could top up the subsidies to honor its original commitment.

Yet as a model of how cities can expand district heating, King's Cross is a success. The Energy Centre was the largest and most impressive system I have ever seen. The project demonstrates that expanding district energy in a city the size of London is a technical problem that is easily solved. Addressing the social aspects of affordable housing is more complicated and potentially contentious.

Innovations in District Cooling

District cooling offers the same savings as district heating. As demand for air conditioning rises in developing and hot-weather countries, district cooling offers a way to provide it efficiently and with lower GHG emissions. Already the United Arab Emirates is building out massive systems. But many questions related to financing and regulation must be answered for investors to be comfortable in building systems. As the technology is applied in Europe and North America, much can be learned about applying and financing cooling systems.

Downtown Austin's Giant Ice Cube

Not many people get a district cooling plant named after them, but not everyone is as forceful on behalf of a vision as Austin's Paul Robbins. Described by the *Austin Chronicle* as "the attack dog nipping at the city's heels,"[46] Robbins and other environmental activists began advancing the idea for district cooling in the mid-1990s. As Robbins explained to me, Austin had old downtown infrastructure, including a couple of power plants, and he thought their waste heat could be used to power air conditioning.[47] A consultant hired by the city examined the feasibility of the idea but concluded that there would not be enough customers to make it cost effective.

The study sat on the shelf for a few years, but was revived when several events converged to meet the needed demand. In the late 1990s, plans for a new city hall were approved that, along with a plan by then-mayor Will Wynn to add 5,000 new residents to Austin's downtown, would add the needed customer base for district cooling. Most important, perhaps, to attract the software giant Computer Sciences Corporation to the downtown, the city offered to provide air conditioning for its two buildings. Suddenly the city, which owns its own utility, needed to find a location and get the plant up and running. As it turned out, the Hobby Parking Garage, owned by the state of Texas, had space for a chilling plant that would have served a future state building. By 2001, the Robbins plant had been built on the site, the first of three district chilling/CHP plants eventually established in Austin.

Austin's district cooling projects dovetail with an energy-efficiency initiative that dates to 1982, when the city started employing building codes that require high levels of efficiency and an energy billing structure that charges higher rates for higher levels of consumption. Taken together, between 1982 and 2016 these measures have reduced power consumption to about 31 percent lower than what it would have been otherwise.[48]

Jim Collins, director of on-site energy resources at Austin Energy, explains that "aggregating the cooling load of multiple buildings into a single plant creates the scale to provide superior energy savings, reliability, and quality. It also facilitates the use of thermal energy where the chilling equipment runs at night, thereby shifting that electrical consumption from on-peak periods to off-peak periods."[49] The Robbins plant stores thermal energy in the form of ice to be used during peak times, acting like a battery. The ability to shift consumption from summer afternoons to the middle of the night saves money for Austin Energy customers. And given that the lowest-cost energy is dispatched into the market first, it is likely that much of the energy that chills the ice comes from West Texas wind farms.

The success of the Robbins plant has led to the development of two others, serving different redevelopment areas of Austin. One of these systems is a CHP plant serving the Dell Children's Medical Center of Central Texas, one of only three LEED platinum hospitals in the United States, and 12 other buildings in the Mueller eco-district. Mueller, the site of the city's former airport, is a 700-acre development of 5,000 single and multifamily homes that uses renewable energy to the extent possible and also employs green stormwater management and water conservation. Another system of note is the University of Texas, Austin, which cools 15 million square feet of space with six chilling plants.

A good part of the reason that Austin can develop so much district cooling is that the city owns its utility, Austin Energy. Municipally owned utilities have a different business model than investor-owned utilities. Both make capital-intensive investments in infrastructure, but the former can recover costs over a much longer period because it doesn't have shareholders expecting a certain rate of return. Collins explains, "We compile our cost of service for each of our systems annually, so we know what we need to charge to ensure that all costs of the program, including capital employed, are returned over the 40-year basis of the program." As a municipal utility, Austin Energy can take a long-term view, knowing all program costs are recovered from the chilled water customers purchase, while the "dividend" of electric demand management reduces costs for all electric customers every year. Chilled-water bills have two components—a capital recovery piece and consumption piece. After 15 years the capital recovery cost drops, which is how Austin Energy ensures the program is self-sufficient.

If the district cooling system has to pay for electricity, unlike systems that use "free" cold water, what makes it energy efficient or renewable? Collins explains as follows: "The electrons we are using are generally from renewable sources, and we are consuming the electrons at off-peak times and reducing demand at peak times when we are more likely to be drawing from nonrenewable sources of energy."[50] That is important in climates like that of Texas, where air conditioning accounts for about half of a utility's peak energy load. With thermal storage in ice, daytime peak demand can be managed—meaning that dirtier peaking plants do not have to be fired up.

Additionally, district cooling plants typically have multiple chillers that can be dispatched as the load increases and declines over the course of a day. This enables the plant operators to "fully load" each chiller so that it operates at peak design efficiency. Individual buildings that rely on their own chillers often have to run at part-load efficiency, which can cause a significant difference in performance.

So what does the future hold for systems like those in Austin? Austin Energy's growth strategy offers an answer. Most new system additions will be made with satellite plants. If one thinks of Austin's growth scenario as a series of centers of dense redevelopment along transit corridors, the concept would be that every center should have a district cooling system. Austin Energy negotiated the first such system with Austin Community College and has obtained city council approval to design, construct, and operate this plant. Austin Energy has three other candidates for satellite systems over the next couple of years. Energy director Jim Collins notes that Austin Energy delivered 15 megawatts of peak demand shift during the summer of 2016, with a goal of 20 megawatts by 2025. Going forward with these satellite systems could double that. Even better, Austin's model should be replicable in many communities across the world.

Chilling in Downtown Toronto

Toronto's commitment to reducing GHG emissions goes back to 1991, when a nonprofit organization, the Toronto Atmospheric Fund (TAF), was endowed with $20.2 million (US dollars) from the sale of city property to test and scale-up strategies to lower GHG emissions. The idea was to use the city as a test bed for TAF funds projects that would have difficulty obtaining traditional financing. TAF currently has assets of approximately $28 million and has provided about $30 million since its inception 27 years ago, saving the city $2.7 million annually in energy and maintenance costs.[51] It funded Canada's first municipal combined heat, power, and cooling system (referred to as tri-generation).[52] This $4.4 million system was completed in 2007 with a $1 million loan from TAF, a $1.75 million loan from Canada's Green Municipal Fund, and $2.3 million from the City of Toronto's Energy Retrofit Program.[53]

Toronto's first climate action plan, put in place by then-mayor David Miller in 2007, established the city as a leader in waste reduction, green building, and land-use regulations that support dense, transit-oriented development. By 2012, Toronto reduced GHG emissions from city operations by 40 percent from 1990 levels. As a result, Toronto has earned wide recognition as a climate leader.[54] Not resting on its laurels, in May 2015 Toronto released Transform TO, a plan to reduce the city's emissions 80 percent by 2050.

Fernando Carou, an engineer and planner in Toronto's Environment and Energy Division, explains that energy use is incorporated into all aspects of planning, particularly in land use. With the downtown population expected to double in 30 years, Carou notes that the city has to estimate future energy demand and figure out how to meet it. The first order of business, he says, is reducing demand through energy efficiency and expanding district energy.

The city's district heating network currently serves 37 percent of its downtown buildings. Started in 1982, Toronto's network was predominantly fueled by natural gas and oil. Toronto Transform TO recognizes that expanding district energy and converting the system to renewable sources is a big part of achieving emissions reduction goals (along with expanding and electrifying the transit system). But it is district cooling that brings planners and energy executives from around the world to study the Deep Lake Water Cooling system. An idea for many years before it was realized, it took a private-public partnership and an approach that could solve two problems at once to make the system happen.

The city had been trying to develop a district cooling system using cold water from Lake Ontario since the mid-1980s, but it was unsuccessful in amassing the capital to build it. In the late 1990s, the city had a problem with foul-smelling water because one of the system's intake lines, located in a shallow part of the lake, was clogged with algae. To solve the problem, the city had to make a significant investment in new filtration infrastructure.

Sharing the infrastructure for deep cooling and water supply reduced the cost of the cooling project from $650 to $170 million and thus reduced the amount of capital that needed to be raised. The chair of the Toronto District Health Council, Dennis Fotinos, initiated and executed the privatization of the utility to raise the capital needed to build a new pipe that would serve a district cooling system and provide clean drinking water, while removing the source of noxious odors.

Fotinos won over investors and the board and became the CEO of the newly created Enwave Energy Corporation.

Enwave refurbished the Island Water Treatment plant, converting it to a full-time operation that draws deep water five kilometers from shore, where the water stays cold all year round. Opened in 2004, the system provides drinking water and, because algae can't survive in the 38-degree deep water, saves the city about $100 million annually in treatment costs because the new intake does not require the activated filters needed with the shallow intake. The trifecta is that the same pipe draws water for the Deep Water Cooling system—the largest lake water system in the world.[55] It pipes cold water to a transfer station, where heat exchangers use it to chill water in a closed-loop system that circulates to buildings downtown. The lake water is cleaned and used as potable water for city residents (figure 3.5). The system, which serves 86 large buildings, saves 92 million kilowatt hours of electricity and eliminates 79,000 tons of GHG emissions annually.

Fotinos emphasizes that district energy can be made commercially viable without government assistance, and estimates that buildings connected to the system can save about 10 percent in annual operating costs. These savings must be what convinces building owners to connect since Toronto, unlike Copenhagen,

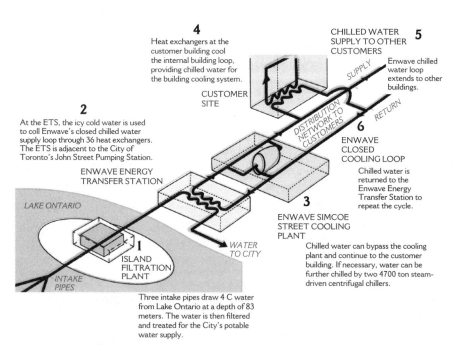

4
Heat exchangers at the customer building cool the internal building loop, providing chilled water for the building cooling system.

CUSTOMER SITE

CHILLED WATER SUPPLY TO OTHER CUSTOMERS **5**
Enwave chilled water loop extends to other buildings.

2
At the ETS, the icy cold water is used to coll Enwave's closed chilled water supply loop through 36 heat exchangers. The ETS is adjacent to the City of Toronto's John Street Pumping Station.

ENWAVE ENERGY TRANSFER STATION

6
ENWAVE CLOSED COOLING LOOP
Chilled water is returned to the Enwave Energy Transfer Station to repeat the cycle.

LAKE ONTARIO

1
ISLAND FILTRATION PLANT
Three intake pipes draw 4 C water from Lake Ontario at a depth of 83 meters. The water is then filtered and treated for the City's potable water supply.

INTAKE PIPES

WATER TO CITY

3
ENWAVE SIMCOE STREET COOLING PLANT
Chilled water can bypass the cooling plant and continue to the customer building. If necessary, water can be further chilled by two 4700 ton steam-driven centrifugal chillers.

Figure 3.5 Deep Lake Water Cooling System
Source: Adapted from NYC Global Partners illustrations.

does not have the authority to mandate connections. The city can, however, promote connection by offering development incentives.

Enwave and the city have ongoing plans to expand the district energy network and to transition it to low-carbon fuels such as solar and sewer heat recovery. The goal is to connect 30 percent of all buildings to low-carbon district energy by anchoring district energy systems and microgrids in 30 nodes across the city. Five nodes will be built by 2020 and another 25 by 2050, under a partnership model through which Enwave contributes cash and technical expertise, while the city provides land and other in-kind resources, such as below-street access for piping.

The Role of Cities in District Energy

Cities are creatures of nations. Even with substantial local autonomy, cities are subject to national laws and regulations that can enhance or frustrate local efforts to improve energy efficiency. Not surprisingly, some of the cities that have done the most with district heating and cooling have benefited from friendly national policies, tax structures, subsidy arrangements, and other economic variables.

In this respect, the United States is very much an outlier, both in its hesitancy to put in place a consistent national energy policy that involves government planning, and in its predominant mode of energy delivery: investor-owned utilities. Also in the United States, there are radical differences between the two major political parties, leading to frequent policy reversals that make it harder for cities and others, whether in the public or the private sector, to develop district energy.

Europe, by contrast, tends to have more supportive national governments, and the differences in policies and outcomes from those in the United States are extreme. They also have support from the EU. As we have seen, the 2012 and 2016 EU directives require member states to assess the potential of CHP district heating and cooling and to develop policies to support feasible projects.[56]

National support underpins Copenhagen's leadership on expanding district energy and advancing it to the fourth generation. The Danish Energy Act was instrumental in mapping the country into heat districts and identifying the most efficient options in each. National legislation that required tapping into district energy facilitated municipal action, and national tax exemptions and subsidies, including a lower fuel tax for CHP, provided the carrots and sticks needed to accelerate district energy expansion. With these measures, the city had support in developing the municipal heat maps. The public-private partnership of the Danish District Heating Association conducts ongoing research that improves district energy technologies and maintains Denmark as an export leader in district energy technology.

The British government provides policy support for cities by setting a goal of achieving 20 percent penetration of district energy by 2030 and 40 percent by 2050, with the broader goal of reducing GHG emissions 80 percent by 2050. A Heat Network Delivery Unit was created to provide cities with funding and technical assistance in building district energy networks. With these national supports in place, the Greater London Authority has followed Copenhagen's approach of creating heat maps and in using district energy as the underpinning of redevelopment. As a result, London is on track to achieve its municipal goal of 25 percent penetration of district energy by 2025.

In Canada, energy policy is left to the provinces, and we see different types of support in British Columbia and Ontario. British Columbia's carbon tax is the highest in North America. When instituted in 2008, the tax was $10 per ton for the purchase of fuel based on its carbon content, and it is currently $12 per ton. Government officials credit the tax with driving investment in clean technology, creating more than 68,000 jobs and reducing emissions by more than 15 percent since it was introduced.[57] Ontario's cap-and-trade system will provide incentives for transitioning to low-carbon energy sources, including district energy, which will support Toronto's efforts. Its first auction, held in March 2017, raised $470 million, and continued auctions will likely raise between $1 and $2 billion annually, all of which will be invested in low-carbon energy across the province. Combined with moving the province's building code to net zero by 2030, building efficiency and district energy have the potential to dramatically reduce energy consumption in Toronto.

It seems clear that from a climate perspective, especially for energy efficiency and the deployment of renewables, district energy should be a critical element in any city's low-carbon planning. In Europe, the incentives line up for public- and private-sector developers to put these city systems in place. In the United States, it is much harder to make the business case for district energy to investor-owned utilities or private developers of energy infrastructure. Who, then, will build district energy systems in the United States, aside from municipally owned utilities such as Austin's? It is helpful to reprise the description of the role of cities in promoting district energy/CHP from the United Nations report *District Energy in Cities*: setting targets for development and expansion; energy planning and mapping; policies to encourage or require building owners to connect to district systems; and waste-to-energy mandates. As we have seen in this chapter, cities on course to successfully meet lower GHG targets have followed this advice—both with and without the support of their national governments.

4

RENEWABLE CITIES

Cities should be at the heart of the energy transition.

—International Energy Agency

HOME TO OVER HALF the world's population, cities can drive the transition to renewable energy, and urban leaders worldwide are stepping up to the challenge. As part of the Paris Agreement in 2015, 700 mayors from across the globe committed to supplying 100 percent of their electricity from renewable sources by 2050. By 2017, the US Conference of Mayors, with some 1,400 members, upped the ante, adopting a resolution supporting the transition to 100 percent renewable energy by 2035.[1]

Although experts debate whether nuclear and carbon capture should be part of the mix and whether biomass counts as renewable, most agree that a transition to 100 percent clean energy by 2050 is doable—albeit technically complex and costly up front. Among the conclusions of an influential study by Finland's Lappeenranta University of Technology and the global Energy Watch Group is that renewables can cover worldwide electricity demand cost effectively by 2050 while creating 36 million jobs, compared with 19 million employed under the current electricity system.[2] This study concurs with Mark Jacobson's widely cited Solutions Project at Stanford University, which further argues that the renewable-energy transition is possible without nuclear energy.[3] Both studies insist that the barriers to transition are political rather than technical. Of course, not everyone in the energy research community agrees that the technical pathway is clear without including nuclear power in the energy mix. Twenty-one scientists published a critique of Jacobson's assumptions and calculations, and the Intergovernmental Panel on Climate Change, the National Oceanic and Atmospheric Administration, the

National Renewable Energy Laboratory, and the International Energy Agency concluded that Jacobson's position on nuclear energy, among other aspects of his modeling, may not hold.[4] They generally agree, though, that the obstacles to achieving 100 percent clean energy are primarily political.

In spite of political haggling, we need to move aggressively now to reach this entirely feasible goal by 2050. It must begin with a rapid transition to clean sources for electric power generation that can support heating and cooling, home and workplace activity, and transportation, a process that involves simultaneously solving multiple problems along the way. One major problem concerns the grid. Meeting all our energy needs with electrical power will almost triple demand for electricity by 2050, putting great pressure on the grid that it currently cannot handle. Simply put, "The electricity grid will have to get bigger, more sophisticated, more efficient, and more reliable,"[5] says climate journalist David Roberts. Relatedly, a lot of utility-scale storage will also have to be developed. We're not there yet on building a smart grid or sufficient storage capacity, but many experts argue that we will be in time to meet 2050 goals. Already, several companies are currently competing to build the world's largest solar and battery farms.[6] Meeting the last 10 to 20 percent of the total-clean-energy target will be especially difficult, since it will involve weaning the system entirely from nonrenewables, but that is no reason to not start.

As we will see in this chapter, cities have an important role to play in getting to 100 percent clean or renewable energy, and they can receive numerous co-benefits in public health, local jobs, fiscal well-being, and social equity in the process, if they do it right. But they also need supportive national and state policy. Relying partly on such assistance, cities have two basic pathways for increasing the production of renewable energy and facilitating its expansion. The first pathway—applied predominantly, if not exclusively, in the United States—is community choice aggregation (CCA), which is authorized by state policies that give municipalities and counties the power to produce or purchase energy on behalf of residents and businesses in a geographically defined area and thus to aggregate demand, leading to cheaper energy contracts than individuals can arrange on their own. Primarily intended to reduce consumers' electricity costs, and proven to be effective in doing so, CCAs are also used to facilitate the transition to renewable energy, although only eight states allow them. Because European energy markets operate differently, mainly relying on feed-in tariffs, CCAs have been attempted in only a few European cities. We will look at two California cities, Lancaster and San Diego, that are using CCAs as part of their strategy to transition to 100 percent renewable energy by 2050 and 2035, respectively.

The second pathway, municipally owned utilities (MOUs), give cities direct control over the source of the energy they produce or purchase. There are about 251 municipally owned electric and gas utilities in the United States (34 are electric only).[7] In Europe, and particularly in Germany, cities are "remunicipalizing" electric, water, and waste-treatment utilities that underwent a wave of privatization beginning in the 1980s. Again, these efforts reduce costs and, in many cases, accelerate adoption of renewable energy.[8] About 90 percent of the European energy utility remunicipalizations are in Germany.[9] We will examine municipal utilities in Austin, Texas, and Hamburg, Germany, to understand their strengths and limitations, as well as the role that higher-government policy plays in both.

A few cities have multiple options—Los Angeles has a municipal utility, a CCA, a feed-in tariff, and other policies that make it a leader on renewable energy. Most cities and states have neither community choice aggregation nor municipally controlled utilities. Many cities with neither purchasing option have made 100 percent renewable pledges and are employing other strategies that I briefly present. I examine the extent to which cities can drive change by themselves and what support is needed from higher levels of government, and differentiate between cities promoting the creation of new renewable production and those facilitating adoption through measures such as solar-friendly permitting and zoning, favorable financing terms, and solar rights policies. Finally, as part of the transition, cities have to ensure that renewable energy is accessible and affordable to residents, and not just a subsidized privilege for those who can afford it. So in the following case studies, I will also examine how cities are incorporating energy justice into their plans.

Is 100 Percent Renewable Energy Possible?

While the European Union began setting renewable-energy targets for its member countries in 2001, and some national targets are even more stringent, the United States has relied almost exclusively on the states to establish renewable portfolio standards (RPS). To date, 38 states plus Washington, DC, have an RPS (or similar program) requiring utilities to purchase a set amount of energy from renewable sources by a specific year (e.g., 80 percent by 2050). Not surprisingly, renewable-energy progress in the United States has therefore been more spotty and less coordinated.

In the United States, a popular strategy for meeting an RPS is to provide homeowners and businesses state subsidies to install solar PV on houses and buildings. A complementary policy, net metering, allows consumers to sell excess renewable energy back to the grid at specified rates. At least 17 states have net metering, though the amount that can be sold back is a point of contention in several states.[10] At the household level, subsidized PV is a great solution. Electricity bills are reduced and, depending on where one lives, unused power can be sold back to the grid at favorable rates. And in recent years, those who can afford it are also installing home-scale batteries that can store up to 24 hours' worth of electricity if the sun isn't shining. So what if we put solar PV on every available roof? The paradoxical answer is that we'd run into problems.

The first problem is that rooftop solar PV can only provide around 15 percent of a transition to 100 percent renewable in the United States and less in European countries, with another 20 percent of the total coming from utility-scale solar.[11] The second problem is that solar is intermittent, as is wind. Lastly, the grid in its current state can only handle about 30 percent renewable energy. These problems are not insurmountable, but overcoming them will take commitment and investment in new technologies.

Solar and wind are nondispatchable energy sources, which means that they can't be turned on and off as needed. Solar only produces when the sun is shining and wind when the wind is blowing. In contrast, dispatchable sources of electricity, such as fossil fuels, hydropower, nuclear, biofuels, and even waste processing can be easily adjusted as demand fluctuates. Utilities need enough dispatchable power to ensure that all customers can be served all of the time. Utilities are required to provide power for peak loads—that is, during extreme hot or cold weather, and in daily cycles.

Unfortunately, solar and wind production peaks do not match demand peaks in most utilities. This mismatch is termed the "duck curve," a phenomenon analyzed by the National Renewable Energy Lab in modeling how the grid could handle increasing amounts of intermittent power (figure 4.1). We know that electricity demand peaks in the morning when people are getting ready for work or school and again in the late afternoon when everyone arrives home. The lines in the duck curve represent electricity demand without renewable energy. As the percentage of renewable energy increases, less power is required from the grid. Solar production declines as the evening peak begins, so the utility has to ramp up energy production with dispatchable sources in the morning and again in the evening to meet demand, an expensive undertaking. The higher the percentage of renewables, the more the cost of integrating dispatchable sources rises.[12] Moreover, as more renewable energy is produced, the more it will threaten to flood the grid in what specialists call overgeneration or spilling—and it will increasingly do so. Potential solutions to these problems include battery storage, energy trading, and demand management.[13]

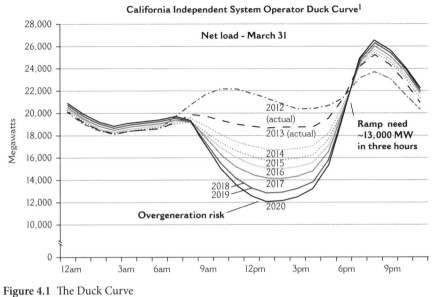

Figure 4.1 The Duck Curve
Source: California ISO and J. Lazar.

Battery storage technology is advancing faster than experts anticipated. The price of battery packs for residential and commercial solar PV systems fell to $187 per megawatt hour in 2018, an achievement that BloombergNEF predicted wouldn't happen until 2025.[14] Thanks to this continuing technical progress, many experts predict that by the time power grids reach the 30 percent renewable mark, advances in battery storage will allow more intermittent capacity to be dispatched. Already, half the solar-energy systems being installed in Germany come with battery storage. The digitally controlled batteries feed power back into the grid as needed.[15]

Another solution is to "trade" excess renewable energy with other grids. Many point to the model developed in Denmark, which produces about 44 percent of its electricity from renewable sources and trades excess energy with Norway, Sweden, and Germany, as evidence that energy trading can work. Using a high-capacity transmission line, Denmark sells excess wind capacity on the Scandinavian grid and imports dispatchable power as needed. But together, their grids haven't been tasked with handling more than 18 percent renewables to date. When trading with Germany, Norway, and Sweden is considered, Denmark's percentage of intermittent power use reduces by almost half.[16] And Denmark, a small country, has one grid operator that effectively manages intermittency, something far more difficult to handle in large countries with many independent grid operators.

California, a leading producer of solar energy, has started to spill some of its PV power because the grid can't handle it, which negates its environmental benefits. A solution would be for the state's grid operator, the California Independent System Operator (CAISO), to connect to other grids to trade excess power. If interconnection balancing authorities were created, CAISO could connect with PacifiCorp, which runs the grids of Wyoming, Idaho, Utah, and Oregon. Multiple regulatory issues would have to be addressed before that could happen, but it is technically possible. Moving across state lines would also affect states' ability to meet their renewable targets. California seeks to become 100 percent carbon free on energy use by 2045, for example, but the PacifiCorp grid uses a considerable amount of coal, which would count as part of California's energy mix and make it difficult to reach its RPS goals.

A move to nationwide high-voltage direct current (HVDC) transmission systems as an overlay to the current AC system would accommodate long-distance transmission of renewables among regions engaged in energy trading and increase the stability of the AC system. AC transmission is limited to about 500 miles or less, while HVDC can transmit much more power over distances two to three times as far, with much better grid stability. Germany and Brazil have already built HVDC lines to accommodate increased wind power and hydropower, respectively.[17] And newer systems are also under development. In addition, electrical engineers and renewable energy advocates have demonstrated that a network of HVDC microgrids could be built for a much more resilient and decentralized energy transmission system.[18]

The National Renewable Energy Lab estimates that we can accommodate an 80 percent renewable grid by 2050 with short-term battery storage and energy trading.[19] The remainder can come from managing demand to smooth out the duck curve. Demand management employs smart-grid technology—two-way communication that allows consumers to make decisions on when to use energy, often automating reduction of peak loads. Recall FortZED in Fort Collins, Colorado, from chapter 2, which tested several technologies to reduce peak energy use and integrate renewables into the grid.[20] By balancing and reducing electricity loads, referred to as "peak shaving," Fort Collins Utilities projected that peak electricity demand could be reduced by 20 to 30 percent.[21] Some utilities and CCAs offer discounts to customers who allow the power provider to automatically adjust their power use during peak times (e.g., turning off air conditioning for brief periods).

While all the technology and regulatory mechanisms are not yet in place, progress is occurring faster than predicted. Most of the path to a clean-energy transition has been cleared. What we need, particularly in the United States, is support from all levels of government to clear the last hurdles. The transition will be easier in some places, such as those with considerable hydro and geothermal assets for dispatchable power. But with energy trading, enabled by new grid technology, regional balance is also possible.

Community Choice Aggregation: A Closer Look

With community choice aggregation (CCA), municipalities or counties buy or produce electricity on behalf of residents, but the investor-owned utility still delivers the power and maintains the transmission lines. Once established, a CCA negotiates a power purchase agreement (PPA), which is a contract with an energy developer for a specified amount of power over a set number of years.[22] CCAs were created to adopt renewable-energy contracts with developers of renewable energy. The long-term nature of the contracts benefits both buyers, who get an affordable source of clean energy, and sellers, who get financing for their renewable-energy projects. Some CCAs purchase renewable-energy credits (RECs)—certificates that verify the purchase of a certain amount of energy from a renewable source. A REC does not mean that the municipality uses the renewable energy—it could be produced and used elsewhere—but the municipality gets "credit" for creating demand for renewable energy. While there are different types of RECs, the important feature is that they produce renewable energy that wouldn't have been developed otherwise.[23] Some CCAs procure the REC with the PPA, but the REC is the only way to certify that a unit of energy purchased is from a renewable source.[24]

Once a CCA is adopted, all residents are included unless they choose to stay with the utility, an option that CCAs are required to make public. California, for example, requires that residents be given four notices on this option. For those who opt in, the state's public utility commission establishes an exit fee paid to the utility to recoup the difference for its long-term contracts to serve a specific number of customers.[25] As we'll see, establishing the terms of these agreements is often contentious, however, for the CCA both supplies power to, and competes with, the local utility.

There is also an indirect social justice element to CCAs in that renters or residents who can't afford to install individual systems on their homes can participate in the renewable-energy transition and the reduced energy costs CCAs typically produce. Further, profits are reinvested back into the community, often giving preference to low-income residents.

California is one of eight states with legislation permitting CCAs, and its cities—San Diego and Lancaster in particular—are making strong use of this strategy to deliver renewable energy and other benefits to their residents.[26] As a result of California's ambitious climate targets—the most aggressive in the country—and extensive bipartisan support for renewable energy, nothing short of a revolution is taking place in how power is purchased in the Golden State. To date, the state has 19 CCAs serving more than 10 million residents, with the largest serving Los Angeles.[27] The California Public Utilities Commission estimates that by 2020, almost 70 percent of the state's electricity demand could be supplied by CCAs.[28] All of them purchase energy at a lower price than the utility, but their popularity is tied to meeting state and city renewable-energy adoption goals. California's legislation calls for relying only on zero-emission forms of energy by 2045. Independently, several California cities have established similar goals.

CCAs are increasing the share of renewables purchased by investor-owned utilities as well. As more customers shift to CCAs, the ratio of renewable energy per customer increases. Analysis by UCLA's Luskin Center for Innovation estimates that the average percentage of renewable energy in the portfolios of the state's three utilities—Pacific Gas & Electric, Southern California Edison, and San Diego Gas & Electric—will reach 67 percent by 2025.[29]

Lancaster, California: A Community Choice Aggregation Greenovator

R. Rex Parris, a Southern California Republican first elected mayor of Lancaster in 2008, has long supported renewable energy. As described to me by Lancaster city manager Jason Caudle, the mayor's position is just common sense: "Climate change is happening. If you have the sun, you should be harvesting it. It makes sense for the planet and it makes sense financially for the city and its residents."[30] And it makes sense for the economy. With a 17 percent unemployment rate in 2009, this midsize city of 160,000 needed a job creation strategy, and Parris decided that going solar should be part of the plan. Currently, about 38 percent of the city's electricity comes from renewable energy—up from about 10 percent when Parris took office—and the city has instituted several policies to get that to 100 percent by 2030.[31] Parris wants other cities to see Lancaster's approach as a template for their renewable transitions.

Under Parris, the city has been on a relentless search for ways to increase solar energy. These efforts would eventually culminate in a three-pronged strategy: increasing rooftop solar, developing utility-scale solar, and creating a CCA to purchase renewable energy. To develop solar, the city council formed the Lancaster Power Authority (LPA), a precursor to the CCA that focused on designing, developing, and operating renewable energy projects in the Southern California region and statewide. Through the LPA, Lancaster established an innovative public-private financing model to install 7.5 megawatts of solar energy on schools throughout Lancaster, as well as 1.5 megawatts on municipal facilities. The LPA also collaborated with the private sector to catalyze utility-scale solar development.[32]

The first step was to install solar PV on all municipal facilities. In addition, the city installed solar PV shades on five municipal parking lots, saving about $50,000 annually and providing the co-benefit of shielding cars from the hot sun. Next, the city partnered with SolarCity to install PV on the city's schools. The utility bill savings from the school installations created a revenue stream for the city that is used to finance the next round of installations.[33] Almost all the electricity needs of the city's 25 schools are now provided by solar at a saving of more than $400,000 per year. At the same time, Lancaster followed tried-and-true strategies for increasing residential solar installations—easy permitting and a spirited public education campaign to disseminate information about state subsidies.

By 2011, Parris and the city council were ready to set a goal of becoming the nation's first net-zero city, meaning that it would produce and procure all the electricity that is uses from renewable sources. City officials quickly realized that rooftop solar could only go so far in meeting this goal. The city had already served as a test bed for new utility-scale solar: in July 2009, Lancaster unveiled a 20-acre 5-megawatt concentrated solar thermal tower plant, developed by eSolar, which uses mirrors or lenses to focus high-temperature heat to the top of a tower or the center of a trough to boil water or refrigerant to generate electricity. This pilot became the prototype for the 377-megawatt Ivanpaw Solar Electric Generating System—the world's largest solar thermal system—operating in the Mojave Desert. To develop utility-scale solar on city land, the LPA provided a 25-acre site for US Topco Energy to develop a 7.5-megawatt solar farm. Lancaster's willingness to rezone land to support large-scale solar development was essential to this component of its three-pronged renewable strategy. Since then, LPA and Topco have developed about 10 megawatts of power.[34]

To expand solar access to low-income residents, Lancaster City Council adopted California's Single-family Affordable Solar Homes (SASH) Program in 2014, which offers rebates for installing PV systems on the houses of income-qualifying residents. The program will continue through 2021. Prior to attracting China-based bus and battery manufacturer Build Your Dreams (BYD) (see chapter 7), Parris supported a partnership between the company and KB Homes to build an affordable solar-energy residential community in 2010. The partnership developed a prototype affordable house that generates more power than it uses. Once KB Homes demonstrated that it could build an affordable energy-plus house, solar became a standard feature of all the company's construction.

For Lancaster, 2014 was a landmark year. In January, the city began enforcing an ordinance passed in October 2013 that required all new houses to have rooftop solar. And in May, Lancaster became the first California city to form a CCA, Lancaster Choice Energy, which is managed by the city council. Kathy Wells, energy projects coordinator for the CCA, estimates that about 94 percent of the city's residents participate in the program, which provides power more cheaply than the utility serving the city. She reports that about 38 percent of the power purchased is renewable (utility-scale solar and wind) and 60 percent is carbon free (including hydro). For a $10 monthly surcharge, customers can purchase 100 percent renewable power. The cost for the basic plan is about 2 percent less than the utility's. Lancaster Choice Energy has been using the profits that would have gone to utility stockholders to reinvest in programs that increase the energy efficiency in buildings and to develop more renewable energy.

Starting in January 2018, the city's ZNE ordinance requires that all new houses have a solar-energy system that produces two watts of power per square foot. Meeting power demands exclusively with renewables requires battery storage, so Lancaster hired Green Charge Networks to install an energy storage system at the Lancaster Museum of Art and History. The system reduces costs for the museum by storing low-cost energy produced at off-peak times for use during peak demand for "demand shaving." Demand charges are triggered when a large facility switches its lights on, thus creating a significant and sudden strain on the energy grid. The battery provides a scaled approach to drawing power from the grid, thus significantly reducing costs for demand charges. So far, it is the city's only battery storage attempt. City manager Caudle points out that storage at the scale needed is a challenge—which is still generally the case everywhere.

To reach a 100 percent renewable-energy target, Lancaster will also have to electrify its public and private transportation system. Attracting BYD allowed the city to create well-paying jobs and catalyzed the Antelope Valley Transit Authority's switch to electric buses. By the end of 2019, all 85 of the agency's buses were electric, making it the first transit agency in the country with an all-electric bus fleet. The purchases made sense to the transit agency because Lancaster Choice Energy could offer an attractive rate, which varies depending on when the chargers are used. The city is building out more charging infrastructure for electric vehicles with grants, public-private partnerships, and funds from the CCA. Starting with a fast charger in the museum parking lot, the city has now installed 23 charging stations throughout the city and streamlined the permitting process to help catalyze the installation of privately owned stations.

Ever greenovating, Lancaster is in the early stages of developing an affordable 67-unit microgrid community with funding from the city's housing agency and the state public utility commission. It will produce all its own energy and can operate independently if the grid goes down. It will also serve as a pilot for flywheel technology, an emerging renewable-energy storage system with significant potential. The flywheel works through a heavy cylinder that floats in vacuum containers by using a magnetic field. The flywheel goes into motion when solar or wind energy is introduced. As the wheel rotates, it stores the energy that started it, which is converted into electricity when needed. Another pilot being developed is a green district that doubles as a power plant: all homes will have solar energy with battery storage that can be dispatched as needed. Both pilots are net-zero communities, meaning that all the energy they need is produced on-site.

To develop economies of scale, Lancaster Choice Energy created another CCA that other communities can join: CalChoice. To date, five communities are operational and five will come online later in 2020. As a unified group, CalChoice communities can make larger purchases and thus bargain for lower prices. And each city keeps the revenue it generates to reinvest back into energy projects.

Some of Lancaster's initiatives, particularly those with far-reaching impacts such as the ZNE ordinance, took several years of planning to ensure that all stakeholders—the Planning Commission, the Architectural and Design Commission, the building industry, and residents—were on board and that implementation would go smoothly. But Caudle notes that the public was on board with the renewable transition from the beginning—mainly because it hasn't cost the city anything, has saved residents money, and has created jobs in solar installation and in cleantech generally.

Lancaster offers an exemplary model for rapid and just transition to renewable energy and a green economy. From the mayor and city council to the municipal administrative staff, all see these projects and policies as demonstrating proof of concept from which other cities with CCAs can learn.

With the city's bent for experimentation, of course, not all initiatives succeed. To address the solar transmission problem, Lancaster joined with Pittsburg, California, to form the High Desert Power Authority to create a local transmission line for solar produced in the region. When the project did not receive federal FERC approval, the city attempted an innovative strategy for creating an alternative route to congested transmission lines, but the issue is not yet settled. Experimentation to figure out large-scale battery storage is ongoing. But the city's pilots for utility-scale solar have been successful. And pilots such as the zero-plus house and microgrid community, conducted with affordability as a top priority, are essential and too-often neglected features of low-carbon planning. Further, the city has accomplished all this with an eye on economic development: its partner, BYD, employs 800 workers and plans to double in size in the near term. It is the city's largest employer.

San Diego: A CCA Overcoming Utility Opposition

San Diego is the only city in the United States whose climate action plan includes a legally binding commitment to obtain 100 percent of its electricity from renewable energy by 2035. Securing that commitment was not easy. Despite the plan's potential for high-tech job creation and energy security, and support from Republican mayor Kevin Faulconer and the San Diego Regional Chamber of Commerce, who view it as a driver of the city's innovation economy, getting to "legally binding" involved an intense political struggle.

The plan got its start in 2010, when the city received $12 million in American Recovery Act funds for energy efficiency and renewable-energy development, some of which was earmarked for creating a climate action plan. A key player in developing the plan was Nicole Capretz, a council member staffer who at the time chaired a citizens advisory committee pushing for a strong plan. Capretz and the city council, dominated by Democrats, wanted the plan to be legally binding, but then-mayor Jerry Sanders, a Republican, opposed making such a commitment. A window of opportunity opened when Democrat Bob Filner became mayor in 2012, but quickly shut when he was forced out of office due to sexual harassment charges the following year. Capretz continued working with city council president and interim mayor Todd Gloria, who hired her as director of environmental policy, and authored the climate action plan with the legally binding 100 percent clean-energy goal.[35]

The city's utility, San Diego Gas & Electric (SDG&E), opposed the 100 percent renewable goal, arguing (as it had with Lancaster) that it was already on a path to rapid renewable adoption and did not need the force of law to continue. It was clearly going to be a fight. Seeking to build bottom-up community support, Capretz left city government with the election of Republican Kevin Faulconer as mayor, and formed the Climate Action Campaign in January 2015. She and others reached out to community planning groups, which were created by the city council in 1966 and given official status as conduits for citizen input into land-use and other planning decisions.[36] Environmental, public health, and labor groups joined the Climate Action Campaign in supporting the climate action plan. Their efforts were boosted when Amory Lovins's Rocky Mountain Institute issued a report on how other California cities were making progress on 100 percent renewable goals. With this groundswell of support, Mayor Faulconer, the chamber of commerce (led by Sanders after he left office), and the Building Industry

Association—all generally Republican—had come on-board, and the city council passed the plan in the fall of 2015. As a legally binding agreement, the city could be sued for noncompliance and placed under a court order to comply.

The question of whether to adopt a CCA to achieve the goal was even more controversial. California utilities had been fighting CCAs ever since state enabling legislation was passed in 2002. Renewable-energy advocates complained that Pacific Gas & Electric (PG&E) had stalled the start of the CCA in Northern California's Marin County by almost a decade, until 2010. The utilities were threatened by the introduction of competition in energy purchasing and argued that under California's RPS, they were already obtaining more power from renewable sources. Further, the utilities and the CCAs disagreed over how much the utilities should be compensated for their loss of business, given that the utility was required to maintain the grid with a smaller customer base to cover the costs.

San Diego Gas & Electric launched a public relations campaign against community choice, but the Climate Action Campaign was ready to take them on. While state law does not permit utilities to campaign against CCAs, SDG&E's parent firm, Sempra, used its marketing division to organize the Clear the Air Coalition to slow the CCA's momentum. Coalition members included the San Diego Regional Chamber of Commerce, the Downtown San Diego Partnership, and the San Diego County Taxpayers Association (which was created to oppose the CCA). The group characterized the CCA as an untested experiment that could lead to higher rates. Capretz's campaign argued that the coalition wanted to get rid of the 100 percent goal and community choice because it would break up their monopoly.[37] After a July 2017 feasibility study concluded that the CCA could achieve most of San Diego's 100 percent renewable goal at competitive rates, the city council passed a resolution to establish the CCA in February 2019 and approved the final documents in the fall.[38]

Eventually, the California Public Utilities Commission granted the state's three utilities, PG&E, Southern California Edison, and SDG&E, an exit fee for CCA customers of 2.3 cents per kilowatt hour. In April 2018, the utilities successfully appealed to the PUC, arguing that the low fee leaves utility customers subsidizing CCAs. CCA advocates argued that exit fees are a disincentive to renewable-energy production and that, otherwise, CCAs operate under the same rules as utilities. Both are required to demonstrate resource adequacy by procuring sufficient energy to meet peak demand for an entire year and on a month-to-month basis.[39] Anticipating higher penetration of renewables, California law also requires CCAs to procure storage capacity equivalent to 1 percent of their 2020 peak load starting in 2024.

Like Lancaster, San Diego had been expanding renewables before passing the 100 percent renewable ordinance. The county's building energy codes required new buildings to be solar ready in mid-2015.[40] By 2016, the Shining Cities report, produced by Environment California Research and Policy Center, revealed that San Diego was first in the nation for solar installations—a 60 percent increase from 2015, representing more than 22,000 PV systems.[41] Capretz estimates that San Diego's CCA will generate at least $50 million in revenue annually, which can be invested in rebates and programs that enable residents to obtain rooftop solar and energy-efficiency upgrades.

In addition, San Diego has an active GRID Alternatives program, a statewide initiative that seeks to include low-income communities in the transition to renewable energy and environmental sustainability. Eddie Price, GRID's community and workforce development coordinator, says that much of his work involves educating residents on energy efficiency and renewable energy, and how they work. He spends a lot of time at community meetings and churches to get the message out.[42] GRID San Diego's Energy for All program helps families reduce their electricity bills by as much as 90 percent and provides job training in solar installation. Executive director Paul Cleary estimates that GRID Alternatives installations will save households that have received them more than $30 million over the next 20 years.[43] In a new program, GRID Alternatives works with affordable housing providers to reduce electricity bills for their tenants by offering free technical assistance and low-cost design and installation services. This program allows renters to be part of the energy transition.

Job training is a core element of the program. Among the groups to which GRID directs training are the incarcerated, formerly incarcerated, veterans, and at-risk youth. The city of San Diego funds GRID to train up to 50 people in these categories per year. One goal is to prepare students for union apprenticeships. GRID's Women in Solar program seeks to increase gender and racial diversity in the solar industry by providing training and pathways to technical careers for women and particularly women of color.

On another front, the Sierra Club and the International Brotherhood of Electrical Workers have been pressuring the San Diego CCA to include specific language on paying prevailing wages, ensuring neutrality in union organizing campaigns, and promoting community benefits such as local investment and hiring. While negotiations with GRID Alternatives to include residents of communities of concern are ongoing, Price questions whether they will be left out if this union commitment is made. As Price notes, "I'm not anti-union, but I'm pro-hood."[44] His goal is to get residents of marginalized communities into jobs with career advancement potential. Similarly, Price is concerned that residents of the communities he represents could be left out of San Diego's push for electric vehicles. Price and colleagues are open to continued discussions with the union to negotiate a more inclusive pathway to union membership.

Faulconer was right about the co-benefits that spring from clean tech. Started in 2007, Cleantech San Diego was already in place when the renewable-energy goal was established. At first an initiative in the San Diego Mayor's Office, it spun off into an independent member-based trade association to support the clean-energy industry in the 18-city metropolitan area. As described to me by Cleantech San Diego's vice president, Shannon Bresnahan, "We are a connector—we accelerate the regional clean-energy industry by connecting businesses, research institutions, and local government smart-cities initiatives."[45]

Cleantech San Diego's 2018 industry study identified 45,000 clean-tech jobs in the metropolitan area, 10,000 of which are solar-related—representing an $8 billion economic impact for the region. A core program is the Southern California Energy Innovation Network, a start-up accelerator that offers coaching and mentoring to more than 30 companies with breakthrough potential. Among its success stories is eMotorWerks, which was purchased by the Enel Group. The company's electric vehicle chargers are smart-grid ready, meaning that they have grid management capabilities that can contribute to peak shaving by feeding power back to the grid when needed to help utilities keep the grid stable with the integration of renewable energy. Another success is Measurabl, a software company that makes a dashboard for analyzing large building energy and water use, among other products.

There is an equity component to Cleantech San Diego as well. Eddie Price of GRID Alternatives has been meeting with Cleantech San Diego president and CEO Jason Anderson about creating an Energy Equity Center that would house energy companies and provide public space for community education. As part of this endeavor, Price plans on developing a sustainability curriculum for the local elementary school that can be replicated throughout the school system.

The battle with utilities will continue, as CCAs have threatened their business model. And utilities have competing internal interests. On one hand, utilities are fighting CCAs over renewable adoption because they have coal and natural gas assets that they don't want to retire, or they are locked into long-term purchase contracts. On the other hand, utilities are major advocates of electric vehicles because they can sell more electricity.

Rapid adoption of intermittent renewable energy, as noted, is already creating challenges for California's grid. As solar and wind penetration grows, CCAs will have to promote policy to build new transmission lines for energy trading, battery storage, the smart grid, and smart EV charging (see chapter 5).[46]

Municipal Ownership

Several cities with municipally owned utilities have spearheaded the transition to renewable energy. Georgetown, Texas; Burlington, Vermont; Austin, Texas; and Los Angeles are frequently cited examples. In Europe, Copenhagen and Hamburg, among others, have led the way.

As with CCAs, municipally owned utilities face political opposition and tension with private utilities. Although many MOUs in the United States are leaders in renewable-energy purchasing, only investor-owned utilities (IOUs) have to follow state RPS requirements. And as with IOUs, the same debates over what constitutes clean energy play out with MOUs. Critics of the speed with which municipals are moving to renewable energy in Massachusetts argue that when MOUs sell renewable-energy credits to IOUs, they are counted by both and that they overestimate the move to renewables by counting nuclear.[47] Municipals invested in nuclear respond to the criticism, arguing that it is a carbon-free source of electricity.[48] Regardless of energy source, municipals generally offer lower rates than IOUs. And because they are locally owned and operated, more consumer dollars stay local.[49]

Here we will focus on two cities with MOUs: Austin, Texas, and Hamburg, Germany. Municipally owned Austin Energy has been increasing renewable-energy purchases for 20 years, but it will have to figure out how to address barriers to achieving ambitious goals. Hamburg has been developing a pathway for "remunicipalizing" a private electric utility that had formerly been publicly owned to achieve ambitious renewable-energy goals.

Austin: A Green City in a Red Renewable State

Texas is a bundle of contradictions, one being that this deeply Republican state is the nation's leader in wind energy and gets about 20 percent of its energy from renewable sources. Austin, the state capital and home to its flagship university, is a Texas outlier both in its politics and in controlling its own utility. Renewable energy is one part of Austin's aggressive climate plan that calls for net-zero greenhouse gas emissions by 2050.

Austin City Council has been requiring Austin Energy, created in the 1890s, to purchase increasing amounts of renewable energy since 1999. At the time, it was one of the first cities in the country to establish an RPS. The city council was concerned that the RPS, considered a bold move at the time, would lead to high energy prices, but it was pressured to pass the measure by the city's Resource Management Commission, an advisory body to the council on alternative energy and water conservation. Additional pressure was applied by Public

Citizen, a national nonprofit public interest organization whose Texas branch was promoting expansion of renewables. Public Citizen organized Solar Austin, a coalition of renewable-energy businesses and advocates, urban planners, and residents, to persuade the city council to embrace renewables. With strong support from incoming mayor Will Wynn, the RPS passed at the end of 2003.[50]

With the political will, the policy, and a commitment from all players—the mayor, the city council, Austin Energy, advocacy organizations, and the public—one would think it would have been smooth sailing to adopting a 100 percent renewable-energy goal. Instead, it has been a story of fits and starts.

The amount of renewables in the system has been increasing gradually, and now stands at 23 percent, but it still has a long way to go. In 2017, the city council passed the Austin Energy Resource, Generation and Climate Protection Plan, which mandates that Austin Energy obtain 65 percent of its power from renewable sources by 2027. The latest mandate, passed in 2018 and supported by a report of the city council's Generation Task Force, calls for Austin Energy to be 100 percent carbon free by 2030. To meet that goal, Austin Energy has made several utility-scale solar purchases from West Texas.[51] In October 2018, the utility approved a 15-year contract that will take it to 52 percent by 2021. Two months later, the city council approved a power purchase agreement between Austin Energy and a solar farm in nearby Pflugerville.

Impressive as these renewable gains are, grid capacity will be maxed out before Austin reaches its goal. ERCOT, the Texas grid, obtained about 18 percent of its electricity from wind and solar in 2017. If Austin and other Texas cities add solar and wind as planned, the grid will quickly reach capacity. As already noted, no grid has been able to handle more than 30 percent of capacity in renewables. Texas also faces an additional challenge: getting wind power from the sparsely populated, wind-heavy west to cities far away in the east. ERCOT has started a major transmission project that will improve grid reliability in West Texas, scheduled for completion in 2021. ERCOT is also investing in battery storage options to defer or eliminate transmission upgrades. Many are relying on predictions that by the time the most advanced adopters reach that 30 percent mark, advances in battery storage will allow more intermittent capacity to be dispatched. But some experts hold that more reliance on concentrated solar thermal with storage would help solve the overcapacity problem in a way solar PV can't.

Enter Paul Robbins, the energy and environmental activist we met in chapter 3 who was the brains behind Austin's district cooling plant. Robbins argues that Austin has to move away from solar PV to utility-scale, concentrated, solar thermal power. He says that "just six-tenths of 1 percent of the land in Texas could provide all of its total 2017 electric consumption." Further, he holds that it can employ on-site compressed air energy storage that uses intermittent or low-cost power to produce compressed air in geologic formations.[52] To draw energy, the air is heated in an efficient combustion turbine. Although the process requires natural gas, the amounts are small. Robbins suggests that as the technology is perfected, waste heat from the compression process could replace natural gas.

We saw concentrated solar thermal power piloted in Lancaster and established in the Mojave Desert. There are at least 150 concentrated solar thermal projects operating worldwide, but very few with on-site storage. Robbins makes the case that Austin should work cooperatively with other Texas utilities, cities, and private companies to develop more concentrated solar thermal with on-site storage to reach its 100 percent goal. The problem is that few want to invest when PV is so cheap and concentrated solar thermal has not reached economies of scale. Although solar technologies other than PV have considerable utility-scale potential if explored, Austin Energy is tied up in natural gas and coal assets that are only at half their expected lifespan. Financially, utilities can't just abandon these energy investments in favor of solar and keep prices reasonable.

With serious investment in utility-scale solar thermal infeasible at this point, Austin Energy has been greenovating in PV. Its Value of Solar Tariff program takes a different approach than net metering to purchasing excess energy from customers with PV systems. Austin Energy calculates the benefits of solar, such as savings from system loss; wholesale energy and new generation capacity; fuel price stability (due to long-term contracts); avoided new transmission and distribution infrastructure savings; and environmental benefits to determine the buy-back rate, which is then adjusted annually according to market conditions.

While the Value of Solar Tariff program benefits those who can afford to install PV systems, the city council emphasized energy justice in its renewable transition by adopting a resolution that earmarks $500,000 of Austin Energy's 2018 budget to install solar on multifamily affordable housing and nonprofit organizations.[53] The nonprofit group Foundation Communities has been installing the systems, which reduce tenant electric bills. In implementing this approach to what is called community solar (sometimes called virtual net metering), Foundation Communities has run up against Austin Energy rules that require each unit of a multiunit building to have its own metered array, which raised costs 15–20 percent more to install.

Further, Foundation Communities pilots innovative projects in low-income communities to demonstrate that aggressive building standards are attainable. One project is built to the Living Building Challenge standard and another to a net-zero-energy goal. All these activities make clear that city government needs organizations such as Foundation Communities and its partners in the community, in the financial sector, and in the construction industry, to both drive change and orient it toward low-income communities.

Hamburg: Remunicipalizing as Energy Democracy

Germany has been supporting the development of solar and wind technologies by funding research and development, and providing direct subsidies, tax allowances, and loans since the late 1970s. These policies were mostly motivated by environmental concerns highlighted by the emergence of the Green Party in 1980. A key policy enacted in 1991, the feed-in tariff, requires utilities to purchase all renewable energy produced at prices set by the government for a specified time, usually 20 years—an arrangement that helps defray high upfront costs. Legislation in 2002 to phase out nuclear power by 2021 spurred even more investment in renewable energy.[54] Key legislation to support the energy transition, known as Energiewende, passed in 2010. It calls for reducing GHG emissions relative to 1990 levels by at least 80 percent and to have 60 percent of energy supplied by renewable sources by 2050. The result is that, today, Germany produces between 40 and 65 percent of its power from renewable sources, depending on time of year.

Cities and citizens have played a big role in Energiewende. German municipalities have considerable executive powers (for example, they are responsible for implementing a large part of national and EU legislation). Progressive cities such as Achen and Freiburg introduced feed-in tariffs and other policy measures in the late 1980s. Due to city and national policy, about half of renewable generation is owned by citizens, co-ops, and farmers.[55] One essential low-carbon strategy introduced by cities is utility remunicipalization, a move with strong citizen support. Historically, municipal utilities (*Stadtwerke*) were common in Germany, but many cities began selling them off in the 1980s due to fiscal crises.

Privatization of public services in Europe started with the rise of Margaret Thatcher in the UK in 1979. The selloff intensified in the 1990s and continued through 2007 with the liberalization of energy markets throughout Europe initiated by the European Commission.[56] Its popularity faded as political parties and citizens alike realized that energy provision should be a public and not-for-profit service. As their contracts with private utilities expired (more than half between 2010 and 2015), cities throughout Europe began repurchasing them. At least 72 cities have taken back their utilities.

At the forefront of this movement is the Free and Hanseatic City of Hamburg, a municipality and city-state with a population of 1.81 million. Between 2000 and 2001, Hamburg sold its electricity and district heating company and gas utility to private companies E.ON and Vattenfal.[57] Before the 10-year contracts were to expire, political officials across parties were beginning to realize that they had given up the ability to guide decisions on energy. In 2009, the Conservative-Green government bought back the utility and established Hamburg Energie to supply renewable electricity (under the ownership of the municipal water company). Hamburg Energie developed a program through which residents could choose locally produced renewable energy. While a movement was in place calling for repurchasing all utilities, the Social Democratic government elected in Hamburg in 2011 decided that obtaining only 25.1 percent of the utility back was sufficient to control local energy decision-making. That decision did not defuse the bottom-up coalition that had emerged in 2010, Our Hamburg–Our Grid, which included international environmental organizations such as Friends of the Earth, church-based groups, and other nonprofit groups that called for a referendum to remunicipalize the city's three utilities and to create a fully public utility with a "socially just, climate-friendly, and democratically controlled energy supply from renewable sources." They proposed a ballot initiative to let the public decide the issue. Despite opposition from the SPD and Christian Democratic Union, Liberal parties, trade and industry organizations, E.ON, and Vattenfall, the initiative passed, though barely, in September 2011.[58]

Our Hamburg–Our Grid raised €50 million in financing. With that support, the city completed repurchase of the remainder of the electricity grid for €495.5 million in 2016, and the gas grid for €355.4 million in 2018.[59] Citizens signed up in sufficient numbers that the utility was in the black within five years of the initial purchase.[60] Jens Kerstan, senator for environment and energy in Hamburg, formed an advisory board as an adjunct to the city's energy agency to manage the utility, with broad representation from Hamburg's citizens and experts.

Hamburg Energie continues to explore transitioning the CHP/district-heating network (see chapter 2) from natural gas to renewable sources. It is currently applying to be one of four federal "real laboratories for the energy transition," which would provide €80 million to develop a geothermal plant with an aquifer storage facility to power the district heating system in the Wilhelmsburg quarter of Hamburg.[61]

As a result of the city's control of its energy utility, a renewable-energy cluster comprising almost 200 firms in wind, solar, and biogas has emerged in Hamburg. In addition, Hamburg Energie, in partnership with Siemens Gamesa Renewable Energy and the Institute for Engineering Thermodynamics at Hamburg University of Technology, received funding from the German Federal Ministry of Economics and Energy for a Future Energy Solutions project in which thermal energy is stored in volcanic rock. When demand is high, the stored energy is converted to electricity. The idea is to demonstrate through the pilot that energy storage can be scaled up to supply more electricity on demand.

With about half of renewable-energy production in Germany under some form of community ownership in which citizens own shares in production, Energiewende has been a democratizing force.[62] Many *Stadtwerke* open renewable projects to individual citizens and cooperatives for investment, a practice stemming from a long-standing tradition that was interrupted in the late 1990s. In addition to these forms of participatory investment, the European Central Bank offered low interest rates for municipal buy-back investments when the private utility contracts ended.[63] Energiewende's goal is embraced by the German people. Even though Germans pay a renewable-energy surcharge of about €18 on their monthly electric bills, 95 percent say that they approve of Energiewende. Still, 37 percent complain that electricity costs are too high.[64]

Replacing nuclear power was a key feature of Energiewende, but Prime Minister Angela Merkel expedited the policy after Japan's Fukushima nuclear plant disaster in 2011, eliminating all nuclear energy (17 reactors) by 2023. It was a controversial move, since GHG emissions rose as more coal came online to replace nuclear power. Yet these concerns were soon allayed. Although a little over a quarter of Germany's electricity is produced from the country's plentiful brown coal and another 18 percent is from imported hard coal, renewable energy (all sources) surpassed coal for the first time in 2018, and in the first quarter of 2019 the country's coal plants produced about 20 percent less power than in the previous quarter.[65] It seems Germany is back on track to achieve its renewable goals.

Can remunicipalization take place elsewhere? Legal obstacles vary among European countries. The first hurdle is obtaining initial financing.[66] But it seems the movement has started. Several UK cities, including Nottingham and Bristol, had established municipal energy utilities by 2016. Nottingham's Robin Hood Energy, like many, focuses on fuel poverty. At the national level, these initiatives are supported by a Community Wealth Building Unit created to support transitioning utilities from the private to public sector.[67] As in Germany, high levels of public support combined with national government funding and other supportive policies are essential to establishing municipal utilities in the UK and across Europe. To date, Boulder, Colorado, is the only US city that has remunicipalized its energy utility.

Cities Facilitating Solar Adoption

Without nearly as much support at the federal level, or an EU-type body, US cities still have many ways to promote solar adoption. One is to lead by example through installing solar on all municipal buildings. Another is to make it easier for residents to figure out how they will benefit from solar PV systems. Both Boston and Cambridge, Massachusetts, have collaborated with MIT's Sustainable Design Lab in developing interactive online maps that allow property owners to determine how much electricity can be produced from a rooftop PV system and how long it would take for the system to pay for itself.

Another approach is to make necessary changes in zoning ordinances, and to simplify and speed up permitting, all of which ease solar installation. Cities can zone solar easements so that property owners can access sunlight across property lines without obstruction from other properties. Cities can also ensure solar rights to install commercial and residential solar-energy systems on properties subject to private restrictions such as covenants, condominium rules, building codes, or other local government ordinances.[68]

Cities can also take advantage of state policies allowing businesses or households with rooftop PV systems to sell excess power back to the grid through net metering. At least 40 states have net-metering laws, and in some that don't, utilities offer these programs. States vary widely in the caps they place on how much net metering is allowed and the rates utilities pay for the power, and a host of other regulations. Cities must pressure state officials to ensure that net-metering rules are fair and caps are expanded to promote solar adoption. Although net metering is available in Europe, many countries use the feed-in tariff to encourage renewable adoption.

Many US cities are also promoting community solar, or what some call virtual net metering, so that renters and people living in multiunit buildings can take advantage of solar. The basic idea is that solar energy generated in one place can be used or credited in another. The arrangement also applies to property owners who can invest in an off-site array if their own roofs cannot generate much solar. Another approach involves installing solar on multiunit buildings to power common areas.

From Energy Justice to Energy Democracy

In the case studies presented here, we have seen varying degrees of concern for fairness and justice in transitions to renewable energy, but it is clearly a recurrent theme. In fact, the energy justice movement emerged out of various environmental activist groups. Energiewende itself, which is attentive to developing renewable energy in an equitable manner, sprang from antinuclear activism.

Energy justice is commonly defined as "a global energy system that fairly distributes both the benefits and burdens of energy services, and one that contributes to more representative and inclusive energy decision-making."[69] Thus, energy-just decision-making must consider availability, affordability, due process, good governance, sustainability, and intergenerational and intragenerational equity and responsibility.[70] The emergent energy democracy movement has a decidedly more political focus, seeking to supplant the dominant fossil-fuel industry with a public, decentralized energy delivery system.[71] The energy democracy movement in the American and European contexts assumes various forms, but in general it calls for broad alliances that include energy but also apply the principles of just access to food and water and more equitable distribution of market goods—or making them public goods.[72] It is a unifying force for many environmental and climate activists, and also includes labor unions.[73]

Energy democracy underpins all the cases presented in this chapter to varying degrees. CCAs embrace energy democracy by definition, since their raison d'être is to reduce energy costs for all residents. Profits are invested back into the community, often favoring low-income neighborhoods. Lancaster's CCA is nested in a broader program of making energy even more affordable for low-income residents. Recall the city's affordable solar-energy community testing and prototype house demonstrating how new construction incorporating building efficiency and solar PV systems can be produced affordably, and its affordable microgrid community now under development. And remember that these projects got underway with bipartisan support.

In San Diego, activist Nicole Capretz mobilized various environmental and justice groups, leading to the adoption of the CCA and the city's legally binding 100 percent renewable-energy commitment. Potential tensions arose within the coalition—in this case between union and community demands. As we see throughout the book, green-blue coalitions support renewable energy and other green technology development, but the partners don't always agree. Historically, some unions have not been attentive to recruiting minorities into training and journeymen positions. Instead of presenting a unified front to the CCA, we see the union and community groups each acting in their own interests.

The European remunicipalization movement has a clearly articulated goal of removing profit from what should be a public good—more so than we saw in Austin. Yet Austin's city council is informed by groups such as Foundation Communities, which is building low-income housing much like Lancaster's. We see a combination of city governments that incorporate justice goals into their energy policy and those that need outside pressure groups to push the justice agenda.

ELECTRIFYING TRANSPORTATION

TRANSPORTATION ACCOUNTS FOR 25 PERCENT of GHG emissions in the United States and about the same amount in Europe. Alarmingly, the overall quantity of transportation emissions is rising worldwide due to increasing demand for cars. While much of the power to decrease transportation emissions lies with state or national governments, particularly in building transit infrastructure or setting national vehicle-emissions standards, cities also play an important role.

Cities can offer incentives to move residents and commuters toward less environmentally harmful modes of transportation, by making public transit more appealing, and biking and walking safer and more attractive. These "carrots" are often offered with "sticks" such as making car travel more expensive with congestion pricing (tolls for entering a defined area of the central city, usually higher at peak hours), reducing parking availability, and making parking more expensive. Cities may also green their fleets and implement city planning strategies to constrain auto travel in city centers, among other strategies.

One increasingly important way to decrease transportation emissions, and the subject of this chapter, is to electrify cars and other polluting vehicles such as trucks, buses, taxis, and trains. In the electric vehicle (EV) policy area, some cities are offering incentives to EV automobile owners by developing convenient EV charging station systems or working with utilities to develop innovative approaches to grid development and storage.

In just a few years, we have gone from only a scant number of electric models on the market to a spate of major plans among auto manufacturers to move away from gas-only cars. GM will produce 20 all-electric vehicle models by 2023, and Ford launched a $4.5 billion, five-year initiative, "Team Edison," to develop 13 new electric models, also by 2023. Volvo (owned by the Chinese company Geely) will phase out production of gas-only cars altogether by 2019. Already, France, Norway, the Netherlands, India, and the United Kingdom have set dates between 2025 and 2040 after which only EVs, or in some cases hybrid vehicles, will be sold.

Cities have a big role to play in accelerating adoption of EVs, particularly in building out charging infrastructure. This chapter examines the efforts of five leading cities, each with a different set of challenges. As we'll see, they have different strategies for addressing regulatory and planning issues that determine what types of charging stations can be placed where and how to charge for electricity. Some cities are electrifying their bus fleets and supporting the transition of taxi fleets and delivery vehicles to electric. Several are examining ways to charge using renewable power. And a few cities are pursuing vehicle-to-grid integration (V2G)—two-way interaction in which cars can push power back into the grid during periods of peak demand. We'll also see that the electrified transportation experiments in these five cities have met largely with success and that their innovations are already spreading to others.

The Pathway to Electric Vehicles

Let's first concede that cars are here to stay. Privately owned vehicles are convenient, comfortable, and time-efficient, allowing drivers to run various errands on the way to and from work (known as trip chaining). Most Americans reside in low-density areas that public transit cannot serve cost-efficiently. Almost 80 percent of Americans travel to work by car—alone. With notable exceptions, the overall EU car commuting rate is about the same as in the United States, although the total number of cars will not likely increase much in either.[1] Rather, it will be in developing countries that the number of cars is expected to rise—and to rise dramatically. As income goes up and the middle class expands in developing countries, so does car ownership. If current trends continue, transportation energy use and CO_2 emissions could increase by as much as 120 percent by 2050.[2]

Emission standards are important, but not sufficient for reducing the pollution caused by cars. In 2009, the Obama administration introduced a national fuel and emissions standard that matches California's strict requirement. The new standard took effect in 2012.[3] Under the mandate, new cars and trucks were required to be almost 40 percent cleaner and more fuel-efficient by 2016. The Climate Action Plan rolled out in August 2015 by the Obama administration took further steps to set emission standards for medium- and heavy-duty vehicles.[4] All these emission standards were a start, but they could be met without the introduction of EVs.

The Obama administration recognized the potential for electric cars. In his 2011 State of the Union address, President Obama said he hoped that a million EVs would be sold in the United States by 2015. To that end, the administration initiated a 2012 federal tax credit for EV purchases, which ranged between $2,500 and $7,500 (depending on battery size) for the first 200,000 vehicles sold per manufacturer. And in 2016, the administration announced an electric vehicle coalition, with federal agencies and private companies signing onto Guiding Principles to Promote Electric Vehicles and Charging Infrastructure.[5] While a start, these initiatives weren't strong enough to convince consumers to purchase EVs or producers to make them. President Trump, as discussed in chapter 1, is moving to roll back fuel-efficiency standards, but the current budget maintains the tax credit for electric vehicle purchases, which ranges from $2,500 to $7,500 [6].

In Europe, mandatory EU targets require that the average emissions of new cars sold must be 40 percent below 2007 emission levels by 2021, a target that cannot be met without rapid adoption of EVs.[7] And as we'll see, several European countries are moving even more aggressively on EV adoption. The EU's 2014 Directive on the Promotion of Clean and Energy Efficiency Road Transport Vehicles focuses on broadening the EV market and considering environmental and energy impacts linked to the operation of vehicles on the roads.[8] The European Clean Power for Transport directive of 2015 recommends that member countries ensure that there is one publicly available charging point for every 10 electric cars by 2020. Further, the EU requires that new and significantly remodeled houses install EV chargers starting in 2019 and that 10 percent of all parking spaces associated with buildings must include EV chargers by 2023.

While European policy is strong, China and India will be the real movers in EV adoption. China has a made a major commitment to EVs, and in 2018 purchased more than half of the EVs purchased in the world.[9] India, through its government-led National Electric Mobility Mission Plan, also has committed to selling six to seven million EVs or hybrid vehicles by 2020, and to sell only EVs by 2030.[10]

A rapid transition to electric automobiles could dramatically decrease GHG emissions and reduce air pollution in cities, which is an immediate threat to public health.[11] But we have a classic chicken-and-egg problem: consumers are hesitant to buy electric cars because the charging infrastructure is not adequately developed, producers won't make more EVs if consumers won't buy them, and the private market won't build charging infrastructure until there are enough cars to make it profitable. It is up to the public sector to correct this market failure.

While electric vehicles have the potential to be nonpolluting, the carbon reduction varies considerably depending on the source of electric power. A vehicle producing zero emissions at the tailpipe could still be responsible for high GHG emissions if the electricity comes from coal.[12] While some economists argue that subsidies for purchasing EVs based on environmental benefits may not be justified in places highly dependent on coal, recent analysis by the Union of Concerned Scientists reveals that even EVs in regions of the United States powered by coal produce fewer GHG emissions than new gas-powered vehicles.[13]

Electric vehicles also have benefits that extend beyond the transportation sector: they have the potential to improve the performance of the electricity grid. One notable innovation involving EVs is vehicle-to-grid integration (VGI), which, in the words of Robbert Monteban of Nissan Europe, allows cars to serve as "batteries on wheels."[14] The idea is that energy generated from vehicles can be fed back into the grid during times of peak energy demand, reducing the need for peaker plants (power plants used only in periods of high demand) or adding new generating capacity. If ongoing research demonstrates that feeding battery power into the grid does not reduce an EV's battery life and allows owners to earn income, EVs could be a relatively inexpensive solution to reducing peak demand and increasing renewable-energy storage.

There are many practical details to be worked out if VGI is to thrive. One problem is that automakers have proprietary communications standards that work only with their models. VGI requires a standardized utility interface and a translation system that allows utilities to communicate with all EVs. Ultimately this will happen; pilots are underway to address these technological shortcomings. And there are other challenges, such as how utilities send demand-response signals to vehicles and then compensate EV owners for energy procured. But if homes with solar power can feed electricity into the grid, it's only a matter of time before vehicles can as well.

Five Approaches to EVs

Three European cities and two in the United States stand out for their attempts to lead in the evolution toward electric vehicles. These cities are delving into practical problems and challenges brought on by the transition to electricity as the source of vehicle power. We begin with Oslo, considered the world's EV capital. It has not only built out an extensive charging infrastructure and provided incentives for purchasing EVs, but it has also experimented with vehicle-to-building and vehicle-to-grid technology. I follow the Oslo story with Amsterdam, which is transitioning taxis, buses, and delivery vehicles to electric and using the city as a living lab for smart charging. In London, we examine a city that is intensively building out charging infrastructure and undertaking policy and programs to make much of the city an ultra-light-emissions zone. We then turn to two sprawled, car-dependent cities—Los Angeles and Atlanta—that are innovating, each in an environment with different challenges. Los Angeles ranks only ninth in the nation in number of EVs, but it is moving aggressively toward electrifying several types of vehicles.[15] Until 2015, Atlanta ranked second.[16] In both cities, widespread adoption was facilitated by state incentives for purchasing EVs. While California offers many types of support to its cities, the state of Georgia pulled the rug out from under Atlanta when a rural-dominated legislature eliminated generous EV tax incentives in 2015. Given that not all cities can count on state support, Atlanta offers lessons in both the precariousness of state support and how to make progress without it.

The five cases covered here highlight questions cities are trying to answer in accelerating EV adoption: Who will install and maintain the chargers? If cities operate chargers, what legal arrangements are optimal for their operation? Where should cities locate chargers? How does subsidizing EVs affect the fiscal needs of other modes of travel? What other transportation policy strategies, both carrots and sticks, might complement EV to decrease non-carbon-based transportation? We will see that the answers to these questions partly depend on the national and state context.

Oslo: The Electric Car Capital of the World

With 61 percent of its greenhouse gas emissions coming from transportation, of which 39 percent is from cars, Oslo has developed an integrated solution for reducing pollution and emissions that features more electric vehicles, better transit, fewer cars, and more bikes and walking. As a start, Norway has exempted EVs from its hefty vehicle tax of almost 100 percent and its 25 percent value-added tax (VAT) since 2001.[17] Oslo has become the world's capital for electric vehicles due to these generous national subsidies, development of an extensive charging infrastructure, and incentives such as free charging, exemption from tolls, and use of HOV lanes. By 2017, half the new-car purchases in Oslo were electric. And by mid-2019, EVs comprised about 60 of all new vehicle sales.

In the beginning, support for EVs reflected industrial policy to promote two Norwegian-made electric cars, the Buddy and the Think City. Although neither of these two-passenger vehicles caught on enough to keep the companies afloat, they did help to increase public acceptance of EVs. But it took the country's biggest pop music group, A-HA, to press the case further. Marianne Mølmen, Oslo's former head of EV infrastructure, told me that the environmental group Bellona raised considerable public awareness through high-profile stunts, one involving

A-HA, which refused to pay tolls or parking fees while driving EVs. Each time the pop group was fined, they generated publicity for the idea that people who drove EVs shouldn't have to pay for tolls or parking. Bellona was eventually successful in convincing elected officials to expand incentives for EVs.[18]

Building on these early incentives, in 2008 the Norwegian Ministry of Transport and Communications, together with several tech companies, created a working group that developed a 10-point action plan for electrifying road transportation. The group established a goal that by 2020, 10 percent of passenger cars would be EVs and plug-in hybrids. Among the policies put in place were exempting EVs from charges on toll roads and ferries. At the municipal level, EVs can park and charge for free and drive in bus lanes, which saves EV commuters 20 minutes each way. Even without the subsidy, charging is practically free (about one dollar a day per charging station) due to abundant hydropower, which also means that EVs in Oslo are truly zero emissions.

While national and municipal efforts were ongoing, two nonprofits, the Norwegian EV Association and ZERO, an Oslo-based environmental organization, pressured Oslo elected officials to step up installations of charging infrastructure. In response, in 2007 the Oslo City Council approved the installation of 400 charging stations by 2011 and then committed to 900 in total by the end of 2014. The city contributed $2.76 million to install the chargers as part of a 10-point plan to reduce GHG emissions. The city council then established a Climate and Energy Fund that subsidizes installations of charging stations in parking garages, shopping centers, and commercial and multifamily residential buildings. Oslo now has 2,000 charging stations, 1,350 of which the city owns, and 20 quick chargers, some owned in a joint venture between the city and private quick-charging operators. The city is leading by example as well: by the end of 2016, 43 percent of the fleet of 1,200 cars were zero emissions. The goal is to transform the entire fleet to zero emissions over the next few years.

These national and municipal incentives worked. By 2011, EV sales began to grow exponentially as more models became available (e.g., the Nissan Leaf in 2011, the Tesla S Model in 2014, and the eGolf in 2015). By the end of 2016, almost 30 percent of new car sales in Norway were EVs. Oslo has more than 35,000 EVs, about 27 percent of the total in Norway.[19]

Since only about 30 percent of vehicle GHG emissions in the city come from private cars, Oslo is working on electrifying taxis and delivery vehicles. In August 2017, the city came to an agreement with taxi companies to make the city's taxis zero emissions by 2022. A nonnegotiable bargaining point for the taxi companies, according to Sture Portvik, Oslo's project leader on electric vehicles, was that the city ensure that enough fast-charging stations would be installed. Several vendors are now ready to meet this need, with apps taxi drivers can use to book their charging time in advance.

In addition to achieving emissions reduction goals, these electric vehicle measures should help reduce air pollution. The city is in violation of the EU Air Quality Directive about five to six days per year because the surrounding mountains create a ceiling over the city that traps particulate matter, nitrogen dioxide, and sulfur dioxide.[20] In February 2017, the city banned diesel on the most polluted days, which occur in winter. Portvik observed that the diesel ban had a psychological effect on people—and got them thinking that it might not be a good idea to purchase a diesel car. He notes that purchase of diesel vehicles has dropped from 82 percent in 2008 to 21 percent currently.

To address the impact of truck traffic, Oslo is participating in a multicity collaboration to accelerate adoption of electric trucks. A European Commission initiative, Freight Electric Vehicles in Urban Europe (FREVUE) seeks to reduce several barriers to wider EV truck adoption, such as high investment costs and limitations of range, payload, volume, and charging. FREVUE has initiated public-private partnerships that involve municipalities, freight operators, energy network providers, vehicle manufacturers, and others in lifting these barriers, particularly on reducing the cost of vehicles.

A second collaboration, SEEV4-City (Smart, clean Energy and Electric Vehicles 4 the City), brings together North Sea region countries in developing locally produced renewable energy to fuel EV cars and trucks. Oslo's SEEV4-City project seeks to link the building and transport sector with computerized demand management. Here Oslo's electric utility, Fortum, is working with the city to build a project called Vulkan, the world's most advanced parking garage for electric vehicles. It is a test bed for managed, bidirectional V2G charging. With so-called smart technology to manage charging of many vehicles, the garage's infrastructure can modulate vehicle charging by delaying, switching vehicles from high- to low-speed charging, or even completely turning off the chargers. If a lot of cars are charging at once, the system automatically switches some cars to a 50-kilowatt battery in the garage.

Vulkan is also pursuing ways of feeding power from car batteries to buildings. Jan Haugen Ihle, country manager of Fortum Charge & Drive Norway, says Vulkan's electrical system is set up to allow apartments on the floors above the garage to be fed electricity from cars in the garage. This form of VGI offers a relatively inexpensive way to reduce peak demand. Elsewhere, researchers are investigating how this technology could also provide storage to compensate for the intermittency of solar and wind power. Perfecting vehicle-to-grid integration is important because as EVs take off, utilities are concerned that they could destabilize the grid by creating high demand at peak times. However, if electric vehicles can offload their excess power at peak times, they could add capacity to the grid. While capacity is not currently a problem in Oslo, Fortum is perfecting the batteries and software for V2G charging (see note for technical explanation).[21] Haugen Ihle told me that Fortum has already deployed the software in several European countries and is in discussions with India, Canada, and other countries.[22]

While national and municipal policies have required tweaking along the way, political support for the transition to subsidized EVs at the national level remains strong in Norway. All political parties agree that more EVs are needed to meet the country's ambitious environmental goals and that it is too early to dismantle incentives. But there are discussions about replacing the VAT exemption with another type of subsidy that would eventually be phased out. Any policy adjustments would follow the "polluter pays" principle and allow the Norwegian parliament to meet a goal that by 2025 all new cars sold will be zero or low emission.[23] A big aspect of polluter pays is increasing gas prices. On January 1, 2017, new fuel taxes kicked in that raised the price to about $7.50 per US gallon for gas, and $7 for diesel.

National policies have not been consistently welcomed by Norwegian cities. Consequently, the national government is turning some EV decisions on subsidies, incentives, and policies back to the cities. For example, some cities complained that national policy decisions resulted in loss of revenue from tolls and parking. To restore that revenue, they have revoked free parking for EVs. In another example, Oslo's bus lanes were slowed because so many EVs were using them as permitted by national policy. In response, Oslo now requires that EVs in bus lanes must have at least two people in them.

Anecdotal evidence suggests that an unintended effect of subsidies may be to encourage people to purchase a second car. The *New York Times* ran a story about a Norwegian couple who mainly got around using bikes, public transit, and a car-share service. Taking advantage of subsidies, the couple bought a Nissan Leaf to replace their traditional car, and when its range wasn't long enough to travel to their country cottage, they took advantage of government subsidies to purchase a second car, an $87,000 Tesla.[24] Indeed, 40 percent of EV owners have another gas-powered car. The reason many drivers cite for not giving up their first car is range anxiety—fear that the electric car won't get them to a distant destination. Others say that the EVs available to date are not big enough for their families.[25] Still, a survey that examined use patterns estimates that the second EV car replaces 82 percent of gas or diesel car use.[26]

It is ironic that Norway can provide generous subsidies for EVs because of the income it derives from oil. Norway is one of the world's largest oil producers and plans to maintain its lead by subsidizing companies to explore new oil in the Arctic. With 12 percent of GDP and one-third of exports from oil, it would be economically difficult for the country to reduce production.[27] But it does create a contradiction in policy when emissions from the country's oil exports are 10 times its domestic emissions.[28] Norway, in short, is reducing emissions at home and disseminating them worldwide. Replicating the level of subsidy that oil-rich Norway provides would be far more difficult politically and economically in many countries.

Going Ultra-Low Emissions in London

London has an air quality problem and, in solving it, aims to become the ultra-low-emitting vehicle (ULEV) capital of Europe. Air-quality-related illnesses cause 9,400 deaths in the city annually.[29] Greater London exceeds legal limits for nitrogen dioxide emissions, about half of which are produced by road transportation. In addition to reducing air pollution, London's 2017 Transport Strategy calls for becoming a zero-carbon city by 2050. With about one-third of trips made by private car, EVs are essential to reducing both pollution and carbon emissions.

Much of what London is doing to reduce vehicle emissions is supported by the UK government, which has a legally binding carbon reduction target of 80 percent by 2050. To decarbonize the transit sector, the UK will be investing £600 million through 2020 so all cars will be zero emission by 2040. A £230 million grant program started by the Labour government under Prime Minister Gordon Brown in 2010 offers £5,000 toward the purchase of an EV. It was refunded in 2014 by the successor Conservative government for another six years as part of a broader £500 million initiative to dramatically expand market penetration. The program has resulted in sales of more than 100,000 electric cars, yet hybrids and EVs still accounted for only 4.4 percent of car sales in 2017, so there is still a long way to go.[30] As in Oslo, consumers are concerned about access to charging, which is why the UK is now placing great emphasis on developing charging infrastructure.

But even before focusing on EVs, London under three different mayors—on the right as well as on the left—had been implementing policies to reduce the number of vehicles in Central London. In 2003, then-mayor Ken Livingstone instituted the world's first congestion pricing zone.[31] Vehicles entering between 7:00 a.m. and 6:00 p.m. are charged a £11.50 daily fee ($15). The policy has reduced traffic by 34 percent and accidents by 40 percent, reduced nitrogen and carbon emissions, and increased cycling by 28 percent.[32] Taking matters a step further, in 2014 then-mayor Boris Johnson issued a Transport Emissions Roadmap establishing an Ultra-Low Emission Zone (ULEZ) coinciding with London's existing congestion pricing zone, in which higher-polluting vehicles are banned or required to pay a substantial fee to enter. The ULEZ was to begin in 2020, but Mayor Sadiq Khan started it in April 2019, 17 months earlier. It requires all vehicles entering the zone to comply with stringent EU standards or pay a daily charge of £12.50 for smaller vehicles and £100 for heavy vehicles (figure 5.1).[33] Such zones are being used by at least 200 cities throughout Europe.

To change the emissions profile of vehicles using the city, London is taking a multipronged approach to promote adoption of EVs of all types. Since 2009, EV owners have been exempted from the congestion charge and have free parking and charging in some boroughs. London also requires that 20 percent of parking spaces in new developments provide EV charging. In addition to cars, London's strategy focuses on electrifying buses and the city's iconic black taxis. If national and local initiatives to increase EV adoption work, London could have between 40,000 and 70,000 EVs by 2020, and 145,000 to 275,000 by 2025.[34] Such rapid adoption requires considerable infrastructure planning, as outlined in a 2015 ULEV Delivery Plan.[35]

In January 2016, London became one of five UK cities awarded funding from the Go Ultra Low City Scheme, a joint national government and industry campaign to stimulate the EV market by improving electric car infrastructure in the United Kingdom.[36] To date it has distributed £40 million, provided by the UK's Office for Low Emission Vehicles (OLEV).[37]

The London Go Ultra Low City Scheme consists of four elements, jointly implemented by the London councils, which represent London's 32 boroughs on policy; the Greater London Authority (GLA); and Transport for London (TfL), a functional body of GLA that manages all public transit and major roads. To address range anxiety, the first element will install rapid-charging infrastructure on main routes and in Central London to serve taxis and private-hire vehicles. Led by TfL, the goal is to install at least 300 charging stations for these vehicles by 2020. OLEV awarded TfL an additional £15 million for these installations.

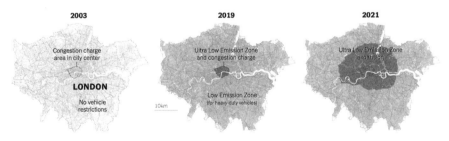

Figure 5.1 London's Ultra-Low Emission Zone
Source: Transport for London.

The second element will meet the charging needs of the anticipated 70,000 privately owned ultra-low emission vehicles (or ULEV—electric, fuel cell, hybrid, or other low-carbon technologies that emit less than 75 grams of CO_2 from the tailpipe) in London by 2020. Since London has few private garages, at least 60 percent of EVs will need access to on-street charging. To address such high demand, about 1,150 charging stations will be installed on borough roads in residential neighborhoods.[38] Already, the boroughs are getting daily requests for charging stations, so planners know that the chargers will be used.[39] Because proximity to and speed of charging are the most important factors in the decision to own an EV, planners expect these installations to motivate ULEV adoption.[40]

The plan's third element will provide car clubs (for-profit shared vehicle rentals) such as Zipcar.[41] This aid is needed because car clubs lease spaces from the boroughs, but are only given five-year contracts. Not knowing if their contracts are going to be renewed, car club owners aren't willing to make the long-term investment in charging stations. TfL views car club adoption of EVs as critical to its goal, so it is aiming to induce at least half of car club fleets to go electric within 10 years, with the added hope that car club membership increases to one million members by 2025.[42]

A program called Neighborhoods of the Future, a localized approach to facilitating EV adoption, is the plan's fourth element. The idea is to test different strategies for making ULEV ownership easy and to replicate successful ones. In January 2017, five neighborhoods working with Heathrow Airport were awarded £1.4 million to test strategies. This funding will be matched by £1.1 million from the London boroughs involved and Heathrow Airport.[43] Among the initiatives are a zero-emission zone, concentrated charging points on streets with EV-only parking and loading points, training for charging point installation and maintenance, and a trial of hydrogen-diesel-powered vans to serve Heathrow's delivery consolidation center.[44]

London also intends to have the greenest bus and taxi fleets of any global city by 2020. The city has the largest electric bus fleet in Europe, with more than 1,300 double-deck, hybrid-electric buses already in use in Central London. TfL has delivered on electric bus purchases ahead of the 2020 goal. The city is also a test bed of innovation in electric and hydrogen buses. If an ongoing test of an all-electric double-deck bus with inductive (wireless) charging is successful, more will be purchased. If another ongoing test of eight electric and eight hydrogen buses is successful, 300 single-deck buses with no tailpipe emissions will be added.

Likewise, plans are underway for transitioning London's 24,000-car black taxi fleet, with a goal of making 9,000 of the vehicles zero-emission capable by 2020.[45]

Already there are 2,450 hybrid-electric taxis operating and in October 2019, the first all-electric taxis started service. With these diesel-fueled taxis accounting for 18 percent of city traffic, electrifying them will have noticeable effects on air pollution. The initial plan required all new taxis seeking first-time licensing in London to be zero-emission capable, but this goal is changing as the ability to produce the vehicles and install sufficient charging is evaluated. TfL is providing grants to decommission older taxis and subsidize purchases of EV taxis. Drivers who trade in their diesel models receive £7,500 and up to £5,000 more if their vehicle is more than 10 years old, and thus more polluting. The ULEV program is installing 50-kilowatt fast-charging stations capable of filling an average battery to 80 percent power in 30 minutes. The national government provided £18 million to upgrade local power grids to support the high-speed chargers. TfL selected five companies to bid on installing 300 charging stations by 2020.

As in Oslo, the Taxi Driver's Association is supportive of the transition, but points out that success hinges on London providing sufficient fast-charging infrastructure. The average taxi travels 125 miles a day, but the new taxis will have a range of less than 100 miles. Many taxi drivers commute 40–50 miles into the city, and because the London taxi vehicles will be hybrid gas/electric they will have the option of using petrol in their vehicles before entering London.

Using a newly released study that identifies where demand dictates charging station locations, TfL is collaborating with UK Power Networks, the electricity grid operator, to design and install a charging system.[46] A problem with expansion is that London's grid infrastructure is at capacity in some areas, and if charging creates high demand at peak hours, it could trigger an overload. Thus, in some places where the city wants to install 50-kilowatt high-speed chargers, new feeder pillars or expensive substation upgrades may be needed.

It could be that locating charging sites will be one of the biggest barriers to rapid expansion of EV infrastructure. Using existing petrol stations is part of the plan, but there aren't enough of them to meet demand. Supermarkets and car parks are other potential sites and already accommodate some of the lower-level charging stations (7–11 kilowatts). But complaints are emerging about the visual pollution charging stations create, particularly in historic neighborhoods. A solution piloted in the borough of Westminster uses traditional streetlights as chargers. A German startup, Ubitricity, is retrofitting the lampposts to hold low-speed chargers, which hang unobtrusively a few feet above the sidewalk. Installation is inexpensive since the power connection already exists. EV owners use an app to sign in and are automatically billed from an electric meter ("smart socket") integrated into the charging cable. Ubitricity's low-speed chargers are designed for overnight use and thus won't tax London's strained grid. Further, the chargers can accommodate two-way power flow so they can feed power into the grid in the future.

A longer-term question is how to manage, maintain, and expand the infrastructure permanently, which is not a role the city wants. Katharina Winbeck, head of transport, environment, and infrastructure for the London councils, explains that the city's current involvement in expanding charging infrastructure is a temporary solution to the chicken-and-egg problem. "Nobody will risk taking on these roles without a revenue stream, which doesn't exist yet," she said.[47] Once there are more EVs on the road and more charging stations come online and charge for electricity, the hope is that a business case becomes viable and a public-private partnership can take over management of the infrastructure network.

Amsterdam: Fewer Cars, More of Them EVs

My first ride in a Tesla was a trip from the Netherlands' Schiphol Airport to central Amsterdam. When I asked how taxi companies could afford Teslas, the driver told me that the Dutch government provided a €10,000 subsidy per car to three taxi companies serving Schiphol—SchipholTaxi, BIOS-groep, and Taxi Electric, which collectively bought 167 Model S Teslas between June and October 2016. By 2019, 70 percent of the million taxi rides from the airport were in Teslas. It's all part of Schiphol's plan, with support and funding from Amsterdam municipality, to become one of the world's most sustainable airports. And there's an economic development connection: in 2013, Tesla opened a factory in Tilburg that does final assembly and testing of the Model S, and serves as Europe's parts and service headquarters. The plant has more than doubled production since it opened, to 450 cars per week. Tesla added a new warehouse at the facility in 2018.

Amsterdam made sure electric taxis took hold by giving them priority in the taxi lines at the city's Central Station and negotiating an agreement with the licensed taxi organizations that increases the percentage of emission-free taxis entering the station each year, reaching 100 percent by 2020. The commitment extends to buses as well. All buses serving the airport are electric and all buses serving the City Region of Amsterdam will be zero emission by 2025, using electricity from solar or wind power produced in the region. There's an economic development connection here, too. Two Dutch companies, VDL and Ebusco, produce the buses.[48] And the Chinese company Build Your Dreams (BYD), which supplied 35 electric buses to serve Schiphol, located its European headquarters in the Netherlands.[49]

In Amsterdam, as in other cities, delivery trucks and vans account for much of the traffic congestion. Already the city's largest grocery chain, Albert Heijn, is delivering groceries with electric trucks and is piloting electric delivery bicycles. But it is harder to transition larger delivery vehicles to electric because the number being produced does not meet the needs of companies serving the metropolitan area. To convert the delivery van fleet, the city periodically meets with a group of companies to discuss strategies for making all vans zero emission by 2025. The city now provides the charging infrastructure and offers subsidies for purchasing electric vans, which will be allowed to deliver from 6:00 a.m. to 11:00 a.m., a time when nonelectric delivery vehicles are banned. A Dutch start-up called Picnic, an online grocery store, is purchasing 2,000 electric delivery vans and will provide free grocery delivery using them. It is likely to become the largest EV fleet owned by a single company.[50]

As for privately owned EVs, Amsterdam began installing charging stations in 2009—well before there was much demand. As EV purchases grew, the city committed to building 1,000 new interchangeable charging points in 2011, and now has 2,800 toward a goal of 4,000 by 2020. But to meet this goal, Amsterdam faced a dilemma: while residents wanted to encourage more EV purchases, they did not want their narrow and crowded streets filled with charging points. Amsterdam's solution was to develop a demand-based system for authorizing new charge points. Drivers who cannot charge on their property (about 80 percent) may request a new charging point for their neighborhood, which the city council grants based on the proximity of already installed chargers.[51] National policy has helped ease the transition: all Dutch cities receive subsidies from the Netherlands Knowledge Platform for Public Charging Infrastructure, which has established national standards that make all chargers interchangeable.

Getting the charging infrastructure right requires accurate information. To this end, the city partners with the Amsterdam University of Applied Sciences (AUAS) to collect data on charging behavior, monitoring about 48,000 sessions monthly. Doede Bardok, a project manager with the city's Amsterdam Elektrisch program, which seeks to expand the charging network and encourage adoption of EVs, explains that knowing where, when, and how long people charge has allowed the city to be strategic about where to place new charging points. The project also examines how high-speed chargers affect owners' charging behavior to determine where to place them in the future. This demand-driven research allows the city to be strategic in placing the exact number and mix of regular and fast chargers to meet present and future demand.[52] In cooperation with other agencies and public-private partnerships, Amsterdam Elektrisch examines how to remove regulatory barriers and update city policies to support EVs, smart charging, and V2G integration projects.

Amsterdam and other Dutch cities are living labs for VGI experiments. The Dutch Living Lab for Smart Charging is using charging stations in 325 municipalities to explore the use of EVs to store peak power produced by solar and wind and feed it back to buildings. The project involves local and regional governments, grid operators, businesses, and universities experimenting with the most efficient ways to use smart charging, and the project hopes to establish international standards that can be replicated.

A three-year running pilot started in 2014 by Amsterdam Vehicle 2 Grid tested whether vehicle charging could be powered by locally produced renewable energy such as rooftop solar. In one experiment, photovoltaic panels were installed on a houseboat and a seven-kilowatt battery from an EV used as storage. Using the onsite battery storage increased the household's energy produced by the panels from 34 to 65 percent of what the houseboat needed. The arrangement also reduced flows to and from the grid significantly. With smart use of the EV battery, the household's grid dependence dropped almost in half.

A larger project (through SEEV4-City) has installed 150 Nissan EV batteries at Amsterdam's Johan Cruijff Arena, which will be drawn on to reduce peaks in demand and thus the need to draw on diesel generators. A related question under investigation is whether EV batteries degrade at an accelerated rate if used to supply energy.

Another EU-funded pilot works at the district level by visualizing all neighborhood electricity streams in real time to determine how and when to charge batteries, and how to incorporate renewable energy generated at the district level. This project connected 25 prosumers (households that produce as well as consume energy) with increased self-consumption between the houses and EV batteries. Examining energy use patterns and exchanges 24 hours a day during all seasons allows the project to determine what the impact of more EVs will be on the grid and how energy production and consumption can interact.

Despite these projects, several people I talked with said that V2G still has a long way to go, partly because bidirectional movement of electricity between cars and the grid has not been standardized and because of the high cost of V2G equipment. Further, even with more EVs, the Netherlands does not have a problem with grid capacity, so tech companies haven't been interested in developing software and hardware for vehicle-to-grid. As Hugo Niesing, the founder of energy and water management consultancy Resourcefully and expert in the city's energy and mobility transition, explained to me, "There is no money to be made nor a problem to be solved at this time. This will change when the share of city-generated renewable energy becomes large enough that peak load (either from EV demand or renewable production) causes grid congestion. The

EV increase is far faster than renewable, already causing charging challenges in parking areas."[53]

Amsterdam's strategy is not just to increase the number of EVs, but to reduce the number of cars overall, so the city promotes EV car sharing. Because of its extensive charging infrastructure and free citywide parking for electric car-sharing vehicles, in 2011, car2go chose Amsterdam to launch its first electric Smart Fortwo car-sharing program with 300 vehicles.[54] The system is not station based—users can pick up and return vehicles where they want. The only stipulation is that drivers must drop a car at a charging station in the city center if its charge drops below 20 percent.[55] The city is also getting polluting cars off city roads. A 2017 measure banned diesel cars from traveling within the A10 ring road circling the city. And in January 2018, Amsterdam banned older and more polluting two- and four-stroke gas scooters in the inner city.

Through national and municipal efforts, the Netherlands followed Norway in achieving the 100,000 mark in electric cars in 2016. Despite these efforts, it isn't clear whether Amsterdam can meet its goal of becoming a zero-emission city by 2025, particularly because the Dutch plan to ban gas and diesel cars won't completely take effect until 2030. Hopefully, the transition to EVs will accelerate. Meanwhile, in addition to lowering pollution and GHG emissions, policy to electrify transportation is enhancing economic development. The Netherlands Ministry of Economic Affairs reports an average of 73 new job openings each month and 2,699 new jobs overall between 2014 and 2017 in the electric transport sector.[56] Agency staff report that being a leader has meant that EV-related businesses such as Segway, Helios (fast-charging systems for electric buses), EV-Box (charging stations), Ebusco (electric buses), Allego (fast chargers), GreenFlux (chargers), and others have located there. All things considered, Amsterdam, Oslo, and London are greenovating cities in the digital and policy forefront of greening the transportation sector in Europe.

In the United States: California's EV Leadership in Cities

About 47 percent of all EVs in the United States are in California, where state leadership has paved the way for its cities to develop effective approaches to accelerating EV adoption. With the nation's worst air quality and six of the nation's 10 most polluted cities, California is seeking to electrify transport as much to reduce air pollution as GHG emissions.[57] Further, with the ambitious goal of reducing GHG emissions to 1990 levels by 2020 and 80 percent below 1990 levels by 2050, the California transportation sector, which produces 37 percent of the state's emissions, has to be a target. And EVs are also connected to California's aggressive pursuit of renewable energy—researchers are investigating how EV storage capacity can help solve the state's growing late-afternoon electricity demand spike.

The California Air Resources Board has focused on EVs since 1990, when it introduced a zero-emission vehicle (ZEV) program that set goals to increase new electric car sales through 2003. Although the program made many adjustments over time, and the goals weren't reached, the program did raise awareness and set the state on a pathway to its current success. By 2010, the board introduced a requirement that manufacturers sell an increasing percentage of ZEVs in the state—reaching 14 percent with 2015 to 2017 models.[58] In 2012, Governor Jerry Brown issued an executive order directing state agencies to accelerate EV adoption, which was followed by a ZEV Action Plan in 2013 that identified the steps agencies should take to reach a statewide sales goal of 1.5 million ZEVs by 2025. The plan was updated in 2016 with additional consumer awareness and education campaigns for EV cars, and measures to increase the commercial viability of ZEVs in the freight sector.[59]

The freight sector is a major polluter, so California provided $398 million in incentives for clean heavy-duty trucks, buses, and freight projects, $190 million of which is for advanced-technology freight equipment such as yard trucks, forklifts, and cranes used in ports.[60] Most of this funding comes from California's cap-and-trade auction proceeds. Other state programs offer funding for school districts to purchase electric school buses.[61]

To stimulate car purchases, California offers rebates up to $2,500 on new EVs, access to HOV lanes, and reduced rates for off-peak charging. The state's Public Fleet Pilot project provides rebates of up to $15,000 for public agencies in disadvantaged and high-pollution communities for purchasing plug-in vehicles.[62] Still, as in most places, it is wealthier people who take advantage of the rebates. There are fewer purchases by Latino and African American residents, even controlling for income.[63] So in late 2016, the state increased the rebates and put an income cap on who could receive them. People with household incomes less than or equal to 300 percent of the federal poverty level ($35,640 or less for an individual, $72,900 for a family of four) can receive $4,500 toward the purchase or lease of EVs, or buying or leasing battery-electric vehicles; $3,500 for plug-in hybrids; and $7,000 for fuel cell vehicles, an increase of $2,000 from 2014.

As for charging infrastructure, the state's public utilities are taking responsibility for some of the buildout. With energy-efficiency efforts reducing consumption, utilities see the EV market as a major source of energy sales growth. Originally banning utilities from participating in the charging market in 2011, the California Public Utilities Commission (CPUC) lifted its ban in 2016 and approved requests from San Diego Gas & Electric's Vehicle Grid Integration Program and Southern California Edison's Charge Ready Program to spend

$22 million on 1,500 EV chargers. Part of the SDG&E program involved installing chargers in communities with multifamily housing to increase accessibility beyond the garages of single-family homes.[64] By 2017, these utilities and Pacific Gas & Electric were on track to invest nearly $200 million in charging infrastructure in multifamily housing, workplaces, and disadvantaged communities. They have also submitted proposals to the CPUC to invest another $1 billion over five years, including chargers for buses and trucks.[65]

While the pace of California's expansion is impressive, an additional 125,000 to 220,000 workplace and public charging stations are needed by 2020 to meet the needs of the 1.5 million EVs the state wants to have on the road by 2025.[66] So in January 2018, Governor Brown issued another executive order launching a $2.5 billion initiative calling for 5 million ZEVs in California by 2030; he continued offering rebates and spurred investment in 250,000 charging stations and 200 hydrogen fueling stations to be installed by 2025.[67]

California is also exploring vehicle-to-grid integration. The CPUC and other state agencies are developing policies and examining regulatory changes needed to support expansion of vehicle-to-grid integration, which helps align EV charging with the needs of the electric grid. In addition, the California ISO (the grid operator) developed the VGI Roadmap with cooperation from California's Energy Commission and the CPUC, and provided opportunities for industry stakeholders to contribute to the process. As we saw in the Vulkan EV parking garage in Oslo, equipping electric vehicle charging stations with timers and automatic switches that can start, stop, delay, and accelerate charging is essential to vehicle-to-grid integration. The US Department of Energy's National Renewable Energy Laboratory (NREL) is partnering with industry and six other national labs on vehicle-to-grid technology that allows EV battery storage of surplus electricity generated from solar and wind during nonpeak periods and feeds power back to the grid when needed.[68]

In another vehicle-to-grid pilot, Southern California Edison and the Los Angeles Air Force Base demonstrated that its EV fleet could send power back to the electric grid.[69] But, as noted earlier, EVs don't yet have the standardized software needed to manage charging to support two-way interaction between vehicles and the grid.[70] This pilot tested software that allows such interaction.

Los Angeles: Beyond Electrifying the Car

With the state's assistance, Los Angeles has supported the construction of an impressive charging infrastructure, with more than 1,500 charging stations in place. The goal is to install 10,000 commercial chargers, 4,000 on city property, by 2023.

In March 2016, the municipal utility, LA Department of Water and Power, started Charge Up LA! The $21.5 million rebate program offers residents up to $500 and commercial properties up to $4,000 for installing fast (240 volt) chargers. Marvin Moon, director of the Power Engineering Division at LADWP, explains that even though 85–90 percent of LA's chargers are in residential garages, people need to see chargers at the workplace and on highways to overcome range anxiety.[71]

With 199 vehicles, Los Angeles has more EVs in its municipal fleet than any other US city, and it will convert its entire fleet by 2030. Leasing rather than purchasing the EVs allowed the city to direct a $1.5 million savings toward installing 104 charging stations.[72] Mayor Eric Garcetti spearheaded a partnership with mayors from Portland, San Francisco, and Seattle, and in January 2017 released a request for information (RFI) to automakers expressing their intent to jointly purchase 24,000 vehicles. As members of the Mayors National Climate Action Agenda, the four mayors invited the other 51 member cities to participate in the RFI. By March 2017, 30 cities had joined in, requesting 114,000 EVs—an order of $10 billion.[73] The mayors sought to use the purchasing power of cities to demonstrate demand and encourage manufacturers to offer a broader range of EVs by creating a bigger market of fleet buyers.[74] They particularly felt the need to let automakers know there is demand after President Trump announced his desire to review and reduce federal auto emission standards.[75] In September 2018, 19 cities signed on to a new initiative, committing to purchase EVs for their fleets.[76] In addition to sedans, the cities will eventually order police cruisers, street sweepers, and trash haulers.[77]

Public transit is also going electric. To reduce pollution, LA completed a phaseout of diesel buses in 2011, and in July 2017 the Metropolitan Transit Authority (MTA) committed to transforming its entire bus fleet to zero tailpipe emissions electric by 2030—the largest commitment of any US transit agency. Once the transition is completed, the city's nitrogen oxide emissions will decline by 20 percent and GHG emissions by 30 percent.

Such an aggressive commitment to new technology is not without its risks. Five electric-battery powered buses manufactured by BYD at a facility located in nearby Lancaster didn't perform well and had to be returned. But Mayor Garcetti, the city council, and MTA leaders agree that it is important for Los Angeles to serve as a test bed to perfect the technology. The city is piloting 95 electric buses on the city's two bus rapid-transit lines (Silver and Orange Lines) and 65 compressed-natural-gas buses to determine a strategy for having a 100 percent electric fleet by 2030. Then, starting in 2019, the MTA will purchase about 19 electric buses a year and has allocated $51 million to replace 35 Orange Line buses and $7.8 million for new charging stations.[78] The buses will likely be purchased from

New Flyer, located in Ontario, Canada. The MTA also committed $66 million for purchasing 60 buses from BYD for the Silver Line, and for charging stations and upgrades to wiring, all of which will be completed by 2021.[79]

There has been some debate over the decision to completely electrify the bus fleet. Denny Zane, former Santa Monica mayor and executive director of the public transit advocacy group Move LA, argues that the city should purchase a combination of zero-emission buses on shorter routes and near-zero renewable natural gas buses for longer routes. Acknowledging that heavy-duty, long-haul trucks are the single biggest air quality challenge for Southern California, Zane claims that electric technologies are not even close to a point where they can be used for long-haul travel. He thinks that if we completely stop using nonelectric bus technologies that can later fill the role of heavy-duty trucks, trucking will default to diesel. But if bus technologies such as near-zero emissions and renewable natural gas are kept in the mix for buses, it will be easier to replace diesel for trucks. Zane argues that buses are the proving ground for trucks: "I'm of course happy that we are deploying electric buses, but I want to keep some percentage that is near zero so that the bus sector is playing the role of developing for the whole trucking sector—which is polluting a lot more than buses."[80] Zane's critics argue that renewable natural gas is the same thing as natural gas—it uses the same pipeline infrastructure, and once it hits the pipes it can't be determined which gas is "renewable," arguing that is why the natural gas industry supports it.

Just as the state has worked to ensure that EV subsidies do not benefit only the wealthy who can afford the high purchase price of cars, Los Angeles is making sure that EVs are available to all. In June 2017, Mayor Garcetti announced BlueLA Carsharing to serve four low-income communities in Central Los Angeles.[81] Blue LA started with a demonstration station that offers community education, outreach, and test-drive events. The goal is to provide 100 EVs and 200 public charging stations to serve about 7,000 participants in the area. Funded with $1.7 million from cap-and-trade proceeds and the California Air Resources Board, it is a subsidiary of the French Bolloré Group, which runs the world's largest car-sharing service, Autolib, in Paris. Several community organizations are involved in education and outreach to residents. Cars can be rented monthly for as little as $10 or hourly at prices ranging from 15 cents to 50 cents per minute. Low-income users get discounts ranging from 25 to 80 percent.[82]

A pioneering form of EV adoption is taking place in the Port of Los Angeles together with the neighboring Port of Long Beach. Collectively referred to as the San Pedro Bay Ports, they receive about 40 percent of the nation's imported goods. They are also Southern California's largest source of GHG emissions and a major source of air pollution, which has been plaguing nearby neighborhoods for years. Plans to expand the use of electric trucks and other cargo-hauling vehicles are about to play a big role in reducing harmful emissions while addressing long-standing economic equity and environmental grievances. According to the California Air Resources Board, Southern California is burdened with between $100 and $590 million annually in health costs caused by freight-truck-related pollution.

Backed by Garcetti and Long Beach mayor Robert Garcia, the San Pedro Bay Ports' 2017 Clean Air Action Plan calls for reducing their GHG emissions to 40 percent below 1990 levels by 2030, and to 80 percent below by 2050. This goal will require a complete switch to zero-emission cargo-handling equipment by 2030 and to EV trucks by 2035. It's an ambitious agenda—currently 91 percent of cargo-handling equipment and 96 percent of trucks at the ports are not even low-emitting vehicles.

Since 2001, when a new terminal to handle increasing shipments from China was approved, community and environmental justice organizations in the neighborhoods surrounding the ports and the Natural Resources Defense Council (NRDC) had been opposing the growth of the polluting ports. The NRDC filed a lawsuit in federal and state courts charging that the environmental impacts of the expansion were not considered. The result of the suit was a $50 million settlement to be used to reduce pollution from the ports.[83] Stunned by the decision, port officials knew they had to address the twin threat of air pollution and GHG emissions.

In 2005, the Los Angeles Alliance for a New Economy (LAANE) and the NRDC organized social and economic justice organizations and unions to create the Coalition for Clean and Safe Ports to maintain pressure. When Antonio Villaraigosa became mayor in the same year, he appointed harbor commissioners supportive of decreasing polluting emissions and addressing job quality issues among truckers. By 2006, the ports had adopted their first Clean Air Action Plan, which called for reducing the ports' emissions (including from ships, trains, trucks, and harbor craft, and cargo-handling and terminal equipment) by almost half in five years. The plan required ships docking in the port to turn off diesel engines and plug into electric outlets. Meanwhile, the ports spent $180 million upgrading electric power systems to accommodate increased demand. A Clean Trucks Program launched in 2008 phased out older polluting trucks by subsidizing the purchase of newer models and charging fees to trucks not meeting standards. The results were impressive. By 2015, the ports' emissions from five pollutants decreased almost 85 percent.[84]

In 2011, the Los Angeles Harbor Department and the Port of Long Beach took a bigger step with the Zero Emission Technologies Roadmap. The Port of Los

Angeles undertook an emissions inventory of various types of handling equipment (e.g., cranes and forklifts) to benchmark progress.[85] Understanding the source of emissions was critical to the design of a road map for reducing them. The road map requires trucks entering the ports to have 2014 or newer engines now, and by 2023 engines will have to be at a near-zero-emission standard. By 2035, only zero-emission vehicles will be exempted from fees collected from noncomplying trucks. The ports also provided more than $7 million for pilots to develop and test zero-emission short-haul drayage trucks and long-haul trucks. Their performance is being evaluated through 2020.

Eugene D. Seroka, executive director of the harbor commissioners, is using what he calls a market-maker concept to achieve the 2023 and 2030 goals. He is working with well-capitalized companies to advance relevant technology so that it becomes commercially available and affordable. Electric versions are not available for all port vehicles, and commercially available equipment has not proven viable in meeting maintenance and repair needs. So the port's drayage operators are working with companies to advance the technology and partnering with other ports along the West Coast to convince manufacturers that there is a large enough customer base to make various electric drayage vehicles profitable to produce.

Critics argue that these small-scale, voluntary demonstrations and pilots are a start, but that more aggressive action is needed to reach the ultimate 2035 goals. NRDC lawyer Morgan Wyenn says that the current port leadership is nervous about being sued again by the Trucking Association, so they are not setting aggressive penalties for noncompliance.[86] She notes that major fines for nonelectric vehicles only begin in 2035—the year the goal of an all-electric port is to be reached. Part of the problem, she notes, is that while Mayor Garcetti is strong on climate change, particularly transportation-related emissions, cleaning up the ports has not been a priority, as it was under Mayor Villaraigosa, a union supporter who was motivated by the Clean Truck Program mandates requiring trucks entering the ports to be driven by employees of unionized trucking companies rather than by independent contractors. While this union mandate didn't hold up in court, the elements mandating cleaner trucks did.

Port leadership is also hesitant to move more aggressively because the port's history of partnering with EV start-up companies has not always been successful. In 2007, the Port of Los Angeles and the South Coast Air Quality Management District partnered to fund a prototype of a short-range, heavy-duty electric truck from start-up Balqon Corporation, providing $527,000 in seed money.[87] In 2008, while testing the truck prototype's speed, range, payload, and charging capabilities, the port issued a purchase order for 20 of the vehicles and associated chargers, for which the city and public agencies agreed to pay $5.7 million.[88]

In early 2009, with an additional $500,000 in seed money from the Port of Los Angeles and the South Coast Air Quality Management District, Balqon began building the electric drayage trucks. But the trucks never performed to the level needed, and Balqon, hit hard by the recession, couldn't raise the capital needed to execute its business plan. The company eventually went bankrupt, so the seed money the city provided in total didn't result in working drayage vehicles or new production jobs.

Still, the payoff to creating an electric vehicle sector makes investment worthwhile. In addition to BYD, headquartered in Los Angeles, Southern California has five other manufacturers of electric vehicles. And the Los Angeles Cleantech Incubator, created in 2011 to advance clean-tech startup companies, has more than 40 companies working on clean-energy and zero-emission transportation solutions covering everything from electric airplanes to energy storage and solar installation.

Los Angeles is one of few climate action plans that integrates strengthening the economy and building equity into its environmental goals. Mayor Garcetti achieved his goal of creating 20,000 green jobs during his first term and providing better access to the jobs to people in low-income neighborhoods. A similar ethos guides the LA Cleantech Incubator. In the words of president and CEO Matt Peterson, "We have values that we want reflected in companies that we are incubating."[89] The EV initiatives are undertaken as part of an overall strategy of providing neighborhoods with several mobility options, as seen in Blue LA. In the end, public- and private-sector concern for the health of people in surrounding neighborhoods—along with neighborhood pressure—solidified a commitment to electrifying most port vehicles.

Atlanta: Making Do without State Support

In a car-dependent, 8,376-square-mile metro area like Atlanta, EV adoption is an essential part of climate action planning. Although Atlanta's Climate Action Plan's goal of reducing transportation emissions 20 percent from 2009 levels by 2020 is not particularly ambitious, the Atlanta metro region was ranked first on ChargePoint's list of regions in the United States with the largest growth in EV sales in 2013. Sales were driven by a generous state tax credit that was rescinded by the legislature in 2015. Since then, sales have dropped by 90 percent.[90] Atlanta's story illustrates that cities are reliant on state and federal policies (there is still a federal tax credit for EV purchases) to achieve climate action goals. But it is also a story of determination to continue to lead on EV adoption—and to do so through an equity lens.

Failure to achieve federally mandated clean air standards motivated the city's first move toward low-emission vehicles. In 1998, Atlanta began participating in the State of Georgia Clean Fuel Fleet Program for cities and metropolitan areas with high levels of ozone or carbon monoxide. The program required government and private fleets to purchase a specified percentage of low-emission-certified vehicles.[91]

Also in 1998, the Georgia legislature created a state income tax credit for zero-emission vehicles that reimbursed drivers of leased or purchased EVs. The credit was expanded twice, ultimately reaching 20 percent of the vehicle's cost (up to $5,000), over and above the federal tax credit of up to $7,500. The legislation was introduced by the Democratic majority leader and co-written by Democratic governor Zell Miller's executive council and was not controversial. It was viewed as part of the solution to Atlanta's air pollution problem (the city ranks particularly high in the amount of pollution from car exhaust). But it wasn't used much, as very few EVs were available on the market. Don Francis, the Georgia coordinator for the US Department of Energy Clean Cities initiative, who has played a role in EV adoption in the state for the past 25 years, notes that utilization of the tax credit increased each year as more electric vehicle models became available.[92] Utilization of the tax credit really took off when Nissan shifted production of the Leaf to Tennessee in 2013 and began promoting a $199 a month, 24-month lease to stimulate sales. With this offer and the tax credit, it didn't take long for Georgia to become the number-one Leaf market in the country. By 2015, the Atlanta metro region was ranked first in Leaf sales, selling 1,000 cars a month.

The Georgia Environmental Finance Agency's Charge Georgia program, which ran from 2014 to 2015, funded 40 level-2 and level-4 DC fast-charging stations statewide—a start, but not enough to reduce range anxiety for people traveling long distances. In addition, the program offered rebates to cities, counties, and colleges to cover half the cost of installing charging stations, including planning, design, permitting, equipment, delivery, installation, inspection, and signage.

Supplied with generous incentives, Georgia drivers quickly saw that EVs have lower operating costs in their area, where electricity costs are low compared with some other parts of the country. An average gasoline vehicle costs $13.57 to operate per 100 miles in Georgia, compared with $3.53 for an EV—and can be as low as 40 cents if charged at off-peak rates. That totals to $1,258 a year for gasoline cars and $388 per year for EVs—a $10 million annual savings on fuel costs for Georgia's EV owners and a 22,000-ton annual reduction in GHG emissions.[93]

But Georgia's income tax credit for EVs was discontinued in 2015, and new EV sales dropped by 90 percent.[94] Francis points out that sales of the mid-market Leaf dropped 95 percent, while Tesla sales didn't go down at all, demonstrating that tax credits are necessary for middle-income working people to afford EVs. But the rural- and Republican-dominated legislature did not see any advantage the credits brought to their districts, where few people bought range-limited EVs. Further, traditional car dealerships lobbied the legislature to stop the incentives, which were hurting their sales.

Despite the loss of the state tax incentives, Atlanta's climate action planning has been successful in promoting EVs as one of several strategies to reduce transportation GHG emissions, which account for 31 percent of the city's total. The city's first climate action plan, unveiled in 2015 under then-mayor Kasim Reed, called for transitioning 20 percent of the city's fleet to electric by 2020, changing zoning ordinances to allow for installation of charging infrastructure, allowing self-permitting for installations from a city website, and offering single-occupancy EVs access to the HOV lanes inside Atlanta's I-285 perimeter highway and free access to I-85 HOT lanes north of I-285. By November 2017, the city council passed an ordinance requiring all new residential construction and 20 percent of spaces in commercial parking structures to be ready and available to install chargers.

To its credit, Atlanta has long addressed range anxiety concerns, a key factor in holding back EV adoption. The city started building out charging infrastructure in 2010. One of its first moves was to require the Office of Buildings to streamline the permitting process for residential and commercial charging equipment. Then in 2011, a large, mixed-use development, Atlantic Station, opened the city's first solar-powered, multiple-outlet charging station—with no charge for using it. In 2014, 18 standard and fast chargers were added at Atlantic Station along with 10 Tesla Superchargers capable of fully charging a vehicle in 20 minutes. This joint venture between CBRE (a property management company), Nissan North America, Tesla Motors, and Metro Plug-In will make Atlantic Station the Southeast's largest EV charging site. Charging rates are low or free and priced by time.[95]

The city has partnered with Georgia Power on much of its charging infrastructure, and in 2015, Georgia Power launched a $12 million program, Get Current-Drive Electric, which installed 37 public DC fast-charging stations throughout the state and offered subsidies for residential and commercial charger installations. In addition, Georgia Power has installed more than 100 chargers at Hartsfield-Jackson Airport and is adding more. The airport charges the same for these spaces as other parking, meaning charging is free. Further, Georgia Power's three-tiered rate structure reduces rates for off-peak hours, so EV owners can charge for just over five cents a kilowatt hour each night between 11:00 p.m. and 7:00 a.m.

The sustainability team of current mayor Keisha Lance Bottoms, whose term started in January 2018, is continuing the push for EVs. Stephanie Stuckey,

Atlanta's chief resilience officer, believes that Atlanta and other cities, even without state tax incentives, can be powerful drivers of EV innovation. She cites the city's partnership with Georgia Power and Electrify the South, a coalition of many partners—Clean Cities-Georgia, Southern Alliance for Clean Energy, Plug-In America, and other stakeholders—that provide education, outreach, and advocacy to keep the momentum going.

Stuckey is supported by Justin Brightharp, Atlanta's alternative fuel vehicle technical adviser. His position is partially funded by the Electrification Coalition, a national nonprofit business organization that works with cities to accelerate EV adoption to both reduce US dependence on fossil fuels and improve the environment. Brightharp explains that he is focusing on transitioning the city's fleet to EVs. A first step, he notes, is right-sizing the fleet, with more car sharing among departments. He stays in touch with fleet managers to learn which types of vehicles work best for different purposes to inform later purchases. "We have to look at the fleet holistically and target opportunities to add electric vehicles within specific departments," Brightharp says. He is also reaching out to the community to communicate the benefits of EVs, including the positive impact of EVs on local economic development.[96]

Ben Prochazka, of the nonprofit Electrification Coalition, puts the challenges facing EV adoption in broad terms: "We're working to disrupt a system where gas vehicles have a 100-year head start." He adds that there is a learning curve for consumers; they need to hear that EVs have a better technology, that the technology is cheaper, cleaner, and has better performance. "Changing the way we drive is a big effort and behavior change is hard," he says, "but we're working on it with the city."[97]

According to Stuckey, equity of access to EVs infuses policy and programs in the Mayor's Office of Resilience. "We heard from a lot of people that EVs are rich people's cars," says Stuckey, "and we don't want that to be the case."[98] One way the office is addressing equity is by working with Common Courtesy, a nonprofit organization that provides rides for those with limited transportation options, on EV ride sharing.

To fund its EV initiatives, Atlanta applied for, but did not receive, round-one funding from Electrify America, a 10-year initiative launched by Volkswagen as part of its 2017 settlement over deceptive emission-measuring practices in its diesel-engine cars. Electrify America will invest $2 billion in the United States on infrastructure and education to accelerate adoption of EVs.[99] Brightharp says the city is applying for round two.

Atlanta is also facing some state policy glitches on the road to EVs. As in Oslo, the HOV lanes are becoming quite congested, partly because of Georgia

Department of Revenue policy that allows flex-fuel (e.g., ethanol-based) cars to purchase plates that allow them to use HOV/HOT lanes. Don Francis, the Georgia coordinator for the US Department of Energy Clean Cities initiative, says he and others are trying to get the rule changed to include only designated alternative fuel vehicles. Another obstacle to EV registration in Georgia is cost—there is a $200 annual alternative-fuel vehicle fee plus $55 annually for the alternative fuel license plate required for HOV/HOT lane access.[100]

An additional policy barrier to EV adoption in Georgia concerns unresolved questions about what utilities are permitted to do within the context of public utility commissions. Georgia Power wants to participate and sees expansion into EV charging as a natural extension of its mission, but without approval from Georgia's Public Service Commission, which regulates railroads and energy providers, the utility cannot charge customers for charging. Stuckey is optimistic, commenting that the city has good relationships with Georgia Power and the Public Service Commission, and all agree on promoting EVs. She adds that one of the five PSC commissioners, Tim Echols, is a big supporter of electric vehicles and solar in the state.[101]

Stuckey acknowledges that cities can't rely on state and federal subsidies for the long term. Still, the city supports a bill pending this session to re-establish a tax credit for EV purchases. In its current form, the rebates would be considerably lower than in the past, maxing out at $2,500, and the program would sunset after five years. She is not hopeful about adoption, however, since it is an election year and the legislative session will be short, meaning not many bills will pass. In favor of the bill, a recent study estimated that lowering or eliminating the registration fee and reinstating a $2,500 tax credit would add $100 million to Georgia's GDP and create $54 million in increased income and 951 full-time equivalent jobs.[102] The city of Atlanta, along with Plug In America, EV Club of the South, the Southern Alliance for Clean Energy, Clean Cities–Georgia, and the Sierra Club support the proposed legislation. Time will tell if Georgia seeks to reclaim its EV leadership status.

Planning and Policy Priorities to Support EVs

Developing charging infrastructure is the most important action cities can take to promote EVs. Yet no city can fund such programs without help from higher levels of government. We have seen how EV sales in Atlanta plummeted when state support for tax incentives was withdrawn. We have also seen the importance of good urban planning to regulate charging infrastructure, determine its best locations, and make sure it doesn't create "visual clutter," a concern expressed to me by planners in London and Amsterdam. For dense cities, providing enough public chargers is essential, whereas in less dense cities where single-family housing prevails, most chargers will be in private garages. In cities like Atlanta and Los Angeles, where most chargers will be in residential garages, there may be less need for public charging. Even so, Atlanta's Don Francis notes that people who have their own chargers still need to see them in public settings to be convinced that they can do more than travel to work and back in EVs. And as we learned from London, companies like Ubitricity are developing charging systems to meet the unique needs of different types of neighborhoods.

Next in importance is facilitating EV adoption beyond private cars and city fleets. Two key approaches to electrifying taxi fleets are London TfL's mandates and Amsterdam's subsidies and prioritization in taxi queues. London's mandates may not work in the US context: when New York's then-mayor Bloomberg tried to require that taxi owners move to hybrid vehicles, taxi owners took the city to court and the mandate was struck down because the requirement was essentially a fuel-efficiency standard, something only the federal government can impose. Meanwhile, the city is being used as a test bed for electric and hydrogen buses— working with private companies to extend their range. The Port of Los Angeles is also playing a test-bed role as companies develop electric versions of various port vehicles.

Cities also can support the transition of delivery vehicles to EV, an increasingly important focus as more and more products are ordered online with expectations of ever quicker delivery. Amsterdam addresses the problem by limiting access for traditional vehicles in congested areas, while allowing electric vehicles to deliver any time. In Amsterdam, electric bicycles are also being used for grocery deliveries—a mode that will work in compact cities, but not in most sprawled North American metros.

Vehicle-to-grid integration is part of a broader move away from centralized, one-way power delivery to distributed and multidirectional energy grids that require a different business model for utilities and different regulations. As we are seeing in renewable-energy net metering, feeding energy from rooftop solar substitutes for power plants in some countries, and the same could apply to EV owners, should vehicle-to-grid integration prove viable. Here too, urban pilots such as those in Oslo, Amsterdam, and California are examining this viability in their quest to speed up adoption of the technology.

These four strategies give cities an important role in facilitating the transition to EVs. They are, however, actions that facilitate adoption. Without national and state or provincial policy, cities cannot go it alone.

LIBERATING CITIES FROM CARS

THE NUMBER OF CARS worldwide will likely double by 2030, and if we continue on the same path, that figure will rise to a staggering 2.5 billion by 2050. Since global population is concentrated in metropolitan areas, the number of cars in cities must be reduced dramatically to achieve the Paris Climate Agreement's goal of reducing GHG emissions 80 percent by 2050, let alone the more aggressive goals cited in chapter 1. Some European cities, as we shall see, have made admirable progress in reducing auto dependency. But making this transition in US cities will be excruciating, as nearly all are built around the car. Even well-promoted high-speed lanes for vehicles with more than one driver, a strategy that is pure carrot, has hardly made a dent in the American penchant for driving to work and perhaps doing errands or picking up the kids on the way home. In fact, vehicle miles traveled in the United States have been rising for the past three years—back up from a 2005 peak that was suppressed as a result of the Great Recession.

Can we reduce America's dependence on cars? Driving less means using other modes of transportation more—public transit, biking, and walking. But options vary depending on a city's population, density, degree of sprawl, and extent of twentieth-century rail removal. The only public transit in most American cities is the bus, which is often associated with inconvenience and poverty. For most people, it plainly takes longer to get to work and to do errands by bus. With the exception of those living in a few large cities with decent subway and light-rail systems and self-consciously green biking enthusiasts, cars are the preferred transportation of most Americans.

In most American cities, cars are given priority while buses, trolleys, bikes, and pedestrians are relegated to the leftover space. Many people in low-income neighborhoods have neither cars nor adequate access to reliable transit, yet equity objectives related to accessibility and affordability of transit are not often integrated into transportation plans in North American cities.[1] Urban planners are enthusiastically rethinking how to design city streets. With fewer cars and parking spaces dominating the streets, the new thinking goes, city lanes can be opened up for other uses and more people can be moved faster, more pleasantly, and with a lot less pollution. These plans need to be evaluated on the extent to which they articulate and deliver on transit equity goals.

In this chapter I begin with a range of actions cities can pursue to deprioritize cars while making room on their streets for transit, cyclists, and walkers. I describe how these strategies work in greenovating cities. The first case presented is Oslo, which is moving toward a car-free downtown. We then examine three American cases that illuminate the technical, political, and cultural barriers to deprioritizing cars. Efforts in Seattle illustrate that even in a liberal city committed to climate action, deprioritizing cars is painful and politically charged. Nashville's two failed ballot initiatives to fund transit infrastructure reveal the challenges many cities will face in trying to introduce public transit. Nashville also illustrates the chicken-and-egg problem facing transit investment: the city is not dense enough to support the transit advocates propose, but if transit is not used to concentrate new development, it never will be. Finally, Salt Lake City has been successful in implementing public transit. With broad public support and constraints caused by mountains and lakes, Salt Lake City has been able to forge new transit links to reduce congestion.

A Range of Action to Deprioritize Cars

Deprioritizing cars is disruptive, particularly in a nation addicted to cars. But some cities are making headway nonetheless. The pioneers are mostly in Europe, although several American cities are also taking impressive steps to stem the auto habit. Strategies and policies on the continuum of necessary action steps are not mutually exclusive; in fact, they are often integrated. While some are positive (carrots) and some punitive (sticks), we will see that views on what is a carrot and what a stick differ. Some combination of the following measures, however, is nearly always in play.

Create Car-Free Areas

Some European cities are going car free. It's hardly a new idea. Florence, Italy, has closed off its 40-block historic center to all but pedestrians, taxis, and buses since the 1970s, as have many other Tuscan towns.[2] Venice is completely car free.

Freiburg, Germany, banned cars in its historic center in 1973 and built extensive bike and trolley infrastructure.[3] Brussels has Europe's largest car-free area, and city officials are continually seeking to expand it. Complementary policies in Brussels include offering free transit rides on high-pollution days and an annual mobility week of public education and outreach on alternatives to car commuting. The week begins with a car-free Sunday, when cars are not allowed on streets in the region. It helps that these cities are both compact and have good alternatives to cars—traits shared by few American cities.

Berlin, Hamburg, Madrid, and Oslo are among the European cities currently taking comprehensive action to create car-free zones and adding bike "superhighways"—physically separated, uninterrupted bike lanes that traverse a city. Berlin's famous Unter den Linden began allowing only buses, taxis, and bikes in 2019. And in April 2019, Berlin senator for environment, traffic, and climate protection Regine Günther announced that the entire city would become car free by 2030, a controversial undertaking. Hamburg's approach is more comprehensive, but slower: pedestrian-only zones will be added gradually to include 40 percent of the city by 2035. Building on the success of a 2005 car ban in Madrid's busy Las Letras neighborhood, all but buses, zero-emission delivery vehicles, taxis, and cars of residents were banned in the entire center city in November 2018. The move is part of Madrid's 2014 Sustainable Mobility Plan that seeks to ban cars from much of the city by 2020.

Provide Less Parking

Too many cities that promote transit and biking don't focus on the role of parking in people's decisions to drive. A considerable body of research demonstrates a correlation between parking availability and driving, and new empirical research found that plentiful parking actually causes more driving.[4] Yet most US cities, far from discouraging parking, establish parking minimums—rules that require developers of commercial and residential projects to build a minimum number of new off-street parking spaces. Parking minimums not only promote driving, but make housing more expensive because its cost is folded into housing sales and rentals.[5] And much of the parking required isn't used. Even mixed-use and urban transit-oriented developments designed to promote walking and transit use create more parking than people use—some by as much as 65 percent.[6] One of the most vocal analysts of this problem, Professor Robert Cervero, a transportation planner at the University of California, Berkeley, holds that the reason so few transit-oriented development projects significantly increase transit use is too much available parking. It's a vicious cycle—plentiful, cheap parking makes it easy for people to favor driving, and vast surface lots in sprawled cities make it more difficult to get around on foot or by bike.

Too many cities have contradictory policies. Cities that want to increase transit—the carrot—will not be effective without the stick of reducing the amount of parking and increasing its cost. A first step is to experiment with reducing or eliminating parking minimums.[7] Among cities pursuing this approach are Buffalo, Columbus, London, Mexico City, Paris, Philadelphia, San Francisco, Seattle, and Washington, DC. Other cities are reducing the amount of free parking on offer. Zurich has taken a comprehensive and highly managed approach. In 1996, the city capped the number of parking spaces—and instituted a cap-and-trade-type system that requires retiring old spaces to match any new spaces. Parking minimums are adjusted depending on proximity to transit. And rather than relying on congestion pricing, the city stops cars en route to the central city when monitors show that the number of cars that can easily move around has been reached. The city has even added traffic lights on routes into town to create congestion. Making life miserable for car commuters is the plan.[8] With a vast tram network, trains, and buses, two-thirds of the city's trips are made on public transit.[9] While few cities will be willing to go this far, Zurich illustrates how complementary policies effectively deprioritize cars.

Institute Congestion Pricing

This approach defines areas in central cities that cars must pay to enter, with higher prices at peak travel times. The idea is to charge drivers for the real economic and environmental costs their vehicles impose on a city. The revenue generated is invested in public transit and related transportation improvements. Although only three cities have implemented such charges—Singapore (1975), London (2003), and Stockholm (2006)—it is currently on the agenda in a few other places. Other cities, such as Washington, DC, have variable tolls on commuter highways leading into the city, with continuously updated electronic billboards displaying fees reflecting current congestion (as high as $40), and well-marked exit lanes diverting would-be car commuters to nearby transit hubs offering plentiful parking.

Congestion pricing is effective in reducing car traffic. In Singapore, the number of cars entering the center city during peak travel times declined 44 percent within months of implementation, a bigger drop than anticipated. Carpooling increased by 300 percent, facilitated by adding more park-and-ride parking spaces, and public transit use increased from by 33 to 69 percent of commuting trips.[10] London's traffic congestion declined by 30 percent. Stockholm also exceeded expectations of reducing traffic by 10–15 percent, with a decline closer to 24 percent. Singapore's GHG emissions have declined by 10 to 15 percent in the inner city, and Stockholm's by 14 percent.[11]

Key to achieving the broad goals of congestion pricing is reinvesting revenue in transit infrastructure. London's program requires that all revenue generated be spent on public transit. London and Singapore increased the number of routes and frequency of buses, and added new park-and-ride facilities. In London, bus delays declined by 50 percent and, as a result, bus ridership increased by 38 percent in the program's first year.[12] These successes have led both cities to adjust pricing along the way to further maximize effect.[13] That said, Singapore's rather draconian measures to limit car use are not politically feasible in many places. Parking prices in the central zone were increased by almost 100 percent.[14] Residents must purchase certificates that cost up to $37,000 to purchase a car, and the number of certificates available is limited by the government.[15]

Even without such severe deterrents, most cities will find that public opinion is against congestion pricing. That is why it had to be introduced on a trial basis in Stockholm.[16] Although almost 80 percent of Stockholm residents opposed congestion pricing at the start, the results—greater ease and pleasure of movement across the city—changed people's minds and the system was made permanent.[17] The only attempt to put it in place in the United States was in New York City, in 2007, and again 2018. Both times it was killed by a state legislature dominated by suburban interests. A more recent "baby step" toward congestion pricing is under debate in Massachusetts. In July 2018, the state legislature approved a pilot study to offer discounted tolls on two major roads for travelers during nonpeak hours. Governor Charlie Baker threatened to veto the measure, arguing that it would be punitive to commuters who didn't have scheduling flexibility. This argument isn't without merit, and low-income commuters with no transit alternatives would be hit hard by it. Evidence to date suggests that this highly effective solution is politically untenable in many places.

Build Right-Sized Bus Rapid Transit

While a main goal of transit, particularly bus service, is to provide mobility for those without cars, transit only works to reduce emissions when buses and trains are full. Many cities are beginning to act on the realization that 40-foot buses aren't always viable in this respect. Here is where experimentation with on-demand vans and other more nimble services could yield more efficient, at-capacity transit solutions. And there is a role for expanding transit in ways that adapt to the needs of particular cities.

While rail dominates in Europe, we have noted that most US cities only have buses. There is renewed enthusiasm and success for light rail and subways in some cities, but as we'll see in our cases, obtaining funding has been difficult. Since only a few US cities have density sufficient for light rail, let alone subways, bus rapid transit (BRT)—buses that move in their own lanes, drive up to platforms, and board like trains—is catching on as a lower-cost alternative to subways, streetcars, and light rail. It's not an either-or choice—even in cities with extensive subways, such as New York, BRT systems keep people moving quickly above ground.

BRT uses modern buses to counter the "loser cruiser" image of buses dominant in American cities, starting with the high school kid who takes the school bus while the cool kids have cars, to the commuter who can't afford a car, to the elderly person who can no longer drive a car. The presumption is that people take the bus only if they don't have another choice. Advocates hope to change all that, with BRT making buses an attractive option, even cool.

The Institute for Transportation and Development Policy (ITDP) rates systems from gold to basic based on how many of the key features a system provides.[18] A full BRT buildout features dedicated lanes, raised platforms for level boarding, enclosed stations, off-board payment, transit signal prioritization, real-time maps, and integration with other transit modes.[19] Transportation planners refer to systems that don't have at least the first four infrastructure-heavy features as "BRT-lite."[20] For the most part, BRT in US cities is at the bronze level, just above basic, with few US systems having dedicated lanes.

BRT has generated enthusiasm because it combines the speed and efficiency of light rail with a cost between 4 and 20 percent less.[21] It can dramatically reduce carbon emissions and particulate matter pollution.[22] Further, many cities are finding that it increases property values, attracts economic development, and helps to revitalize blighted areas.[23]

The first BRT system dates to 1974 in Curitiba, Brazil, a city of more than 1.8 million. It was the brainchild of then-mayor and architect Jaime Lerner as a cost-effective way to decrease car congestion. The Rede Integrada de Transporte to this day is only one of three BRT systems worldwide that has achieved the ITDP gold standard. Large articulated (double or triple cabin) buses run in separated lanes with local traffic lanes on either side. The system also includes higher-speed express lanes.[24] Five radial busways between 5 and 7.5 miles long converge at the city's center from various districts of the city. The system carries about 2 million riders daily.[25]

Curitiba's experience reveals that zoning and land-use planning are integral to the success of BRT. The blocks adjacent to the five busways are zoned for high-rise buildings, both commercial and residential. Building heights taper off on streets further from the busways, ensuring that development occurs along each busway, rather than just in the center city. As a result, about 40 percent of the population lives within three blocks of one of the main busways. Observers of Curitiba's long-term commitment remind cities wishing to implement a gold-standard system that it takes "political leadership, innovation, pragmatism, technocracy, and continuity."[26]

BRT has spread to other large, dense South American cities. At least 56 European cities in 14 countries have BRT.[27] Worldwide, at least 150 cities have implemented systems.[28]

Provide More Room for Bikes and Pedestrians

The Institute for Transportation and Development Policy estimates that biking could reduce emissions from urban transportation by about 11 percent, but it would require increasing urban miles traveled by bike to 11 percent by 2030 and 14 percent by 2050—a big jump from the current level of about 1 percent in US and Canadian cities. It would take a massive investment in building safe bicycle lanes, more bike-share services, land-use planning that emphasizes transit, and reducing or ending subsidies for driving—from fuel to parking.[29]

This investment isn't likely to happen in more than a handful of North American cities. Although bike rental ("sharing") systems are popping up in many North American cities, they are unlikely to have much impact on moving people out of cars. As evidence, consider Portland, Oregon, a leader in promoting bike travel. Portland has been building its biking infrastructure since 1973, and still only about 6 percent of work commutes are done by bike. Compare that figure with 50 percent in Copenhagen, 63 percent in Amsterdam, 30 percent in Malmö, and 28 percent in Freiburg.[30] While the popularity of bike rental systems perhaps reflects a growing American desire to break the car habit, few US cities have installed separate lanes in which bikes can travel safely. Instead of separated, dedicated lanes for bikes and buses, we get what transportation planners have dubbed "sharrows"—lanes marked confusingly with a bike symbol—that are used by both cars and bikes.

My Northeastern University colleague Peter Furth explains that polls reveal that 30 percent of the public wouldn't ride a bike in a city under any circumstances; 60 percent would bike more if they felt it was safer (interested but concerned); 8 percent would ride with only minimal separation from faster car traffic; and 2 percent would ride in a city regardless of the infrastructure. The problem, Furth notes, is that most cities are building bike infrastructure for the 8 percent. These unsafe lanes dominate national planning and engineering guidelines.[31] Furth and colleagues study the stress and connectivity of bike lanes in different cities, finding that in many cities it is difficult for a potential commuter to get across the city—say from home to work—without traveling on high-stress streets, defined by high speed limits, sharrows or no bike lanes, or wide intersections.[32] While Furth estimates that the price of developing safe and connected urban bike infrastructure would be about $1.50 per person annually over a decade, most cities are not making anything close to that level of investment. And given the level of sprawl in most American cities, the distances many commuters have to travel are too long for bike infrastructure to make sense as a practical alternative to driving.

"Complete streets," an approach to designing and operating streets that safely accommodates pedestrians, bicyclists, drivers, and transit riders of all ages and abilities, is gaining popularity in many American cities. Complete streets are focused on improving intersections to make crossing safer. The movement got its start in 2004, and currently about 25 percent of American municipalities report having complete-streets policies. The problem is the policies are often ignored. A recent study of 125 complete-streets policies found that most are aspirational and don't grant clear legal authority for implementation or provide requirements or processes for balancing the trade-offs among the different uses that the streets are supposed to accommodate. The study concludes that most policies are weak and "do not create a solid foundation for transforming deeply institutionalized auto-oriented street building practices."[33]

Further, comprehensive complete-streets policies tend to be in places that are white and wealthy, according to a 2017 report examining policies across the country.[34] Some evidence suggests that complete streets can lead to gentrification.[35] More recently, a rekindled demand for urban living has turned transportation innovations like modern streetcars and complete streets into amenities sometimes used to attract real-estate investment and high-end "creative class" workers and consumers. In 2017, the National Complete Streets Coalition adapted its evaluation framework to include the equity impact of projects and encourages creating more projects in underserved neighborhoods. It is a loop that is proving hard to break—low-income neighborhoods often reject complete streets projects, fearing that they will cause gentrification.

Connect Transportation and Land-Use Planning

Historically, there are strong connections between transportation and land use. Highway construction led to sprawled patterns of commercial and residential development.[36] Transit-oriented development (TOD) focuses development and redevelopment of urban areas around transit stations. The idea is to create dense, vibrant, mixed-use neighborhoods that are walkable and bikeable and to increase transit ridership.[37] While it has been standard practice in many European and Asian cities and with bus rapid transit in Bogotá and Curitiba, it has only been promoted in the United States since the late 1980s as a way to curb sprawl and decrease auto congestion.[38]

Implementation has not been easy—land assembly is expensive and financing is a challenge. It requires considerable coordination—government from local and regional to federal is involved, along with transit agencies. Many of these issues have been addressed as TOD becomes a standard approach to planning. Since property values generally rise for housing located near transit,[39] TOD needs to focus on preventing gentrification.[40] There are notable successes. Denver has increased urban densities and created a surge in downtown development around new transit stations.[41] Notably, Denver's TOD strategy includes a fund to preserve or create 1,200 units of low- to moderate-income housing. And in Oakland, community organizations are leading development initiatives around transit stations that include affordable housing, local business development, and social services to benefit existing residents.[42]

We will see various combinations of these "carrot and stick" approaches to deprioritizing cars. Oslo stands out for comprehensively embracing all of the strategies. Seattle has as well, though congestion pricing is just now being considered. Nashville is struggling to add BRT and rail against political opposition, but it has done little to promote transit adoption. Salt Lake City is adding light rail and also beginning to promote walking and biking along with more transit-oriented development.

What about Uber and Lyft? A lot of people think of Uber, Lyft, and like services as a transportation revolution that will continue to evolve to serve urbanites better. But we are a long way off from such a future. Uber and Lyft operate in a highly concentrated urban environment—representing less than 4 percent of all trips in the United States. Only a small percentage of the country will be served by cars for hire. Further, all evidence to date suggests that Uber and Lyft are displacing walking, biking, and transit. A recent UC Davis survey found that between 49 and 61 percent of people using ride-hailing would have otherwise used transit, car-share services such as Zipcar, biking, or walking.[43] The business model of Uber and Lyft is to get people hooked with low company-subsidized fares to establish market share and then to move on to market pricing power. Moreover, newer ride-hailing services such as Uber's Express Pool—van services with multiple riders—will eat further into transit agency revenue, making it difficult to maintain service.[44]

It is hard to predict how the future of autonomous vehicles will unfold. Some promoters contend that cities shouldn't make investments in "nineteenth-century" transit, meaning mass transit in general. But autonomous vehicles might carry 10,000 passengers per lane per hour, versus the current 2,000 for highways, while transit can move 50,000 passengers per lane per hour.[45] One concern is that Uber, Lyft, and advocates of an early shift to autonomous vehicles are becoming something of an antitransit lobby, urging cities to become more car-friendly rather than less. This would only lead to more congestion. Whether or not autonomous vehicles win broad acceptance in the near term, transit remains essential for cities.

The View from Oslo

We learned of Oslo's place as the electric vehicle capital of the world in chapter 5. Sture Portvik, Oslo's project leader on electric vehicles, tells me that expanding public transportation and making it cleaner are also key priorities along with making biking safer.[46] More transit and biking ultimately requires deprioritizing cars, and Oslo is moving on that front as well.

Oslo's success is rooted in land-use planning from the 1980s to contain the spatial expansion of the metropolitan area. The result was an increase in population density in both the metropolitan area and in the city by about 11 percent. The "compact city" policy and densification have continued, setting the metropolitan area up for efficient transit.[47]

Transit ridership has been rising steadily for years, up 4.6 percent during 2016 alone. Oslo's five-line metro, the T-banen, carries 118 million passengers annually and provides 44 percent of all motorized trips.[48] Frequency of service on the tram system has been increased, and in 2016 Ruter, Oslo's public transportation company, announced an unprecedented 10-billion-kroner (US $1.3 billion)[49] expansion to be built over eight years. Ruter also aims to be completely fossil free by 2020, quite achievable since the tram and metro run on renewable hydropower. About 35 percent of city buses are powered by biodiesel, hydrogen, and biogas. Battery electric buses pilots began in 2017, and major bus charging infrastructure installations started in 2018. By 2025, 60 percent of the bus fleet will be fully electric. Five hydrogen buses are being tested as part of a European hydrogen bus demonstration project. Portvik adds that more park-and-ride solutions are being developed to reduce the number of cars coming into the city. And tolls for entering the city on ring roads are higher during the morning rush hour. Combined with highly subsidized fares, he expects car traffic to be reduced significantly. And all of this was initiated under a conservative government.

In 2015, Oslo citizens elected a progressive government made up of the Labour, Green, and Socialist Left parties. This coalition doubled down on efforts of previous conservative city governments by proposing to create Europe's largest car-free city center. The city's announcement was met with considerable opposition from residents and businesses, which was a bit of a surprise to planners, given that only 12 percent of the area's residents owned a car and 93 percent commuted by public transit, bike, or on foot. But the business community was concerned about losing shoppers and street life generally. Residents were concerned that their neighborhoods would become isolated.

After several months of planning, the city council devised a gradual three-phase plan to minimize cars in the city center by 2019. The idea is to reduce cars by shrinking parking. As of June 2017, most cars (even electric) must park in garages outside of the city center. Spaces for the disabled and delivery vehicles are being preserved. By early 2019, 700 parking spaces were eliminated. [50]

The city plans to add 60 kilometers (nearly 40 miles) of bike lanes, on which construction is underway, and it has begun closing off a few streets to cars with the aim of converting 35 streets to bike-only. With a recently improved city bike program, the added lanes will help the city to reach its goal of 25 percent commuting by bike by 2025. Given that Oslo is hilly, the city council appropriated 5 million kroner ($645,800) to subsidize electric bike purchases, and it is piloting a small freight terminal where goods are dropped off for distribution by electric bicycles. Kari-Anne Isaksen, political adviser to Oslo's vice-mayor on environment and transport, told me that planners are also working to improve the pedestrian network by adding amenities such as playgrounds, trees and foliage, and cultural events in the pilot areas.

In Norway, where cars are taxed at 100 percent and government subsidies for transit are plentiful, cities don't have to go it alone. Further, a 2011 European Union transport plan called for eliminating gasoline-powered cars in cities by 2050. But in the United States, cars rule, and historically federal transportation aid has supported highways nearly to the exclusion of public transit. So American cities trying to reduce car traffic and promote transit, walking, and biking have a far tougher job.

Seattle: A Virtuous Cycle of Building Transit

As a major international port and air transportation hub with a flourishing tech economy, Seattle has been one of the fastest-growing cities in the United States for several years. It is also one of the nation's most ambitious cities in addressing climate change, with a goal of becoming carbon neutral by 2050. [51] With 66 percent of Seattle's GHG emissions produced by road travel, getting people out of cars must be a priority.

Seattle leads the country in its efforts to expand public transit. With a population of about 725,000 and the metro numbering more than 3.5 million, Seattle has the density to do so.[52] The city broke ground on its first light-rail project in 2006.[53] But rail projects have long timelines, so turning bus routes into BRT has been a priority. Seattle now leads the nation in BRT growth, with about 20 percent of workers using it each day. According to the Federal Transit Administration, Seattle bus and rail ridership increased by 60 percent between 2003 and 2017, while it has decreased in most US cities.

How does Seattle do it? Everyone I talked with told me of Seattle's virtuous cycle of building and improving transit based on rider input and incentivizing ridership by providing transit access as a job benefit. And Seattle planners are linking land-use planning to transportation so more people in this rapidly growing city can get around easily without cars. Increasingly, the agenda includes linking transit growth to developing more affordable housing.

Much of Seattle's new transit infrastructure has been funded by taxes raised through citizen-approved ballot initiatives. Three successful ballot measures since 1996 have raised the funds to build and expand the regional light and commuter rail network. Move Seattle, the city's 2015 transportation plan, details how to accommodate the expected growth in downtown jobs and population over the next 20 years without increasing capacity for vehicular traffic. Instead of accommodating more cars, Move Seattle focuses on expanding transit, walking, and cycling. Its initiatives include adding 7 to 10 corridors with designated protected lanes for bikes, buses, and transit; developing seven BRT corridors with designated lanes; more frequent inner-city bus service; adding 50 miles of new protected bike lanes and 60 miles of greenways; providing bike routes to all schools; adding 100 blocks of new sidewalks, and improving crossings at 225 intersections.[54]

It is an ambitious agenda, and implementation has not been without bumps. To understand the obstacles the city has encountered, along with its accomplishments and the lessons they teach, we now turn to a political, economic, and cultural analysis of Seattle's public transit buildout.

The Rail Connection: Light Rail and Streetcars

Like most US cities, Seattle abandoned its nineteenth-century streetcar system in 1941. With ever-growing traffic congestion, conversations about linking downtown to Sea-Tac Airport with rail began in 1961. They went nowhere until 1996, when residents of the region's three-county transit system, Sound Transit, voted to increase sales and vehicle excise taxes to fund a north-south light-rail route as the core of a new metropolitan rail system called Link. Of the $3.9 billion raised, $1.7 billion was earmarked for a 25-mile stretch consisting of two lines—one going south to Tacoma and Sea-Tac and another to the University District of the city. The project got off the ground slowly due to cost overruns, debates over stop locations that resulted in route changes, resignations of key officials, lawsuits, and unsure federal funding due to these delays.

But the plan was eventually realized. The airport line began service in 2009, and an extension from downtown to the University of Washington opened in 2016. Jonathan Hopkins, executive director of Commute Seattle,[55] an organization that works with employers to reduce car commuting, explained to me that much of the trouble was due to the inexperience of the newly created multi-billion-dollar Sound Transit agency, which had never before undertaken a large capital project.[56] First-time efforts can sometimes result in "rosy predictions while under-estimating cost," he said, which affected planning for the Sea-Tac project. He noted that every rail project since Sea-Tac has been completed on budget, and that two later rail projects came in 10 percent under budget and ahead of schedule.[57] Indeed, it is a testament to Sound Transit's success that residents have repeatedly voted for transit initiatives despite their making local sales taxes relatively high—the current rate is 10.1 percent in Seattle and Tacoma.[58]

Inexperience and early cost overruns with these maiden north-south projects were not the only trouble facing Seattle's transit buildout. Flagging ridership on two newer rail lines led to debate over supporting rail or less-expensive BRT lines. It is still unresolved, and has stymied development of an important connector line key to unifying the entire system.

In the 2000s, transportation planners saw the need to link existing light rail, commuter rail, buses, and Amtrak to streetcars in densely settled outer neighborhoods. Two streetcar lines were developed to fill that role. The South Lake Union line, opened in 2007, connects this growing neighborhood to downtown. The First Hill line, opened in 2016, also connects to downtown. Seattle Department of Transportation data reveal that ridership in both has been lower than expected. The First Hill line boarded only about 840,000 riders of the predicted 1.24 million in 2016, its first year of operation. Cars with capacity to carry 100 passengers average only 40 people per hour on the South Lake Union Line, and 32 on the First Hill line. Thus, it is no surprise that fares cover only 34 and 18 percent, respectively, of their operating costs.

The plan to address these fiscal and ridership shortfalls is to build a Center City Connector, which would connect the two other streetcar lines to downtown and operate in a dedicated lane. Construction of underground utilities for the connector began in January 2017 after receiving a $75 million federal grant, for a projected total cost of $155 million.[59] City officials anticipate that the connector will quadruple ridership on the two existing streetcar lines, with five stops at popular locations bringing passengers downtown.[60]

The project, however, is on hold. Due to cost increases associated with design fees and the need to relocate a utility, the original estimate of $155 million jumped to $177 million. When project estimates were pushed to over $200 million, Mayor Jenny Durkan put the brakes on the project in April 2018 and commissioned a new study of ridership projections and operating costs compared with bus alternatives. The study will factor into current debates between those who believe that flagging ridership does not support investing in streetcars over buses and those who think new rail buildout still has a place in Seattle. The *Seattle Times* is leading the charge in supporting buses rather than fixed rail.[61] Several transit advocates and a former Seattle Transportation Department planner told me that they didn't think the project would be restarted. If not, the $75 million in federal funding would have to be returned.

Although the streetcar connector is in doubt, the general direction of transit in Seattle is up. When three light-rail stations were added in 2015, ridership increased by 91 percent in 2016 and another 9 percent over that in 2017. The proportion of Seattle residents living within a 10-minute walk of a frequent transit stop increased to 64 percent. Almost half (48 percent) of commuters to downtown Seattle used transit in 2017, while only 25 percent drove. A combined 11 percent walk or bike, and 10 percent use car or vanpools.[62]

Off the Rails: Bus Rapid Transit

Buses are the workhorses of Seattle's transit system. Investing in more frequent service on all 200 bus lines and changing routes to connect with two light-rail stations has paid off. Seattle is one of only two cities in the country (Houston is the other) in which bus ridership increased in 2017. Former director of Seattle's Transportation Department Scott Kubly explains three choices that made buses work so well in Seattle. First was building a bus tunnel through downtown in the mid-1980s, which allowed a huge increase in the number of buses that could provide reliable service. Second is state legislation. The Washington State Growth Management Act of 1990 established urban growth boundaries and requires cities in fast-growing metropolitan areas to coordinate transportation and land-use planning with the goal of containing new development in compact areas.[63] The 1991 Commute Trip Reduction Law calls for employers to reduce drive-alone rates by supporting public transportation, carpools, cycling, and walking. This was strengthened in 2006 with the Commuter Trip Reduction Efficiency Act, which required large employers across the state to reduce drive-alone trips by 10 percent by 2011, by offering employee benefits for not driving alone.[64] The third was making Third Avenue, the city's central corridor, a bus-only lane while a light-rail line was being constructed in the downtown tunnel, which habituated residents to bus travel.

To keep the momentum going, King County Metro, which operates Seattle's buses, is improving on RapidRide, the BRT "lite" system. The system has six routes and plans to add seven more by 2024. The percentage of residents near a high-frequency bus route (every 15 minutes) has increased from 25 to 64 percent since 2015. Another improvement to bus travel was banning cars on Third Avenue during morning and afternoon peak-commute hours. At least 250 RapidRide and regular buses travel the thoroughfare per hour during the peak morning and evening commute, with about 52,000 boardings in the corridor daily. It has worked so well that the bus-only rule was applied all day in the fall of 2018. The improvements demonstrate the virtuous cycle—ridership on the RapidRide C and D lines increased by 40 and 28 percent, respectively, between June 2015 and June 2017.[65]

Biking: An Aspirational Plan

Biking has had a rough history in Seattle. The city's first bike master plan was released in 2007, but as in many cities, there are still more sharrows (lanes shared by bikes and cars) than protected bike lanes. As more unprotected lanes were added, drivers rebelled against what they called Seattle's war on cars. By 2009, a full-blown controversy was underway between bikes and cars. A lot of that anger was directed at then-mayor Mike McGinn, and it played out in the mainstream and alternative press.

The death of three cyclists in 2011 diminished the bikes-versus-cars debate and brought safety to the forefront. A new organization, Seattle Neighborhood Greenways, formed to advocate for more and safer low-traffic streets. McGinn was on board with redirecting the debate from bikes versus cars to creating safe streets for all. Dialogues between biking advocates and detractors helped to reduce the animosity. And the city began implementing projects from the 2007 bike master plan to increase safety. In 2014, Seattle's first downtown separated bike lane opened on Broadway. And a three-quarter-mile Second Avenue protected bike lane opened with another nine-tenths mile completed in 2018. Road diet projects throughout the city are reducing car lanes to accommodate pedestrians and bikers. And an ordinance was passed to reduce speeds to 20 miles per hour on side streets and 25 on arterial roads.

Seattle's 2014 bike master plan calls for significant additions to the bike lane network.[66] The plan's main author, Steve Durrant, describes it as "very aspirational" in its goal of creating separated bike lanes for all ages and abilities. It also stands out for its emphasis on equity. Durrant tells me that the plan is based on analysis of neighborhoods that are not well served by biking infrastructure and an intention to focus on these areas. The goal, he says, is to create new demand by building the infrastructure in these neighborhoods.[67]

Several people I interviewed described implementation as "painfully slow," consisting mostly of piecemeal improvements here and there. Worse, it now appears that the whole bike agenda is in jeopardy with the controversial five-block extension of the separated bike lane on Second Avenue in 2018. The project was portrayed in some media as a $12 million one-mile bike lane, but it was just one part of a $12 million complete-streets program with a larger set of improvements that included additional loading zones, streetlights and signals, and fixing water drainage problems.

Another major project, a protected bike lane on Fourth Avenue, which was greenlighted under Mayor Murray, has been postponed until 2021 by Mayor Durkan, out of fear, she says, that the bike lane will delay cars. Yet according to two people I interviewed, the bike lane, combined with other improvements, would have resulted in faster travel for buses than today, and have very little impact on cars. Bike advocates are concerned that the real trouble is cost, and that the project won't be restarted after the road construction is completed. Installing bike lanes in Seattle has cost between $1 and $2 million per mile, well above the $860,000 per mile estimated in Move Seattle. Now the Seattle Department of Transportation says it only has funding to build half of the 50 miles of bike lanes approved in Seattle's 2014 bike master plan.

While there is some pushback against specific projects, expansion of bike lanes will continue—what's at issue is the pace. In July 2018 the city council unanimously passed a nonbinding resolution that holds the Seattle Department of Transportation to a 2020 timeline for building six already budgeted protected bike lanes through the downtown. With the Washington State Convention Center under construction, buses will move from the downtown transit tunnel, congesting streets even more, so SDOT officials are concerned that bike lane construction can be speeded up. A $92 million community benefit from the developer of the $1.7 billion convention center expansion includes about $16 million for building new bike lanes, in addition to affordable housing and other benefits.

Business Support for Transit-User Incentives

A key reason transit ridership is high is that Seattle companies offer their employees transit discounts and price parking high enough to discourage car commuting. The groundwork for employer transit subsidies was laid with the state's 1991 Commute Trip Reduction Law (mentioned previously), which obliges employers of 100 or more to complete a biennial survey that identifies how their employees get to work. Companies also are required to appoint a transportation coordinator to work with the city on reducing car commuting. But employers are given quite a bit of leeway in figuring out how to reduce car commuting. Subsidizing transit and vanpooling while charging more for parking is typical. Some employers have offered discounts on mortgage rates for employees who move closer to work and have purchased home office equipment so employees can work at home some of the time.

The incentives offered by the Bill & Melinda Gates Foundation illustrate how an employer can reduce driving. Compelled by state law, the city negotiates legal agreements with large companies such as the Gates Foundation to achieve a "drive-alone rate" that varies depending on location in the central city. In 2008, the foundation applied for a building permit to move its offices downtown, which would add 1,200 new commuters to the densest part of the city. As a condition of the permit, the foundation will hold the number of employees who drive to work alone to 34 percent.

To meet that obligation, the foundation offers two employee benefits to discourage driving. Along with a shower room and bike storage facilities for bike commuters, it provides the ORCA Passport, an annual transit pass. The second benefit changed how parking is priced. Gates Foundation employees receive a $3 daily payment for not driving. And rather than offering a monthly parking rate, the foundation charges a daily rate of $12 to park on its premises. Hopkins explains that once employees have paid for a monthly pass, the incentive is to get one's money's worth by driving every day. But with a daily rate, commuters must decide each day whether to pay the daily rate or to take the $3 for not driving.[68] When the Gates Foundation building opened in 2011, the drive-alone commute rate was 42 percent, but within a year it was down to the agreed-upon 34 percent.

Similar benefits are offered by almost all downtown employers and by some in other parts of the city. Businesses provide different levels of subsidy for ORCA Passports. Companies must pay for at least half of the card's cost and provide the cards to all employees at a worksite. Some employers choose to subsidize the full amount. Employees get unlimited rides on the entire regional system. The Passport also covers the costs of vanpools and offers a guaranteed ride home program for participating employees who need to get home to handle emergencies. It is quite an asset for businesses and employees—a Passport costs downtown employers about $700 per employee for a pass that would have cost about $1,200 a year at the fare box.

These combined approaches to reduce car commuting are working. A 2016 survey by Commute Seattle revealed that 96 percent of the approximately 270 companies employing 100 or more, and 56 percent of smaller businesses, offer a commuter benefit. As a result, over 60 percent of King County Metro's fare box revenue comes directly from employers paying for part or all their employees' transit access. In the same year, downtown businesses invested $100 million in commuter benefits and infrastructure.

Seattle has also been proactive in reducing "ride sharing" services, which contribute heavily to traffic congestion and compete with public transit for passengers. Seattle acted early to limit Uber, Lyft, and Sidecar with a 2014 ordinance that limits each service to 150 drivers on the streets at a time, a considerable drop from the 2,000 cars that the services estimated they had on the streets at that time. To protect taxis, Seattle City Council passed a resolution to consider raising base fares on Uber and Lyft from $1.35 to $2.40, the base rate charged by taxis.

Another disruptive business model, internet retail delivery services, is clogging city streets with delivery vehicles. In response, the University of Washington's Urban Freight Lab partners with the city of Seattle, the US Postal Service, United Parcel Service, Costco, Nordstrom, and Charlie's Produce to use the city as a learning lab to identify solutions for reducing home-delivery traffic. Professor Anne Goodchild, who directs the lab, is leading its Final 50 Feet project, which is running pilots that aim to reduce the time delivery trucks spend on streets. A solution being tested is shared lockers for goods delivery in apartment buildings to reduce the amount of time drivers spend in buildings. The project is also mapping the city's capacity in loading zones and bays, and establishing measures of efficiency.

Finally, congestion pricing was put on the agenda by Mayor Jenny Durkan in April 2018. The city is studying the issue, but Commute Seattle's Hopkins points out that implementation is years away because the metropolitan area doesn't yet have the transit capacity to support it. He suggests it might be an option in 2023–2024 when additional light rail comes on line, but it could be pushed out as far as 2030–2035, when the Ballard / West Seattle extension line opens.[69] Discussions on equity impacts of the charge, how it would affect tradespeople, and whether Uber/Lyft drivers would be exempted are ongoing.

The Land-Use and Parking Link

Seattle's coordination of transit and land-use planning is creating more neighborhoods in which people don't need cars. Seattle's comprehensive plan's urban village strategy focuses residential and employment growth near transit stations.[70] The strategy directs new development away from single-family neighborhoods and into three types of centers at increasing levels of density. As we'll see later, the city is attempting to link the urban village strategy to greater equity in transit access and more affordable housing.

Working hand in glove with its comprehensive plan, the Seattle City Council has been reducing parking requirements for new construction in transit-rich areas, defined as being within one-quarter mile of a frequent transit stop, since 2006. In 2012, the parking minimum was reduced to .5 parking spaces per new unit. Even at this level, a 2015 study by King County Metro found that only about 70 percent of apartment parking spaces in the county were being used, which gave the city council the evidence it needed to expand the areas of the city in which the parking rules would apply in April 2018. A related goal is to lower the high cost of housing, since each parking space costs about $30,000 to build and buildings with parking charge about $250 more in monthly rent than buildings without it.[71] Data published by the *Seattle Times* show that since 2012, 30 percent of new apartment buildings near frequent transit have no parking.

The Transit-Affordability Connection: Who Does Transit Serve?

Like most rapidly growing cities, Seattle's development pressures have fostered inequality, and the public sector needs to do more to make both transit and housing more affordable. In addition to the business Passport ORCA card program, owners of multifamily buildings can offer residents passes. But a 2016 study found that 68 percent of residents in market-rate buildings have ORCA passes compared to 22 percent in affordable housing. A one-year pilot that offered ORCA passes to low-income residents for less than $20 per month was well received, but it has not been extended. Several affordable housing advocacy organizations are calling for making it permanent. A motion has been introduced in the city council and a cost assessment is underway.[72]

Seattle is facing an affordability crisis in housing.[73] While eliminating parking can reduce housing prices at the margins, the city's growing areas have little moderately priced housing. The city has been addressing the problem in several ways that connect to transit.

In 2011, Seattle received federal Housing and Urban Development Sustainable Community program funds to combat displacement of low-income residents by new transit stations. Funds were used to purchase land near the stations to build affordable housing and to work with residents to identify place-based investment strategies. The $3 million grant was leveraged with $5.9 million from local public and private sources.[74] The project, named Community Cornerstones, has created 300 units of affordable housing along with office space, childcare, community meeting rooms, local retail space, a cultural center, and support services for residents.

State legislation may help to make housing more affordable while increasing transit-oriented development. The state's 2016 "80-80-80" policy requires Sound Transit to offer 80 percent of its surplus property that is suitable for housing to affordable housing developers who make at least 80 percent of units on the site affordable to people earning 80 percent or less of area median income, rather than selling it off to the highest bidder. And in March 2018 the state legislature amended the law to allow any public agency to discount the price of property if used for affordable housing.[75] With the law in place, King County donated land near the Northgate light-rail station to a nonprofit developer, which will open in 2021. King County and Seattle have donated $10 million to the project.[76]

Further, in 2018, a coalition of housing, transportation, and community groups pressured Sound Transit to adopt an equitable TOD policy informed by broad community participation. The policy supports local businesses against displacement and aims to stem gentrification that has occurred around several transit stops. It was informed by the process of planning affordable housing near a transit station in the Capitol Hill neighborhood that opened in 2016. Sound Transit sold the air rights above to build mixed-use housing and the city broke ground on this long-awaited project in June 2018. The building, which aspires to be LEED Platinum, will have 428 apartments, of which 178 will be below-market rentals priced according to income.

The Long Road Ahead

Cars rule in American cities. Seattle's efforts to emphasize trains, buses, bikes and walking while deprioritizing cars has created a culture shock. To some extent it is a generational difference—driving and parking have been perceived as rights for a long time. Paying for both is disruptive. Younger people prefer transit and bikes to cars, but as in many cities, enthusiastic embrace of Uber and Lyft is creating a disruption of its own, and Seattle is one of the cities that is taking them on. Seattle has been reducing and eliminating off-street parking requirements in areas with good public transit access since the 1980s, but it has gotten more controversial as policies have expanded. Deprioritizing cars and trucks over buses also creates upset. As Gordon Clowers, a senior urban planner with the Seattle Department of Construction and Inspections, points out, "Adding signals with first priority to high-occupancy buses is good policy, but in practice may be very unpopular with automobile commuters and freight haulers by adding to their delay at key congestion points." Further, he comments regarding limiting parking, "We are sensitive to pushing it too far."[77]

While Seattle is a liberal, environmentally conscious city, not everyone is on board with investing in public transit and biking while deprioritizing cars. The *Seattle Times* editorialized against Sound Transit 3, as did the state Republican Party on the grounds that it would cost taxpayers too much without clear benefits. And while the city is attempting to address transit and housing inequities, Seattle still has a long way to go. How it plays out in Seattle will be the harbinger of whether cities in a less politically supportive environment, such as Nashville, can replicate its approach.

Nashville

Nashville is Tennessee's largest city, with 691,000 people in a metro area of 1.9 million.[78] Like many Sun Belt cities, its pattern of rapid growth has been low density and sprawled. The metro area is projected to grow by one million residents over the next 25 years, adding more cars to already gridlocked streets and highways. While Nashville is in no sense a climate action leader, it has been attempting to expand its bus system and add rail. The city's business elite is relatively public minded and friendly to mass transit, but two transit proposals for BRT and light rail have failed in the past four years.

Nashville's story reveals the complex political, cultural, and social factors that make deprioritizing cars difficult in many, if not most, American cities. At bottom, mass transit is a hard sell for car-dependent, medium-size cities, especially when they are fragmented culturally and racially, and laboring without state policy support.

Amping It Up

Nashville's bus system hasn't been keeping up with growth, and riders complain of inconsistent and infrequent service. Expansion and improvement of the system was on the agenda of Karl Dean when he was sworn in as mayor of Metro Nashville and Davidson County in September 2007.

Working with Dean, the Metropolitan Transit Authority (MTA) and the Nashville/Davidson County Council appropriated $7.5 million for improving the system. Staff from the city and MTA visited several cities, including Charlotte, Denver, Salt Lake City, and Seattle, to learn how to develop transit in bus-only cities and to understand potential roadblocks to implementation. Dean sought federal funding for a route that he hoped would connect the racially divided city. Proposed in 2012, the Amp, named to acknowledge Nashville's reputation as a music city, would create a 7.1-mile BRT route at a cost of $174 million. The project sought $75 million in federal funding and $35 million from the state, with the remaining $65 million to be funded from the city's capital budget. The proposed route would have extended across the city, connecting the poor but gentrifying east (40 percent African American) side and wealthy west side (92 percent white) through the downtown.

But the seemingly straight line across Nashville had several fault lines. Supporters included the Nashville Chamber of Commerce and the Convention and Visitors Corporation, Vanderbilt University, several hospitals, and many downtown businesses, who saw transit as essential to continued economic development. Members of the opposition group, Stop Amp, were against using tax dollars for transit generally and had specific objections related to their businesses. Key among them were Rick Williams, the owner of a limousine company, and Lee Beaman, who owns a large car dealership.[79]

The plan's east-west route, which would have served several rapidly growing neighborhoods across the city, was controversial. Residents of largely African American North Nashville didn't support it because they preferred improvements in the regular bus lines serving their neighborhood. Some complained that its path was designed to serve big employers (such as downtown corporate headquarters and the universities) and to increase property values of those anticipating the development it would create, rather than serving people most in need of transit.[80] The downtown entertainment and tourism industry opposed the dedicated lane, which they thought would ruin the character of the neighborhood and scare off tourists with years of construction. Wealthy West End residents worried about "riffraff" from East Nashville coming to their neighborhood.[81]

Despite the critics, the project seemed to have sufficient popular support. When the Obama administration committed $27 million in federal funds in March 2014, Beaman determined that the Amp would have to be killed at the state level. He enlisted Americans for Prosperity, the right-wing political advocacy organization financed by the Koch brothers. Andrew Ogles, director of the Tennessee chapter of Americans for Prosperity, worked with state senator Jim Tracy, chair of the Transportation and Safety Committee, to draft legislation that banned BRT from using dedicated lanes or rights of way.

The compromise bill that passed the state legislature allowed dedicated lanes, but only with the approval from the state legislature and the state highway commissioner (regardless of whether state funds were used).[82] By then Dean, near the end of his term and term limited, figured a new mayor would be unlikely to take up the divisive issue, so he announced in October 2014 that he would not seek financing for the project. Three months later, Steve Bland, new CEO of the MTA, called for halting the ongoing design work. But Bland was not giving up on transit—he authorized using $750,000 in unused Amp funds for strategic planning for transit on multiple corridors.

Trying Again with Light Rail

Bland followed up on his promise: the MTA and the Regional Transportation Authority (RTA) developed a 25-year strategic plan, nMotion, released in September 2016, which laid out three scenarios for improving transit. One called for modest improvements in the existing bus system, a second for expansion of the bus and BRT system, and a third built on bus and BRT expansion to add light rail to serve the entire region. The MTA obtained considerable community input on the scenarios, and resident polls conducted by the Mayor's Office indicated broad public support for developing light rail, according to Erin Hafkenschiel, director of transportation and sustainability in the Mayor's Office.[83] But as a visionary plan meant to guide development, nMotion had neither funding nor regulation authority for implementation. It would be up to the mayor to develop a specific transit development plan and find the funding to support it.

The next steps were up to then-mayor Megan Barry, a liberal Democrat with close ties to the city's business community and a transit supporter. Working from the third scenario of nMotion, Barry assembled a group comprising the Nashville Chamber of Commerce, real estate developers, and property owners to develop a transit proposal. The plan, Let's Move Nashville, was released publicly in October 2017 to go on the ballot in May 2018.

It called for expanding the service hours of the bus system, creating four "rapid bus" routes (BRT-lite that would have signal priority, but dedicated lanes and level-boarding platforms on only limited stretches), 26 miles of light rail along five corridors, 19 transit centers, and sidewalk and bike infrastructure improvements. The $5.4 billion in capital costs for the plan, totaling $9 billion, would be financed through four tax increases (sales, hotel, car rental, and business and excise) that would start in 2023 and end in 2068, raising about $100 million annually.[84]

The proposal only covered Davidson County, one of ten counties comprising the metropolitan area, because state law only allows transit referendums at the county level and only for counties of a certain size. Although the MTA and the RTA and several county mayors supported the plan, Bland told me that most of the region's mayors took a wait-and-see position, saying that they would consider connecting to the system once it was up and running.[85]

The Nashville Chamber of Commerce started the Transit for Nashville campaign to promote the initiative and quickly raised $1.3 million to sell it to voters. The business community seemed to be in agreement that it was essential to continued economic growth. The *Tennessean* editorial board supported it, as did many politicians in the region.[86]

On the opposing side, Lee Beaman launched No Tax 4 Tracks in January 2018 and the state chapter of Americans for Prosperity launched a "Stop the Train" campaign. Its website encouraged residents to voice their disapproval of what they called a waste of tax dollars.[87] They ran a very effective door-to-door campaign, calling the plan a $9 billion boondoggle. All told, the campaign contacted about 42,000 people by phone and visited about 6,000 households.[88]

Initial support seemed to be strong, but by April, a *Tennessee Star* poll revealed that 63 percent opposed the initiative.[89] The May referendum failed by almost the same margin—64 percent voting against and 36 percent in favor.

What happened? It's a story of death by a thousand cuts.

While the Americans for Prosperity campaign was one factor, everyone I talked to—whether for or against—said it was only one of several factors that did the proposal in, starting with the behind-closed-doors approach to developing it. The announcement of the Let's Move Nashville proposal came as a complete surprise to most members of the city council and the public, feeding suspicion that it would benefit developers and those whose property values would increase more than it would benefit commuters.

Skeptics were concerned that the plan was too ambitious. Council member Angie Henderson told me that she voted against it for fiscal reasons: "With a $30 million budget shortfall, starting with five light-rail lines in a city that doesn't use the transit we have didn't make sense," she said. Henderson sees the middle scenario of nMotion—improving the bus system by adding more BRT—as the first step in improving transit.[90]

Critics also argued that the city isn't dense enough to support light rail. The density along the light-rail corridors is about 5 to 10 housing units per acre, well below the minimum of 12 to 25 suggested by the Federal Transit Administration.[91] But Hafkenschiel pointed out that job density along the corridor, at 40 employers per acre along most of the routes, was high enough. Further, she argued that density would be increased as transit-oriented development concentrated growth along the rail lines.[92]

Another aspect of the proposal that was greeted with skepticism was the tunnel to divert buses and trains from downtown streets. The nMotion plan hadn't provided detail on how to alleviate congestion. As council member Freddie O'Connell told me, "The solution for downtown congestion in nMotion was a gray box. Mayor Barry's proposal lifted the lid and showed us a billion-dollar tunnel."[93]

The coup de grâce came in March 2018, when Barry resigned after pleading guilty to felony theft of city funds and having an affair with her bodyguard. But she already had been losing credibility among her base in the African American community with proposals to reduce a hospital's services and to use a historic park, Fort Negley, to develop low-income housing. One official told me that her November 2017 surprise announcement to close inpatient services at Nashville General Hospital, the city's only safety-net hospital, and turn the property into an ambulatory surgical center, was a key turning point. Although a compromise was reached, council member Erica Gilmore told me that in both cases, community members were as much upset about the surprise of the announcements as the actual proposals.

Gilmore says that lack of trust is why she ended up not supporting the transit plan. Jackie Sims, a community organizer in North Nashville, told me that she didn't support the plan because it didn't go where transit-dependent residents needed it to go.[94]

Concern that the plan would not serve the historically black North Nashville community runs deep. Fifty years ago, a 100-square-block area of the neighborhood was razed in preparation for construction of Interstate 40, displacing about 1,400 people and causing housing values to decline by 30 percent. In fact, Interstate 40 was purposely located there to create a physical barrier between black and white neighborhoods.[95] Community organizations fought the interstate in a battle that ultimately went to the Supreme Court, to no avail.[96] Now North Nashville is gentrifying. Recent census data indicate that the African American population in several historically black neighborhoods, including North Nashville, declined by 20 percent in the last decade as whites moved in.[97] Concerned that transit would accelerate the gentrification that was already underway, many were skeptical of the proposal, and the opposition deftly exploited this mistrust in its advertising.

People's Alliance for Transit, Housing and Employment (PATHE), a coalition of several organizations, including Homes for All Nashville, Music City Riders United, and Amalgamated Transit Union Local 1235, organized to campaign for connecting transit with low-income housing. But in any effort to require affordable housing near metro stops—which PATHE argued was key to alleviating gentrification—the city and metro government's hands were tied by the state. Officials knew that the state legislature was working on a bill that would preempt Nashville's inclusionary zoning policy passed in 2016. The bill, passed in March

2018, bans local governments from requiring affordable or below market-rate housing when granting incentives, building permits, or other authorizations.[98] Although Tennessee's Improve Act, passed in April 2017, raised the gas tax to fund transportation and allowed cities to pass taxes for transit, the funds could only be used for the transit itself. And while the state legislature also passed the Redevelopment District Law, which permits the creation of transit-oriented development (TOD) districts and can include affordable housing, the city's historical misuse of TOD by creating redevelopment districts for things like a ballpark left many community organizers skeptical that it would ever be used for building affordable housing in transit-dependent neighborhoods.

Several advocates of the program told me a big lesson learned was that messaging matters. Transit for Nashville didn't have a persuasive story about how transit would benefit everyone, particularly for those living in the outer parts of the county.[99] The campaign focused on "dark money" channeled to the opposition through Nashville Smart, a nonprofit 501(c)(4), which isn't required to disclose its donors under federal law. Council member Freddie O'Connell notes that "people wanted to hear about the real costs and benefits, not about outside influence." O'Connell's honest assessment of the campaign: "We brought knives to a gun fight." In a city where few used transit, a campaign such as one used in Salt Lake City, "Some of Us Use It, All of Us Need It," would have been more effective.

Another political miscalculation was choosing to run the ballot measure during a low-turnout election in May rather than waiting until November. The campaign was short, leaving little time to explain to skeptical voters.

The Nashville experience shows that major local funding for mass transit is an uphill climb, even when the local business community supports it, and there is little margin for political miscalculations, of which there were many. But other cities in red states have been successful.

Salt Lake City: A Surprising Leader in Transit Expansion

Utah hasn't had a Democratic governor since 1985 and has had a Republican trifecta since 1992. Yet the Salt Lake City region, which has a mix of Democratic and Republican mayors, has been building transit since the 1990s—much of it funded locally. Salt Lake City itself has been led by Democratic mayors since 1976. Politicians and the business community are united on the need for transit to fuel the area's economic growth. Surrounded by mountains the length of the metro area on the east and west and two lakes north and west, they realized early on that there is no room for more highways.

A 1992 ballot initiative to fund transit failed. But when the Utah Transit Authority (UTA), which serves the Salt Lake City metropolitan area, received federal funds for 80 percent of a light-rail line, it jumped on the opportunity. The first line of what became the TRAX system, a 19-mile north-south line, opened in 1999, and transit has been expanding ever since.

A growth-planning process undertaken in the late 1990s by Envision Utah, a nonprofit organization that works with cities and towns to plan for healthy expansion in Salt Lake City, called for 300 miles of light rail and created a vision of how denser growth would create better neighborhoods and a better downtown than unchecked, sprawled development. Envision Utah sought considerable citizen participation, so its recommendations were well regarded by the public. Once the first line was built, residents who were skeptical about transit saw the benefits and wanted it in their neighborhoods. A second line, spanning east-west, opened in 2001 to connect the downtown to the University of Utah.

An 89-mile commuter rail, FrontRunner, opened in 2008 and was expanded in 2011. In addition, the city's nine-mile BRT line, MAX, opened in 2008. It operates in segregated lanes and has off-bus fare collection. Another BRT line is scheduled to open in 2019, and others are being planned.

In August 2013, a project that added 70 miles of rail connecting suburbs to downtown and a line to the airport was completed two years ahead of schedule and $300 million under budget. A streetcar line also opened in 2013 to connect neighborhoods to TRAX and bus services. The line has been so popular that an additional track is being built to allow more frequent service. In 2013, Salt Lake City was the nation's only city simultaneously building light rail, BRT, streetcars, and commuter rail.

The TRAX light-rail system now has three lines with 50 stations along 42.5 miles of track. It has created a virtuous cycle—the more residents see transit, the more they want it and the more businesses want to locate near transit stations. The UTA estimates that 25 percent of downtown workers arrive by public transportation.

Transit planning is widely supported. A plan developed by all of the state's transit agencies was unveiled in 2010. Its state funding formula called for spending one-third each on transit, state roads, and local roads. Unity on the importance of transit from the state on down has translated into success in obtaining federal dollars. State funds along with dedicated local sales taxes approved by voters in ballot initiatives make up the difference. As a result, Salt Lake City has been one of the nation's leaders in per capita transit investment for most of this century.

Following Envision Utah's commitment to transit-oriented development, a walkable suburban development with connection to transit has been built.

A planned development called Daybreak is a mixed-use community of about 12,000 that will ultimately have 20,000 homes.

Yet the Salt Lake City area also has had bumps in the road in transit planning. Voters rejected Proposition 1, a $58 million sales tax hike for mass transit and road improvements, in 2015. While 62 percent of Salt Lake City voters, representing about 17 percent of the county, supported the increase, it was not popular in much of the rest of the county. But rather than being a vote against transit, many saw it as a vote of no confidence in the UTA, which was under scrutiny for problems of mismanagement, bloated salaries, and questionable deals.

In November 2017, a ballot initiative proposing to raise $87 million from a 0.25 percent sales tax increase was rejected by seven of 17 counties in the region. In March 2018, the state legislature passed a transportation bill with a clause that allowed counties in which the proposition failed to approve it or place it back on the ballot. In May, Salt Lake County passed an ordinance to enact the 0.25 percent sales tax increase to fund transit and other infrastructure improvements if cities and towns representing 67 percent of the county's population adopted it as well. A month later, that threshold was reached, allowing a 0.25 percent countywide tax. And in June, the proposition from 2015 passed, which will be spent on roads and transit.

So it appears that transit is back on track in Salt Lake City. A new transit master plan was unveiled in 2017. When its projects are completed in 2040, at least 73 percent of Salt Lake City residents will live within two blocks of a high-frequency bus or rail service. The lesson of Salt Lake City is that broad public support is crucial and that success builds on success. Once a transit system is valued by actual users, popular backing is reinforced. The constraints imposed on highways by those mountains and lakes didn't hurt either.

Deprioritizing Cars Won't Be Easy

Building a comprehensive urban transportation system that deprioritizes cars requires political support from state and or national government, particularly for building expensive rail infrastructure. Such support is evident between Oslo and Norway and Seattle and Washington. In Nashville, the Republican state legislature actively sabotaged efforts to develop both BRT and light rail. Although Utah's legislature is Republican, there has been less opposition to planning in general and a recognition from the legislature that the physical barriers to expansion of the Salt Lake City metropolitan area necessitate public transit expansion.

Business community support helps, too, particularly in the US context, where there is relatively recent transit development in some cities. In Seattle, state policy that supported asking businesses to take actions to reduce car commuting of their employees and asking them to pay for transit passes was essential to increasing transit commuting in Seattle. Further, many downtown employers are part of Seattle's 2030 District (see chapter 2), through which building owners voluntarily commit to reducing the transportation footprint of their buildings. In Nashville, many major employers were on board for building light rail, but some weren't, and they were more effective in mobilizing state government to subvert the transit agenda. The business community was on board in Salt Lake City, seeing transit as essential to continued economic development.

Public support can make or break transit initiatives. Even in environmentally conscious Oslo and Seattle, planners had to slow or back down on initiatives due to public concerns about parking or costs. Envision Utah engaged citizens in the planning process and created a common vision among residents and the business community that transit would improve gridlock on the roads and quality of life in general. That message was effectively marketed.

Particularly in the US context, it's a tough time to be selling transit—whether rail or bus or BRT—when ridership is down in almost every city. And there's a new element that we saw play out in Nashville. Naysayers argue that our traffic gridlock can be solved with Uber and Lyft van services and autonomous vehicles. All three will play a role in transit in the future, as will more electric vehicles, as discussed in the previous chapter. But Uber and Lyft, whether cars or vans, will only add to highway congestion.

The problem is that in most newer cities, the transit grid, if it exists at all, is so partial that too few citizens use it and trust it. So cars keep begetting more cars. Mass transit is likely to reach critical mass only with significant federal funding that deprioritizes adding more roads, something that awaits a massive infrastructure push from a future progressive administration.

7

HOW ECO-INNOVATION DISTRICTS CAN
ACCELERATE URBAN CLIMATE ACTION

WE HAVE SEEN IN several chapters that action taken at the district scale—in building efficiency, district energy, transit-oriented development, and renewable energy—offers a way for cities to ramp up their climate action and to experiment with different technologies and planning strategies. While *eco-district* is the term most commonly used to describe these approaches, I use the term *eco-innovation district* to capture their potential for innovation in product and process. With that in mind, eco-innovation districts are defined areas in which cities concentrate state-of-the-art technologies in green building, smart infrastructure, and renewable energy to create sustainable, resilient, and inclusive districts that accelerate action on climate change and sustainability.[1]

Urban climate action is relatively new and planners need to experiment with new approaches, new technologies, and new ways of organizing the planning process to establish what works. There are several reasons for implementing climate/sustainability plans at the district level. It is often not politically or economically feasible to implement policies or technologies at the city level. For example, cities have shown willingness to apply LEED requirements on some new construction, but they are less likely to impose stringent energy codes on all construction throughout the city because of opposition from developers. In some cases, new green infrastructure systems that are untested could be piloted in a district before being applied citywide. A city with aggressive climate action goals can also use district-level sustainability to expand the base of support for its actions, while a city that does not have political support for aggressive climate action can use district-level sustainability to build support for developing goals. Finally,

151

district-level sustainability initiatives can be integrated with neighborhood-based planning to achieve multiple goals, such as green affordable housing development.

The challenge for city planners and elected officials is to learn from experimentation by sorting out what works, what doesn't, and why. In previous work, Jennifer Lenhart and I examined how Malmö city government became a learning organization in the process of developing the Western Harbour eco-innovation district. In this chapter, I recap the basics of this work and apply it to Stockholm's Hammarby Sjöstad, an eco-innovation district that integrates several aspects of the city's climate action planning and serves as a test bed for green technologies and then to another eco-innovation district in Stockholm, the Royal Seaport.

But green technology isn't the only concern. A trait common to these widely acclaimed districts is that they are largely green oases for relatively wealthy residents. It is therefore essential also to examine the extent to which inclusion of affordable housing is integrated into the planning process. Thus, the four questions I address in this chapter are:

- Does the district perform better than or as well as the rest of the city on per capita carbon emissions?
- How well does the district serve as a test bed for green technologies that can reduce GHG emissions?
- Does the city employ a deliberate process of organizational learning that allows city planners and elected officials to apply effective practices and lessons learned from district-scale experimentation?
- What measures have been put in place to ensure a diversity of income levels?

I further examine whether the experimentation undertaken in European eco-innovation districts can be replicated in the United States.

The Value of District-Scale Climate Action Planning

Several types of eco-innovation districts are being implemented in cities throughout the world. Some seek to be powered exclusively by renewable energy (Vauban in Freiburg; Western Harbour in Malmö). Some are created around district infrastructure, particularly district heating and cooling systems (Vancouver's Southeast False Creek). Others focus on how neighborhood revitalization can embrace sustainability and resilience. Most integrate several aspects of sustainability into their planning, both mitigation and adaptation measures. Definitions of what constitutes an eco-district have proliferated.[2] For all the differences among them, however, they share one characteristic: the level of implementation is the district, rather than the entire municipality at one extreme, or the individual building or a cluster of buildings at the other. Many urban practitioners and the foundation officers that fund district-scale initiatives, particularly in the United States, see this approach as the "sweet spot" between the building scale and the city scale in achieving sustainability, community development, and climate action goals.

The first eco-districts, broadly defined, were established in European cities in Germany, Sweden, England, Denmark, Spain, France, and elsewhere in the 1990s.[3] They represent attempts by municipal governments to integrate multiple aspects of sustainability. There are now approximately 420 eco-districts worldwide.[4]

Under the umbrella term "district-scale sustainability," there are at least eight distinct approaches in the United States.[5] While in European cities eco-districts tend to be led by city government, in the United States almost all of them are promoted by nonprofit organizations that provide technical and in some cases financial assistance to cities or the community organizations developing them. Another is led by a nonprofit organization, EcoDistricts, which was created in 2012 to provide technical assistance to cities in the United States and Canada to create eco-districts that are "resilient, vibrant, resource efficient and just." Started as the Sustainability Institute in 2009 in Portland, Oregon, the EcoDistricts brand uses a participatory framework for designing an eco-district, covering strategies and metrics in eight principal areas: equitable development, health and well-being, community identity, access and mobility, energy, water, habitat and eco-system function, and materials management. Its participatory building approach is intended to ensure that equity is integrated into each project's planning.

An important distinction, in both practice and policy, exists between districts developed on regenerated brownfield sites and those in places where most property is already developed. Going even further, San Francisco's Department of Planning devised a four-part typology for the eco-districts it has developed. Blank slates are on undeveloped land or cleaned brownfield sites. Patchwork quilts have a mix of land uses and multiple owners. Strengthened neighborhoods focus on greening established neighborhoods while creating community development opportunities. District-based industrial networks attempt to align production, distribution, and repair uses. Of these, the blank-slate approach has considerable potential for greenovation—for interconnecting infrastructure and exploring green technologies.

A small literature documents the practices in various eco-districts, but given the range of definitions and contexts, there is little assessment of their effectiveness. Although some of it is a bit outdated, the limited literature analyzing eco-districts suggests that they have fallen short of achieving environmental goals. A key critique is that the environmental discourse is not backed up by performance measurement. In particular, this critique is levied against Stockholm's Hammarby Sjöstad.[6] Similarly, critics argue that Vancouver's widely acclaimed Southeast False Creek eco-district has made limited progress toward GHG reduction.[7]

Another line of criticism argues that eco-districts foster ecological gentrification, or development under the rubric of sustainability that drives out low-income residents for high-end housing and related uses.[8] Ecological gentrification also takes place with the expansion of exclusively middle-to upper-middle-class housing into previously undeveloped land or in postindustrial areas such as in the Stockholm, Malmö, and Vancouver eco-districts. Some argue that Vancouver's citywide eco-density policy has brought ecology and gentrification together as explicit government policy.[9] While the Southeast False Creek eco-district originally required that one-third of the development be designated as low income, the city council dropped the requirement. Similarly, a conservative change of government shifted the split in private and municipal housing for Hammarby Sjöstad from 50-50 to 70-30, ensuring that it would be a green middle-class enclave.[10] Critics of Malmö's Western Harbour argue that it has transformed a postindustrial landscape into a middle-class enclave built to meet economic development goals.[11] Jennifer Lenhart and I (2016) maintain, however, that the city did increase affordability requirements in later phases of the Western Harbour development and succeeded in uniting equity and environmental goals in one of the city's poorest neighborhoods and in other areas.

For all this analysis, most of it critical, there is evidence that technological innovation and economic development occur in eco-districts through their functions as test beds. Among such innovations are Western Harbour's district heating and cooling system, which relies partially on aquifer storage and is essentially a centralized heat pump. During the summer, solar thermal energy heats water that is pumped into limestone cracks 70 meters (230 feet) below ground. A wind-powered pump brings it back up for heating in the winter, while cold water from the Oresund Sea is pumped back down into another storage area for cooling in the summer. Similarly, Southeast False Creek's innovation was to use heat from a sewage treatment plant for energy. At a more general level, research on Hammarby Sjöstad suggests that eco-districts have positive effects on the clean-tech sector in the surrounding city-region, which will be discussed in more detail in this chapter.[12]

Related to this test-bed function, my research on Malmö's Western Harbour finds that city planners and elected officials can apply what is learned from eco-innovation districts and apply it to other areas of the city. Planners and city staff in Malmö undertook a deliberate process of experimentation, re-evaluation, and adaptation of practices that organizational theorists Argyris and Schön refer to as double-loop learning, which includes an ongoing modification of organizational values, policies, and norms to incorporate new practices.[13] My analysis of an eco-innovation district concluded that effectiveness is as much about changing the planning process as it is about new technology. Further, the willingness to experiment and to learn from failures inherent to experimentation allowed Malmö planners to adopt the technologies that work best in the context of the local culture. Without the creation of an eco-innovation district, these learning opportunities would not have occurred.[14]

Eco-Innovation in Practice: Stockholm's Hammarby Sjöstad and the Royal Seaport

Stockholm, one of Europe's fastest-growing metro areas, has a long history of environmental urban planning, with the goal of eventually becoming fossil free. Its first environmental program was initiated in the 1970s, and the city is now amid its ninth program, with goals in transport, energy, land and water, waste treatment, and building materials. In addition, the city has a Sustainable Energy and Action Plan, which lays out a strategy for becoming fossil free by 2040.

District energy is essential to the fossil-free goal. Stockholm's district energy system provides 80 percent of the city's heating needs. Over time, the system was switched away from oil- and gas-fired plants to renewable energy. Now 90 percent of district energy is produced from renewable sources (mostly wood for heating and harbor water for cooling). The Värtaverket CHP plant, opened in 2016 and one of Europe's largest, runs on wood chips and can heat 190,000 apartments and provides enough electricity to power 150,000 vehicles.[15]

The ninth plan calls for halving the energy use in the entire building stock by 2050. Major renovations of existing buildings must reduce use of energy for heating, cooling, electricity, and hot water by 30 percent. As stipulated by the EU, Stockholm seeks to halve energy use in buildings relative to 1995 by 2050. Like Malmö (see chapter 2), Stockholm has a dialogue with developers and construction companies on reducing building energy use to 45 kilowatts per square meter per year. To that end, all new construction on city-allocated land must be at 55 kilowatt hours per square meter per year.[16]

Stockholm's transportation planning deprioritizes cars to emphasize public transit, biking, and walking. The region's extensive subway system opened in 1950 and underwent a major expansion in the 1970s. In 2014 another major expansion was planned to better serve the growing metropolitan area, with construction starting in 2018. About 78 percent of rush hour trips in and out of the city are made by public transportation.[17] Inner-city buses, trolleys, and regional trains are powered exclusively with renewable energy.[18]

The safety of bikers and walkers is a priority. In 1975, the city began building more lanes as part of a plan to add 300 kilometers of separated bike lanes. In 1998, Stockholm implemented a ridership and safety plan that further separated bike lanes from traffic, making cycling safer and encouraging greater bicycle use. If they prove safe, the lanes become permanent. Many streets are car free, and the city pilots programs to reduce car lanes while increasing bike lanes. Perhaps Stockholm is seeking to rival Oslo in creating car-free zones. Stockholm transit commissioner Daniel Helldén has plans to transform swaths of the waterfront into a promenade for walkers and bikers.[19]

Car ownership in Sweden is predicted to rise based on population growth, so city efforts to discourage individual ownership are essential.[20] Stockholm takes a two-pronged approach to reducing the number of cars on city streets. The first strategy is to reduce their impact by promoting carpooling and electric vehicles. The idea is to promote nonprivate car pools (e.g., Zipcar) as "supplementary public transit."

Stockholm aims to be a world-leading city on clean vehicles by 2020.[21] The bus system has been using electric hybrid vehicles since 2008. And by 2015 a goal of making 90 percent of public buses fossil free was achieved (five years ahead of schedule). The city served as a test bed for a line of hybrid buses that can charge wirelessly in seven minutes. The pilot used one charger on an eight-kilometer (4.9 mile) route. The KTH Royal Institute of Technology estimated that installing the chargers on all the city's 94 bus routes would halve CO_2 emissions and lower energy consumption by 34 percent.[22] In addition, the buses have lower maintenance costs.[23] In 2014, representatives from three city departments, the Environment and Health Committee, Stockholm Parkering AB (a city-owned company that operates and maintains the city's parking infrastructure), and the Traffic Committee, and three municipal housing companies formed a working group to build out EV charging infrastructure.

With the carrots are a big stick (the second strategy): a congestion-pricing program that was introduced in 2006. The expectation was that traffic would be reduced by 10–15 percent, but the actual figure is 22–25 percent. Carbon dioxide emissions were reduced 2–3 percent overall in Stockholm County, and 14 percent in the inner city.[24] The city has supported freight consolidation centers to decrease the number of delivery vans and trucks entering the city.[25]

These and other measures have reduced Stockholm's GHG emissions from 5.5 tons per capita in 1990 to 2.5 in 2015 (compared to 4.47 in all of Sweden in 2018).[26] The city is well on the way to achieving its fossil-free goal.

Stockholm has also acted on climate adaptation, particularly with stormwater management. Stockholm's green stormwater strategy, developed in the late 1990s, requires developers to handle stormwater locally, and the Stockholm Water Company offers a discounted rate on water/sewer fees for doing so.[27] The city is moving toward on-site infiltration and detention of stormwater. Open systems—bioswales, canals, and tree pits—are favored for drainage over combined stormwater sewers.

Development of Hammarby Sjöstad

Two city priorities converged to create Hammarby Sjöstad. In 1995, the city council decided to bid on hosting the 2004 Olympics and to develop the Olympic Village in this fading industrial area. While Stockholm didn't win the bid, the desire to revitalize the area remained and fit well with the city's goal of reversing sprawl by building the city inward to accommodate rapid population growth. The city's offices of planning and environment developed a plan for the district with the goal of being twice as efficient as the rest of Stockholm on several measures of sustainability, and to expand the use of renewable energy.[28] In clearing the brownfield site, an opportunity arose to lay out infrastructure—extend district energy and transit to existing systems—but also to test new approaches. Construction began in 1999. The district now has about 24,000 residents.

The city of Stockholm provided Hammarby Sjöstad's developers a strong foundation of climate metrics in building efficiency, energy production, and water use to expand upon. In 1995, planners in three Stockholm city departments—Real Estate, Streets, and Traffic; Environmental Health Protection; and City Planning—had established criteria for ecological building. The goals they put in place would further reduce energy usage, promote renewable energy, and create demand for green products. One of the goals was that nonrenewable energy should account for no more than 30 percent of a new building's total energy need. On building energy use, city planners asked developers to build to a standard of 60 kilowatt hours per square meter per year—including space and water heating and electricity, compared with the city's standard at the time of 100. Hammarby Sjöstad's developers asked to increase the standard to 120 and they reached a goal of 80–120.[29]

The model for Hammarby Sjöstad's water system redevelopment was created by planners in the water and waste administrations working with the energy company Fortum. The Hammarby Model is a closed-loop system in which water and waste are recycled and returned to the community in the form of renewable biogas, heat, and compost (figure 7.1).[30] The heat from water treatment and burning

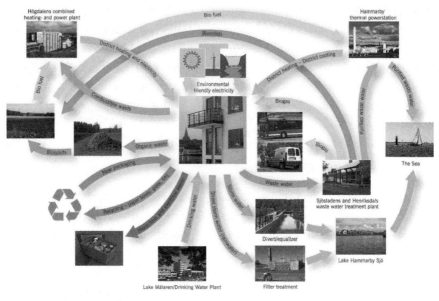

Figure 7.1 The Hammarby Model
Source: City of Stockholm

waste is returned to the district heating system. Hammarby's greenovation is the vacuum system for getting waste to a centralized processing system. The Swedish company Envac developed a system in which waste is transported underground in one of three openings. One is for recyclables, one for organic waste, and the third for all else, which is incinerated. The openings feed into underground vacuum tubes that transport the waste to a central processing facility where the organic waste is converted to compost and biogas. Waste that is not recyclable is burned and the heat feeds the district-heating network, as does heat from the sewage treatment plant.

Another aspect of Hammarby's closed-loop approach is that all stormwater from the district is managed on-site. As the soil on the brownfield site was cleaned, it was prepared for filtrating stormwater. A planned system of green spaces collects rainwater, and bioswales collect and purify it. Runoff from roads drains into separate treatment pools and then infiltrates back into the ground. Canals throughout the district collect water in case of very heavy rain.

Consistent with Stockholm's transportation policies, Hammarby Sjöstad is well connected to the rest of the city and deprioritizes cars. A tramline with four stops that connects to the city's subway was built early on in the district's development. Three new bus routes were added to serve the district, and the buses run on biofuel. A free ferry service to the central city leaves every 10 minutes. Bicycling and walking are also given priority. About 45 kilometers of walking paths and 18.5 kilometers of safe bicycle paths make getting around without a car easy.

Hammarby Sjöstad also follows transit-oriented development principles. Buildings of higher density are located near public transit stations, which are centrally located. All residences are within 300 meters of a tram station. Further, all residences have at least six types of amenities within 500 meters of their entrances so that people can access services on foot or by bike.

These "carrots" were accompanied by the stick of reduced parking. The initial goal was to limit parking spaces to .5 per housing unit, but planners increased the number in the second phase of development to .7 after early residents complained that more parking was needed. Looking ahead, the city, working with a resident group, is currently seeking to make the district a showcase for electric vehicles.

We see in Hammarby Sjöstad a model of how a city can integrate multiple aspects of its climate agenda. Having a clean slate allowed the city to build into the development infrastructure needed to achieve climate goals—particularly in transit and district energy—creating a reduced-emissions environment. Although not discussed in detail here, recycling and district-scale stormwater management also were key elements of the model that contribute to sustainable living.

Planners, architects, developers, and builders in Stockholm are using district-scale developments to pilot green technologies, but the districts are one part of a broader national and municipal strategy to become fossil free and to advance the technologies to get there. A partnership between Stockholm and energy provider Fortum is using waste heat from data centers, attracted to Stockholm for its cold climate, to feed the district heating system. Digiplex, a Nordic data center operator, is supplying enough heat for 10,000 apartments. Ferroamp focuses on solar storage. CorPower Ocean invented a technology that perfects producing energy from wave action. It is located in Stockholm, even though there is no wave action there, because the city is a such a strong supporter of greenovation. Thomas Öström, CEO and cofounder of Climeon, a company that invented technology to turn hot water, often from industrial processes, into electricity, describes what Stockholm provides: "We have a safety net here. There's a system to help you out if you fail, which allows you to take a chance and start a company like this," he says. "It creates an environment that is healthy for taking chances."[31]

The Four Questions Considered

Let's now consider how well Hammarby Sjöstad performs with respect to the four questions raised at the beginning of this chapter. In general, the results are decidedly mixed.

It is difficult to do an accurate comparative analysis of district-versus-city performance on per capita carbon emissions. Few cities have any, let alone up-to-date, GHG inventories, and that is also the case for Stockholm. A critique is that project goals were not systematically assessed during construction.[32] So proxy measures have to suffice. If all or most of the buildings in a district are nearly zero net carbon or passive house, then it is reasonable to conclude that they produce lower GHG emissions than buildings built to a lesser standard.

Besides, there are other ways of determining eco-districts' value in bringing down GHG emissions. If more buildings in a city are built to higher standards due to lessons learned from the district, then one can conclude that developing the eco-innovation district contributes to accelerating a city's climate action. This line of analysis can also be applied to transportation. If the measures in place result in decreased reliance on cars among residents of the district, then it can be assumed that those measures, if applied throughout the city, would decrease GHG emissions.

Urban planners in Stockholm estimate that Hammarby Sjöstad has a 30–40 percent lower environmental impact than the rest of the city. While that may be true overall, the average energy consumption for all buildings in the district is a relatively high at 165 kilowatt hours per square meter per year.[33] Interviewees in the architecture community noted that building performance varies considerably, obscuring the fact that many buildings are very efficient. Several interviewees said that the energy use goal was unachievable without adding considerable cost to construction.

Both my interviews and other studies reveal that another reason building energy use has been relatively high is that the mostly wealthy residents may have less incentive to save money on utilities by reducing indoor temperatures or using less hot water.[34] In addition, builders knew that the intended residents would want large windows with views, which compromised efficiency.[35] My interviews with a member of a local resident organization confirm that people think they are "being green" just by choosing to live in Hammarby Sjöstad. The head of communications for the district notes that a lesson learned is to "engineer in" building energy conservation, as residents cannot be relied upon to change habits. This view was repeated in interviews with architects and representatives of building companies, and it is now standard practice in Stockholm construction.

By design, Hammarby Sjöstad contributes to the city's efforts to reach goals on reducing car use. Residents have four transportation options: the tram connecting to the subway, bus, the free ferry, and biking. Almost 70 percent of trips by Hammarby Sjöstad residents are by public transit, walking, or biking. Even though the number of parking spaces per unit was increased, there are only 210 cars per 1,000 residents, compared with 370 per 1,000 in the rest of the city. The mode share of all trips by car in Hammarby Sjöstad is 21 percent versus 32 percent for the city.[36] Almost 20 percent of residents participate in car sharing, which the resident organization promotes.[37]

Determining whether Hammarby Sjöstad serves as a test bed for GHG-lowering green technologies is more straightforward, and the answer is an unqualified yes. Experimenting with different systems and technologies for efficient buildings has made meeting higher standards achievable. Although the closed-loop system used existing technologies (e.g., district heating and cooling, waste to energy), connecting them and using Envac at the district scale was new. At the time, almost all of Envac's systems handled only one general waste stream. Hammarby was one of the first installations with multiple waste streams. Jonas Tornblom, a senior vice president at Envac until 2017, told me that the innovation in Hammarby Sjöstad was not so much the Envac system per se as its integration with other infrastructure installations. He notes that pneumatic waste collection became a standard in Stockholm and is now the norm for all major developments. It has also become standard in Singapore, Barcelona, and Seoul.[38]

The city, working with the resident organization, is seeking to make the area a showcase for electric vehicles. Residents are involved in a project, Elbil 2020, which promotes car sharing and building charging infrastructure so that shared cars will be electric. The resident group studying strategies for expanding charging infrastructure concluded that people need to be able to charge at home-based parking locations to make the shift from traditional cars to electric cars. The group is now working with at least 10 district housing cooperatives to help them install infrastructure in their garages and is preparing a national "charge at home" campaign to spread the message and the practice.

A group of Hammarby residents is collaborating with tech companies in an economic association, ElectrCITY, an innovation platform of 40 members and partners from business, academia, the city of Stockholm, and NGOs founded by resident Allan Larsson. In order to meet Paris Accord and Stockholm goals, ElectriCITY hosts several pilots in energy and sustainable transportation. Part of ElectriCITY is Hammarby Sjöstad 2.0, in which residents meet among themselves and with city officials to find ways to improve on the energy performance of the district.[39]

A deliberate process of organizational learning is a key part of Stockholm's strategy for increasing standards. Several planners discussed with me various ways in which developing Hammarby Sjöstad was explicitly part of the city's climate action agenda. This is evident in applying the lessons learned both to already developed areas of the city and to new blank-slate developments. Further, they have done so fully aware that considerable financial support was available for Hammarby Sjöstad, and that applying its integrated model in other parts of the city would have to succeed on market principles.

Urban planners offer numerous examples of how they have used knowledge gained from Hammarby's missed goals to develop even more aggressive goals in other parts of the city, with highly successful implementation. Interviewees reported that they have particularly learned a lot about building efficiency in the process of developing Hammarby Sjöstad, and they offer as evidence that Stockholm now requires close to passive-house standard (maximum of 55 kilowatt hours per square meter per year) for all new developments on city-owned land, compared with 80 kilowatt hours, the national standard for the region.

And the city is trying to remedy lower-performing buildings in the district. An ongoing initiative comprising about 50 housing co-ops in Hammarby Sjöstad is working with ElectriCITY Stockholm to dramatically lower the use of energy for heating. A resident involved in the initiative, called Sjöstadsföreningen, reports that it has benchmarked 96 high-performing buildings and found an average energy usage of 118 kilowatt hours per square meter per year, with a range from 55 to 185. The group has developed what members define as a new innovative approach, which tests "target-oriented energy management." In addition, the group is working with four housing organizations, the city of Stockholm, and the National Energy Authority to spread this form of management to housing cooperatives throughout Stockholm.

Developers and planners of a second district-scale development, Stockholm's 236-hectare (583 acres) Royal Seaport, actively studied what went wrong (and right) in Hammarby Sjöstad when they began planning redevelopment in 2009. Recognizing the lack of performance data, planners developed SRS-M, for rigorous measuring, monitoring, and feedback of energy and material flows.[40]

The plan for Royal Seaport—a former industrial area 2.1 miles from the city center—calls for 12,000 new residential units, 30,000 workplaces, and considerable commercial space to be completed by 2030. The overall climate goal is for per capita CO_2 emissions to be 1.5 tons per person (workers and residents) by 2020, and to be completely fossil-fuel free by 2030—and eventually climate positive.[41] To get there, city planners revised the closed-loop model used for Hammarby Sjöstad, making it even more comprehensive.[42]

On building energy efficiency, the goal is passive house, with 30 percent of energy from renewable sources. Much of the area's energy will be supplied by a biofuel CHP system. On transportation, the goal is for 70 percent of work-related trips from the Royal Seaport to be by public transit. Bikes get more space than parking, with a requirement of 2.2 bike parking spaces per unit.

The Royal Seaport serves as a test bed for green technologies even more than Hammarby Sjöstad did. A key one involves smart-grid technology that includes grid integration, household real-energy meters, and an energy quality hierarchy that allows high-quality energy use only for needs that require it.[43] This smart grid will link 170 apartments with a smart lab and seeks to be a global showcase for more sustainable electricity production and distribution systems, and for new market-based approaches to supplying electricity.

Recognizing that there was little outcome measurement in Hammarby Sjöstad, the city is piloting a system for measuring energy, water, and waste flows in real time in Royal Seaport. Two key performance indicators are kilowatt hours per square meter per year and percentage of energy from renewables. After a long process of obtaining the data from utilities, building owners, and other sources, the system allows building owners, residents, and city officials to see the output and to make improvements when needed.[44] Several city planners I interviewed confirmed that this experiment or proof of concept has led to a deeper understanding of how to achieve aggressive building-efficiency goals and promotes resident participation in the process.

What measures have been put in place to ensure a diversity of income levels? While there are many green social spaces throughout the development, criticisms that the district is a middle-class, if not upper-middle-class, enclave are valid. The goal in this regard was not particularly ambitious—that half the housing units would be rental—and has not been achieved. Although as a nation Sweden gets high rankings on Oxfam's Commitment to Reducing Inequality index, these measures are related to education, healthcare, and worker protections. There are no national or municipal requirements for including low- or moderate-income housing, and with high construction costs, developers build to the market. Since 2010, Sweden has absorbed many migrants, particularly from Syria, Iraq, and Iran, and integrating them into the country's society and economic life has been difficult. Riots have occurred in the suburbs of Stockholm, where immigrants tend to live, and in other cities. As in many cities throughout the world, residential segregation by class prevails.

Is Stockholm's Experience Replicable in the United States?

Two institutional factors could make it difficult to replicate the successes of Stockholm in most US cities: stronger powers of municipal government in Northern Europe, and European national and regional policy and funding to support climate action.

Extensive municipal power over land use in Swedish cities is a key factor in their ability to get developers to comply with tough standards.[45] When the city sells properties to developers, leasehold agreements maintain ownership of property with the city, giving it power to negotiate and plan with potential lessees.[46]

Stockholm planners also note that the city owns the energy, water, and waste companies and can simply require them to cooperate on goals. Vestbro (2005) also points out that the city has sometimes paid more than market value for properties it didn't own so that all land being developed would meet its standards. Also, in Sweden most income tax is collected by municipal governments, placing spending decisions on climate action under local control. As one observer notes, "The abundance and relevance of government agencies and state-owned companies creates a governing and institutional framework whereby the state itself provides, owns, and recovers direct revenues from a significant portion of the 'systems and processes' of sustainability, thus enabling implementation and construction of sustainable communities."[47]

Second, layers of policy at the level of the EU and nationally provide strong policy and financial support to cities. Both the EU and the Swedish government invested heavily in Hammarby Sjöstad (and the Western Harbour in Malmö). Both received funding for initial cleanup of the site: Malmö received $2.1 million from the EU and about $33.4 million from the Swedish government, and Stockholm $79 million from the Swedish government, of which $26 million went to Hammarby Sjöstad.[48] The city invested about $2 million in the cleanup. In total, about $685 million of public and private funding was invested in Hammarby Sjöstad.[49]

The Unique Role of Eco-innovation

This chapter suggests that eco-innovation districts can play a significant role in advancing a city's climate action planning. We have seen that an important factor in their success in Europe is policy and financial support from both their national governments and the EU. We have also seen that local policy has been more aggressive than it is in most US cities, partly because municipalities have much more authority to make policy.

Local and higher levels of policy interact and also reflect public attitudes. We have seen that this is particularly true with transportation. Financial support for public transit is essential, but banning parking in a central city, reducing it in a neighborhood, and reducing traffic lanes in favor of bike lanes require high levels of public support, which exists in Stockholm but not in many North American cities. When public support does not exist, city planners need to change views, back down, or some combination of both. When residents complained about the low parking ratio in the first phase of Hammarby Sjöstad, for example, it was increased from .5 to .7—a standard still not achieved in most cities.[50]

Rather than being accepted, the elements of urban climate change are highly contested in many American cities. We have seen this throughout the book in adopting high building-efficiency standards, implementing policies to support expansion of renewable energy, and investing in public transit. Even in places that support policies on renewable energy we see external opposition being fomented by conservative anticlimate groups such as the American Legislative Exchange Council and Americans for Prosperity, both of which receive considerable funding from the Koch brothers and other fossil-fuel interests. And at the federal level we see the dismantling of environmental regulations and climate-change denial, rather than ramped-up support to states and cities in their climate mitigation and adaptation strategies.

The different eco-district models being implemented in the United States have varying degrees of focus on building efficiency, transit, renewable energy, and stormwater management. Cities in states with strong state legislation in these areas are at an advantage. Currently, they rely mostly on foundation funding, making it more difficult to operate at the scale we see in European districts. Further, because these projects are led by external nonprofit organizations, they aren't always well coordinated with a city's climate action efforts. There are many benefits to eco-districts, but if they are truly to accelerate urban climate action planning, they need to be integrated into the city's broader agenda.

CITIES AND A GREEN NEW DEAL

CAN A LOW-CARBON ECONOMY be a major source of economic development and jobs? The latest grand plan for transition to renewables is touted as a Green New Deal, a catchphrase invoked by at least a dozen policy proposals. Transition to a green economy is urgently needed for its own sake, but the evidence on jobs is mixed. There are some jobs in explicitly green industries such as wind and solar, and more jobs to be had if the United States becomes a leader in related manufacturing as well as installation. But to achieve serious scale, this would require major shifts in trade and industrial policy at the national level, as well as massive investment in modernizing infrastructure generally, well beyond what cities can do locally.

My research on how cities and states have attempted to build a green economy suggests that we need to learn from past failures. In my previous book, *Emerald Cities*, I wrote of efforts to develop solar manufacturing in Austin and Toledo, among other case studies. All the elements of smart economic development practice were seemingly in place. But the local businesses succumbed first to competition among the states and then to subsidized competition from China. Yes, there are still lots of jobs in solar installation, but a Green New Deal should include federal investment in developing next-generation solar and a trade policy to support producing this round domestically.

It's a different story for wind energy. Although about half of the components for land-based turbines are imported, with a new round of offshore wind farms about to be installed on Lake Erie and the eastern seaboard, a coherent industrial policy could create a domestic supply chain. This outcome would also require national policy restructuring, as well as state and city policy inducements.

Production of railcars and electric buses offers more promise of job opportunities. The United States ceded leadership on bus and railcar production decades ago. But as we will see, this is beginning to change. Progressive cities such as Los Angeles, pressured by jobs and justice groups, are mandating local production and supply chains as a condition for winning their electric bus and railcar contracts.

Perhaps the greatest job creation potential, at least in the near term, lies in retrofitting buildings for greater energy efficiency, which perhaps has more job creation potential than any of the other categories. To do this right, we'll have to learn from many programs that aren't working as well as expected, but one program in Philadelphia demonstrates that energy-efficiency retrofits can reduce energy demand and create well-paying job opportunities for un- and underemployed people.

A massive overhaul of public infrastructure, which would cost well into the trillions of dollars, also holds great economic development and job-creation potential. Some of this, such as a shift to solar, is explicitly green. Some of it, such as replacing aging water and sewer pipes, bridges, and highways is simply overdue public investment. And some, such as constructing a nationwide smart grid, is implicitly green in that it replaces an aging grid and supports more efficient use of electricity. There is no point in splitting hairs about whether all such investment is a deep shade of green. Large-scale public investment would create millions of jobs and help shift the economy in a more sustainable direction.

A Green New Deal?

The idea of grounding new domestic industries and jobs in a green energy transition has been around for a while. The Apollo Alliance, created in 2006, evoked the expedition to the moon in calling for an Apollo-scale investment in green technologies and energy efficiency. Initiatives were proposed in the UK as early as 2007 by the New Economics Foundation's Green New Deal group (now called the Blue New Deal to avoid confusion). Amid the Great Recession, the Obama administration also kept alive the link between renewable energy and economic development. The 2009 stimulus package invested $90 billion in cleantech, of which about $20 billion was on tax incentives for solar and wind, and about $50 billion for energy technology research and deployment programs, mostly focused on the grid and energy efficiency. Several other proposals were made during the Obama presidency, although as the economy improved, none were enacted. President Trump, despite his nominal commitment to infrastructure investment, has been aggressively moving America backward on the green technologies of the future—favoring coal instead of solar and wind and gas guzzlers rather than electric vehicles.

However, there has been great interest on the Democratic side. Data for Progress, a new Washington, DC-based progressive think tank, proposes a Green New Deal agenda to transition to a low-carbon economy. It calls for 100 percent clean and renewable electricity by 2035, net-zero building energy standards by 2030, zero-emission passenger vehicles by 2030, and fossil-free transportation by 2050. In addition, it identifies goals for wetlands, forest, and soil restoration; urban brownfields development; and resilient infrastructure. Data for Progress analysis reveals that this agenda would create 10 million jobs over 10 years.[1] Likewise, the International Trade Union Confederation estimates that, depending on the level of investment, a green jobs agenda in the United States could create between 15 and 21 million jobs.[2] In late 2018, Democrats began working on a Green New Deal, which at this point supports the broad idea of a major investment in clean-energy infrastructure, particularly a smart grid, to decarbonize the economy. Freshman House member Alexandra Ocasio-Cortez has been its most vocal advocate in the new Congress sworn in January 2019. The goal is to decarbonize the agricultural, manufacturing, and transportation sectors, while creating a more general fair new deal with job guarantees, minimum basic incomes, and healthcare. Other proposals have emerged since then, including a June 2019 Blue-Green Alliance Solidarity for Climate Action plan that focuses on creating union jobs and workforce training programs.

No matter how ambitious or well structured, however, a Green New Deal will have to contend with China, which has a national industrial policy to establish leadership in solar, wind, and electric vehicle production. In contrast, the United States not only lacks a national industrial policy, but its states compete with one another to offer subsidies and tax concessions in an inefficient zero-sum game in search of jobs. Without a national commitment to building the green economy of the future, China is likely to dominate both production and development of new technologies, leaving the United States mainly with lower value-added installation jobs. And cities will be left playing David to China's Goliath.

As the politics of the original New Deal demonstrated, the United States does not like to engage in explicit economic planning unless it is under conditions of wartime emergency. Direct government pursuit of industrial objectives violates both our professed belief in free markets and our global commitment to liberal trade devoid of national favoritism. Nonetheless, the United States has been willing to use tax credits to subsidize wind and solar production. In addition, the federal Department of Energy has underwritten research on renewable energy and even operates as a venture capitalist. But these efforts have been piecemeal and erratic, making it difficult to put renewable energy on a path that is cost com-petitive with fossil fuels, which are themselves subsidized by federal tax policy.

The federal tax credit for solar and wind energy installation is one of the most important stimulants for private investment. The tax credit has been in place since 2005, but only for short periods and with no guarantee of renewal. Investment slows when the credit's future is uncertain. Fortunately, in 2015, Congress ex-tended the tax through 2021. GTM Research estimates that this extension alone will result in more than 50 percent net growth in US solar installations from 2016 to 2020. The credit will be eliminated for residential installations perma-nently in 2021, and reduced to 10 percent for commercial installations. But what will happen when that window closes? And who will manufacture the energy-harvesting products readied for installation? A Green New Deal has answers to these questions that would benefit American cities and the US economy, but it's not yet clear that the stalemate in American politics will allow it to prevail.

The Rise and Fall of Solar Manufacturing in America—and the Role of China

Because of the uncoordinated nature of solar planning US-style, the American effort to become a leading producer of solar PV panels has essentially been dis-placed by a player that has no compunctions about using as much subsidy and as much government direction as necessary to capture the world's solar produc-tion industry. That, of course, would be China. The United States has lost the first round. The question is whether America can lead again in next-generation solar—and what that means: PV production, installation, advanced R & D, or all three? It also requires much clearer policy guidance on linking these three aspects of a solar transition, along with more supportive trade policy.

The current era of solar includes lots of false starts, whose lessons should in-form policy for the next era. In my 2010 book *Emerald Cities,* I wrote enthusiasti-cally about how states and cities were building a new solar production industry in the United States. An improbable story I told concerned two solar manufacturers in Toledo, Ohio. Toledo was long a center of glass production. Research at the University of Toledo used expertise in glass to create an advantage in solar cells. When First Solar opened its first factory in nearby Perrysburg in 2000, it was the country's largest PV solar panel producer.

Another manufacturing success out of Toledo was Xunlight, using flexible thin-film solar technology. The company was started by a University of Toledo physics professor, Xunming Deng, and his wife, Liwei Xu, in 2002. With $3 mil-lion in start-up funds from the university's Innovation Enterprises, $2 million in state and local tax credits, and a $4 million state loan, the company began producing its flexible stainless steel solar cells. Xunlight also received $34.5 million in tax credits from the stimulus in 2010, in addition to a $3 million grant from the National Institute of Standards and Technology, a typical case of how solar entrepreneurs in the United States cobble together diverse subsidies.

In 2007, Xunlight raised $7 million in financing followed by another $22 million from major technology investment firms. It seemed on track to becoming an international leader in thin-film flexible solar modules. In 2010, Xunlight invested $2 million to open a production facility in Kunshan, China. The idea, or so CEO Deng said, was to assemble panels at a lower cost while expanding the Toledo plant. Two years later, the plant was sold. By the end of 2014, Xunlight filed for Chapter 7 bankruptcy and closed all operations, a victim of China's pricing advantage.

In my home state of Massachusetts, Evergreen Solar was the darling of the solar industry. Started in 1994, Evergreen expanded in 2008 into a $450 million facility in the former Fort Devens Army Base, outside of Boston. With more than $50 million in various state and local subsidies and land deals, Evergreen's claim to fame was its patented string ribbon technology that used considerably less silicon than other panels. But silicon prices dropped, undermining Evergreen's market advantage. By August 2011, Evergreen too had filed for Chapter 11 bankruptcy and sold its assets to pay off hundreds of millions of dollars to its creditors. Evergreen, along with Solyndra (also a recipient of stimulus funds and casualty of the silicon price drop), has become a favorite whipping boy of conservatives warning against the perils of industrial policy.

Georgia-based Suniva also struggled, but it seemed to be coming back after China-based Shunfeng International Clean Energy bought a controlling stake in the company. It moved production from overseas to a new domestic plant, which opened in 2014 in Saginaw Township, Michigan. The company was given a five-year $15 million tax credit from the Michigan Economic Growth Authority, and it pledged to create 350 jobs and produce 170 megawatts of monocrystalline modules a year by 2017. Instead, the Michigan plant closed that year, citing "continued downward market pricing pressures."[3]

Other companies have fared better, but they have not been without trouble. In 2012, SolarWorld (headquartered in Germany), the largest crystalline PV solar producer in the United States, closed its California operation and shut down lines in Hillsboro, Oregon. Then in 2014, when market demand had increased, the company announced a new $10 million production line in Hillsboro with capacity to increase production from 380 to 530 megawatts annually and increase employment from 700 to 900. Demand for the company's 72-cell bifacial solar panel technology, which is up to 25 percent more efficient than other models, is growing, with an increase in shipments of 62 percent in 2015. But SolarWorld still imports panels it produces in Germany for installation in the United States.

Displacement by other countries, and particularly China, isn't just an American story. Freiburg, Germany, was another solar success story featured in *Emerald Cities*. During the 1990s and into the 2000s, Germany was the place everyone was looking to for lessons in how to build solar capacity—both in increasing share of the electricity load and in manufacturing prowess. Germany's 1991 feed-in tariff, which required utilities to purchase all the renewable energy produced at an established price, quickly made it a leader in solar production.[4] But Germany's solar industry was hit by Chinese domination of the market as well. Solar giants Gehrlicher Solar, Q-cells, and Conergy were bankrupt by 2013.[5] As in the United States, project planning, installation, and maintenance are all that's left of Germany's solar sector. Employment in manufacturing of solar panels, at about 80,000 at its peak, is now down to several hundred. In September 2018, the European Commission decided to let tariffs on Chinese panels expire with the rationale that it would create more jobs in installation (some estimate 40,000 for the EU).[6] So, as in the United States, growth in solar energy infrastructure in Germany and the European Union will be with Chinese panels.

What happened? How could these promising companies go bankrupt when worldwide solar installations are growing? Solar is expanding internationally and, in the US utility-scale sector alone, comprised 18 percent of new generation in 2019.[7]

The main explanation, again, is China. To establish a solar industry, beginning in the 1990s, China offered huge subsidies, low wages, and free land to induce US solar companies to locate there. The only stipulation was that they couldn't sell their products in China. This happens to violate free trade principles and arguably trade law, but many US companies took the deal and the US government did not make an issue of it. Then China started developing its own solar industry and dumping products on the world market at below-cost prices—something that also violates trade law. Chinese policy and then production reduced the price of solar panels by 80 percent between 2008 and 2013.[8] Many US and German producers couldn't compete. Installers of solar panels liked the low prices and became part of the lobby urging the US government not to take a harder line against China.

In 2012, US solar manufacturers sought relief from Chinese dumping, and the Department of Commerce imposed tariffs averaging 31 percent. By 2014, Commerce had closed loopholes and imposed tariffs averaging 52 percent (ranging from 26 to 165 percent) on PV panels from both China and Taiwan (because China had been using Taiwanese inputs to avoid tariffs). After review in January 2015, the department set the tariffs at an average of about 20 percent.

But the tariffs came too late to save much of the US industry. At least 14 US solar manufacturers went out of business by 2012, and almost 60 worldwide. With its explicit industrial policy of state-subsidized production and discrimination against imports, China is playing by its own rules and demolishing other nations' efforts, even as it depends on their imports of Chinese products. By 2015, seven of the top ten PV producers were Chinese, and by 2018 only one US producer, First Solar, remained on the list.[9] And although First Solar is building solar farms in the United States and throughout the world, almost all its highly efficient panels are made in Malaysia, where much Chinese manufacturing has moved in light of rising wages.

And now China has created a huge internal market. China's first big push in solar was an investment of $221 billion in renewable-energy development as part of a stimulus package in 2009. This investment would help China meet a goal of producing 11.4 percent of its primary energy from renewable sources by 2015, and 15 percent by 2020. The five-year plan that started in 2011 originally had a goal of producing five gigawatts of solar energy, which was increased several times. A 2015 goal of adding 17.8 gigawatts was exceeded by 20 percent. The plan covering 2016 through 2020 calls for 100 gigawatts. China's solar producers are building huge solar farms to meet the renewable goals of the five-year plans. To put this in perspective, in 2017, China added 53 gigawatts of solar energy—more than Germany installed in the last 30 years, and more than the total capacity of 51 gigawatts in the United States in 2017—and added another 40 gigawatts in 2018.[10]

The good news is that solar PV is still growing in the United States. And with solar providing only 1 percent of our electricity in 2018, growth will continue.[11] But most of it, as in Germany, involves installing Chinese panels. And this creates a perverse politics antithetical to a recovery of US manufacturing, in which companies that use made-in-China panels become lobbyists against any crackdown on Chinese subsidies, for fear that retaliatory tariffs would raise their prices.

The tariffs imposed by President Trump in May 2019 were not part of any strategic plan to reclaim US manufacturing leadership in solar (or any other particular industry). Rather, they were a blunderbuss approach expressing general opposition to China's mercantilist model. If America is to recapture manufacturing leadership in solar, it will require better coordination of energy, industrial, and trade policies.

Although solar panels on private residences are what is most visible to the public, about 60 percent of current generating capacity is utility-scale, mostly in California.[12] Solar growth is based largely on state subsidies of incrementally better, tried-and-true crystalline solar PV panels and not cutting-edge technologies considered to be "next generation" solar. With this innovation-less strategy, in the words of Varun Sivaram, who follows the solar industry at the Council on Foreign Relations, "Solar is headed down a path of profitless prosperity."[13]

The issue of where production is located is related to the question of the solar industry's rapidly evolving technology. Will the US lead in developing next-generation technology, and if so, how? A related question is whether US manufacturers truly need to be producing PV products using current technologies to keep moving to more advanced technologies.

MIT's "Future of Solar" report maintains that considerable R & D needs to focus on achieving large-scale expansion of thin-film solar ("second-generation" solar), integrating increasing amounts of solar power into the grid, and developing technology for large-scale storage.[14] Further, reducing costs requires innovation in manufacturing technologies for producing solar.

Why thin film? Because the first-generation monocrystalline silicon cell technology that is currently being installed will not get much higher than 25 percent efficiency (the percentage of radiation hitting the cell that is converted to electricity). Many experts following the field argue that we need to double or triple the long-run performance of solar cells. Achieving these efficiencies will require third-generation solar cells, which use advanced materials in multiple layers. These cells are under development, but cost has to be reduced, and efficiency and longevity increased, before they are viable solutions. We need to incubate companies that will be able to produce high-value-added solar products at low cost.

The globalized nature of the industry makes it challenging to target domestic production as well as R & D and installation. A typical company may have its headquarters and some research in one country and its production in various locations. Even with the lure of subsidies, these corporate decisions are often beyond the reach of state or national policy, as in a recent attempt to promote solar manufacturing in Buffalo, New York.

A Cautionary Tale: The Buffalo Billion and the Gigafactory

The story of New York State's attempt to build solar production in Buffalo illustrates the difficulty in bringing solar production back to the United States. In 2012, New York governor Andrew Cuomo tried to build an economic development strategy around a single US company, SolarCity. Cuomo's "Buffalo Billion" economic development program promised to invest $1 billion to create jobs and investment in targeted growth industries. The state committed to paying $750 million of the $900 million cost to build a "gigafactory" for SolarCity, which promised to spend $5 billion on the operation over a decade and to create some 1,500 production jobs, and almost as many in regional suppliers and services. What made this subsidy a gamble is that SolarCity, an installation company, had no experience in manufacturing. But SolarCity had a successful record and thrived on subsidies, having received close to $1 billion in domestic tax subsidies and grants for installing Chinese panels throughout the United States. The payoff for the company and upstate New York seemed likely given that SolarCity's panels would combine elements of crystalline and thin-film technology, and thus be the most efficient ones on the market (though not next-generation solar technology). Further, SolarCity promised a state-of-the-art production process that would take many fewer steps than other producers.

Instead of opening the plant in 2016 as planned, the company reduced its projection of 1,400 factory employees to 500, calling into question whether it was necessary for the state to build a 1.2-million-square-foot facility. And there was reason to question SolarCity's employment commitment. When given an $11.8 million subsidy for a $27 million project to install solar panels at Oregon State University and the Oregon Institute of Technology, SolarCity originally partnered with SolarWorld to produce the panels in Hillsboro, Oregon, which would have generated $10 million in wages. Instead, the panels were produced by convict labor. SolarCity gave the contract to Suniva under a subcontract with Norcross, which employed workers from Oregon's Federal Correctional Institute. These inmates were paid 93 cents an hour, compared with the $11 starting wage at SolarWorld. This was not exactly the job creation envisioned by the Oregon Department of Energy's Business Energy Tax Credit program, which has since been shut down.

In 2016, Tesla bought SolarCity (which was cofounded by Elon Musk) for $2 billion, and took on its investment and job creation commitments, calling it Gigafactory 2.[15] The intention was to build solar roof tiles that take the place of roofing shingles. But so far, production problems have prevented a full rollout. Apparently, Musk hasn't okayed the appearance of the tiles.

Tesla claims to employ 800 people at the plant, 300 more than the contract requires at this point, but half of them work for Japanese manufacturer Panasonic, which subcontracts part of the factory. Panasonic is producing solar cells there that Tesla agreed to buy to supply its solar retrofit arm. Because of difficulties in getting panel production up and running, Panasonic has had to sell the components that were to be sold to Tesla to other companies. Musk promised that production will increase in 2019.[16] In the interim, the state dropped the requirement that Tesla would have to create 1,500 supplier jobs. But the company still faces fines as high as $41.2 million each year if the 5,000 direct jobs are not created.

Subsidizing new industries is politically risky. Adding to the problem, Governor Cuomo's "signature initiative" has been marred by scandal—exactly the sort of conflicts of interest that lead conservatives to conclude that government should avoid industrial policy. In 2018, a politically connected developer who donated to Cuomo's campaign was convicted of rigging bids for several state-funded contracts, including SolarCity, to companies with close ties to the governor.[17] Still, it seems likely that Gigafactory 2 will go into production and, if nascent attempts by workers to bring in the United Steel Workers and the International Brotherhood of Electrical Workers succeed, the Buffalo region will support good jobs in the green economy for decades to come.

Is Solar Panel Production the Goal?

This saga raises the bigger question of whether states should be subsidizing solar production facilities to compete with China, especially when domestic production represents only modest technical innovation.

The good news is that solar provides more jobs in the United States than oil, coal, and natural gas combined. According to the Solar Foundation's 2018 survey, there are about 242,343 solar workers in the United States, a 3.2 percent decrease over 2017, but a 159 percent increase since 2010. Only about 14 percent, however, are in production; with automation, that share is not likely to increase much, even if the United States stays in the game. Of the remaining jobs, about 64 percent are in installation and project development, with the rest in sales, operations and maintenance, and distribution.[18]

Solar—both installation and manufacturing—epitomizes the technology of the future economy. But further action by China may dash all hopes for American and European panel producers. In June 2018, China reduced domestic quotas and subsidies for solar, exacerbating the glut on the worldwide market and reducing prices by as much as 35 percent. *Forbes* predicted that this price drop would wipe out the protection US producers receive from Trump administration tariffs on crystalline panels.[19] There is no doubt that cheap Chinese panels are behind the rapid decline in the cost of solar energy. The debate will continue about whether America truly needs to produce solar cells to ramp up generation of solar power. But one thing is clear. If we want US companies to stay in the production business, we will need more coherent national policies—on trade, on subsidies, on technology, and on the connection between production and installation—than anything we've tried so far.

Tilting at Windmills

Despite the huge advantage fossil fuels have had in securing federal subsidies, wind energy has become cost competitive. Currently, wind energy, at $29–$56 per megawatt hour (unsubsidized), costs less than natural gas, at $41–$74 per megawatt hour.[20] Offshore wind is changing the scene even further. The Department of Energy's 2016 *National Offshore Wind Strategy* report is a road map for achieving its 2015 *Wind Vision* report goals: that wind power (land-based and offshore) supplies 10 percent of the nation's electrical demand in 2020, 20 percent in 2030, and 35 percent in 2050.[21] The DOE estimates that wind energy off the Atlantic Coast could supply about 35 percent of the country's electricity and that this level of development would create 160,000 jobs in coastal regions. The amount of wind energy that can be captured and used (the capacity factor) for offshore wind is much higher than for onshore. Because offshore turbines are higher and bigger, and the winds steadier, they can produce more energy and do so less intermittently than onshore turbines—typically between six and nine megawatts of electricity annually. The DOE's National Renewable Energy Lab estimates the United States has about 2,000 gigawatts of offshore wind energy capacity, which is roughly double the nation's current electricity use.[22]

Although there have been ups and downs, wind turbine manufacturing and its associated supply chain have done better than solar manufacturing. In 2017, wind energy, broadly defined, employed 105,500 in the United States and 344,000 in Europe.[23] About 38 percent work in construction, development, and transportation, 25 percent in manufacturing, 19 percent in operations and maintenance, and the rest in other categories.[24] With all the current projects and pending commitments, the potential is many times that. The DOE estimates high levels of domestic content in the three largest components of a turbine: more than 85 percent for nacelles (the housing for the gearbox and other generating components), between 70 and 85 percent for towers, and between 50 and 70 percent for blades and hubs.[25] But it is difficult to track the rest of the vast supply chain. The DOE estimates that fewer components are made in America than the American Wind Energy Association (AWEA) claims. The difference, as a source from the Lawrence Berkeley National Laboratory told me, is that "the AWEA is permissive in how they define a supplier." Regardless, wind employment will continue to grow; wind turbine technician is the second-fastest-growing occupation in the United States, only behind solar photovoltaic installer.[26]

But there's a cautionary tale here, too. Wind supply chains are also highly competitive internationally, and how the game is played matters. The next section examines how Cleveland and the northeastern Ohio region and several northeastern states are cooperating to develop a regional supply chain to support offshore wind production, one that gets a leg up on the global competition.

Cleveland: A Long-Term Strategy

Cleveland has been trying to develop offshore wind turbines on Lake Erie since 2004. After many political and funding challenges, construction on a pilot program for a six-turbine wind farm will begin between 2019 and 2021. The pilot, Project Icebreaker, seeks to surmount obstacles to year-round generation in a large body of water that is partly frozen each winter. Should it be successful, a new wind-powered energy grid could be developed along the southern shores of all the Great Lakes. Given shifting political support at various levels of government and the threat from rival producers that benefit from more consistent government policy, it's a small miracle that the Cleveland project is still alive.

Soon after arriving as president of the Cleveland Foundation in 2003, Ronn Richard began exploring offshore wind on Lake Erie as an economic development engine for this declining manufacturing city. The foundation funded feasibility studies that were encouraging enough for it to underwrite an initiative to create an advanced energy cluster in northeast Ohio. The effort started with a $200,000 grant to the Cuyahoga Regional Energy Development Task Force to examine the legal, technical, environmental, and financial issues involved in developing offshore wind farms. The foundation supported wind more broadly by granting $3.6 million to Case Western Reserve University's Great Lakes Institute for Energy Innovation to research energy storage, and $250,000 to the Lake Erie Energy Development Corporation (LEEDCo) to coordinate a demonstration project.

LEEDCo, established by Cuyahoga and Lorain Counties, the city of Cleveland, and NorTech Energy Enterprise, also aimed to promote the development of offshore wind energy along the Ohio coastline of Lake Erie. Lake and Ashtabula Counties later joined, as did Erie County in Pennsylvania in 2015. Dave Karpinski, vice president of operations at LEEDCo, cites a long-term goal of generating 20 percent of Ohio's electricity from offshore wind. The first step would be the proof-of-concept pilot program to demonstrate that a turbine could function in the seasonally frozen lake.

While offshore wind is well established, development on Lake Erie presents distinct engineering challenges. Think of a wind turbine as a big sail on a mast: it wants to bend in the wind, so it needs a strong foundation. On land, turbines usually are embedded in huge concrete blocks. The towers of offshore turbines in the ocean are anchored into heavy steel tubes driven as much as 100 feet into the seabed and fixed with concrete. But Lake Erie is not very deep and has a shallow bedrock floor with clay underneath, which would not support a turbine adequately. There would be several false starts before solving this problem.

In 2010, LEEDCo selected Freshwater Wind as the lead in a partnership with some 20 companies internationally to continue developing the pilot. By this time, however, the political winds were shifting. Several state economic development programs that promoted renewable energy during Democrat Ted Strickland's tenure as governor were eliminated when Republican John Kasich was elected governor in 2010. In 2014, Governor Kasich signed legislation that put a three-year freeze on the state's push toward renewable-energy adoption. A second Kasich-approved law increased the distance turbines must be located from abutting properties, which halted the construction of 11 previously approved wind farms.

So, rather than state support, it was the federal DOE under President Obama that kept the project alive. At the end of 2014, DOE gave LEEDCo $3 million to continue its engineering work. Fortunately, in December 2016, Kasich reversed course and vetoed a bill to maintain the freeze, citing the jobs and advanced technology being created in both the wind and solar industries. In May 2016, LEEDCo received $40 million from DOE, to be delivered in three smaller grants as engineering, permitting, and construction goals were met. The total cost for the pilot project, including $1.7 million from the Cleveland Foundation, is between $120 million and $128 million, about a third of which will come from private investors.

The last hurdle for the pilot was approval by the Power Siting Board, which held hearings to evaluate claims for and against the pilot. Some expressed concern about potential bird kills and effects on boating. In addition, Ohio-based Murray Energy Corporation, the largest privately held coal company in the United States, funded opposition consultants. The National Audubon Society, the Sierra Club, and the Ohio Environmental Council testified in favor of Icebreaker.[27] In July 2018 the board granted tentative approval, pending the results of studies monitoring the turbines' impact on birds. In October 2018, DOE released the environmental assessment, which concluded that there were no significant impacts associated with Icebreaker and that the project would not require an environmental impact statement. The expected construction date is now 2021.

With first-mover advantage, Ohio's manufacturers could supply wind turbine producers as more capacity is built across the Great Lakes, notes Lorry Wagner, LEEDCo's president. "This is about building an industry from the science and engineering to production," he says.[28] Already, Ohio has about 60 plants producing components for onshore wind. The Cleveland-Cuyahoga County Port has reinforced its docks to become a staging area for blades. So it seems that Icebreaker is on track and that Ohio will capture some of the manufacturing supply chain. The offshore foundations will require lots of steel, fabricating, and welding. Assembly of the turbines has to occur locally due to their size, and time will tell how much of the offshore supply chain is in Ohio.

Shifting Winds: The Costs of Inconsistent Policy

The multiple obstacles and veto-points in the Cleveland project provide a vivid example of why development of new energy technologies is often so slow in the United States. While there are obstacles in Germany or in China, they are nothing like those in the United States, where incumbent industries have more raw political power. China is a one-party dictatorship that can move fast once the elite makes a decision and provides resources. Germany is a democracy, but it can move with far greater speed and clarity than the United States once a decision is made by the federal government. Although it was controversial, Germany was able to end nuclear power almost overnight.

It's instructive to compare federal government subsidies for fossil fuels, which are permanent and immense, with subsidies for wind energy, which are modest and intermittent. Federal energy subsidies for domestic gas and oil production began in 1916 and continue in various forms today. The oil industry receives a huge tax subsidy, known as the depletion allowance, to compensate for the value of a company's assets over time. The Department of Energy began funding research into fracking in 1978 and maintained it for at least 14 years, totaling $137 million. In 1980, Congress passed a generous tax break to stimulate the unconventional natural gas drilling, providing drillers $10 billion between then and 2002. Despite record-breaking profits, oil and gas subsidies have continued to the present, totaling $470 billion in tax breaks over a century. And if that's not enough, the 2003 Bush-era energy bill exempted fracking from EPA drinking-water regulations, and in 2005 exempted it from parts of the Clean Water Act.

The production tax credit for wind energy, like solar, was authorized for one or two years at a time, with frequent renewals. Each time its renewal was in doubt, private investment in wind and other renewables dropped dramatically. In December 2015, Congress extended the credit for five years with a plan for phasing it out. Projects started through 2016 received the full credit, but in each subsequent year, the credit drops by 20 percent until it reaches zero for projects starting in 2021. The production tax credits will be phased out gradually by 2019. Renewables received about one-fifth of the support of oil and gas during the early years of development, when strong investment can make a big difference.

As if the federal government's preferential treatment of oil and gas producers weren't a big enough problem for the fledgling US wind industry, China blocks development on a different front. It not only subsidizes domestic production, but places domestic content requirements on wind producers entering its market—all but eliminating foreign competition. Spain's Gamesa and other turbine producers seeking to move into China's expanding wind market agreed to manufacture there in the early 2000s and went along with China's demands that they only use Chinese suppliers. These suppliers then worked with Chinese turbine producers, cutting the foreign producers out. By 2005, China required that 70 percent of components for Chinese wind farms be produced domestically, causing Gamesa's market share in China to plunge.[29]

Chinese competition later affected the US wind industry in another way. Gamesa and several European turbine producers, such as Vestas (Denmark) and Siemens (Germany), set up plants in the United States in 2007 and 2008 when natural gas prices were high. Although domestic content requirements were not in place, there were hopes that these turbine producers would locally source many of the approximately 8,000 parts that go into a turbine. But global overcapacity—much of it Chinese—crushed many of them. In 2006, Pennsylvania invested heavily in three Gamesa turbine plants. By 2014 all three had closed. Nordex ended US production in Arkansas in July 2013 after only two years, and since then it has been supplying the US and Latin American markets from its home base in Germany.

As in the case of solar, the United States may be losing wind production, but installation continues to accelerate. State renewable portfolio standards (RPSs), which require utilities to produce specified percentages of their power from renewable sources by a specified year, are driving the current round of offshore development. Almost half of all US wind capacity built between 2000 and 2017 was delivered to meet RPS obligations. These standards will drive renewable-energy additions of about 4.5 gigawatts annually through 2030.[30] The 16 gigawatts of electricity in development in 23 East Coast offshore wind projects were all motivated by state RPSs and climate action goals.

The Search for Consistency in Three Northeastern States

New Jersey made the first offshore commitment in 2010, when then-governor Chris Christie signed the New Jersey Economic Development Act. The legislation sought to develop 1,100 megawatts of offshore wind and create 4,300 direct jobs in the construction phase and 80 in operations and maintenance. But in his 2016 Republican-primary presidential run, Christie changed his position on renewables, and nothing happened until Democrat Phil Murphy was elected governor in 2018. Shortly thereafter, he signed an executive order to develop 1,100 megawatts of offshore wind and a total of 3,500 megawatts by 2030 to help reach a commitment to reaching 100 percent renewable energy by 2050 (Table 8.1).

Table 8.1 Offshore Wind Commitments of Eastern Seaboard States

State	RPS (amount and target date)	Offshore wind commitment (megawatts)
Connecticut	40% by 2030	200 by 2023
Delaware	25% by 2025	Under discussion
Maryland	25% by 2020	400
Massachusetts	35% by 2030, increasing 2% annually through 2029	3,200 by 2030
New Jersey	50% by 2030 (100% clean by 2050)	3,500 by 2030
New York	50% by 2030	9,000
Rhode Island	38.5% by 2035	400
Total offshore		7,700

Massachusetts became the next significant offshore-wind frontier. A 16-year-long battle to get approval for Cape Wind, a proposed 468-megawatt wind farm in Nantucket Sound, failed in 2017, but in 2016 the legislature passed a bill to develop 1,600 megawatts of offshore wind by 2027. At the time, this was the largest mandate in the country. In 2018, the Democratic legislature and Republican governor Charlie Baker called for another 1,600 megawatts by 2035. While adding more offshore wind solidified the Commonwealth's commitment to renewable energy, this compromise bill was much less ambitious than a bill passed by the state senate a month earlier calling for increasing the RPS 3 percent annually and procuring up to 5,000 megawatts of offshore wind. A greenovating aspect of one project being developed for Massachusetts, Revolution Wind, is that the 144-megawatt offshore wind farm will be linked to a 40-megawatt Tesla battery storage system, making it the world's largest combined offshore wind and energy project, according to Deepwater Wind CEO Jeffrey Grybowski.[31]

New York has plans for even more offshore wind than Massachusetts. In January 2017, Governor Andrew Cuomo announced that the state would construct six offshore wind projects totaling 2,400 megawatts. Cuomo then announced an additional 9,000 megawatts in January 2019, for a total of 11,400 to date.

Maryland is developing lower offshore-wind capacity, and getting that was a struggle. In January 2017, the state legislature overrode Republican governor Larry Hogan's veto of legislation to raise the renewable portfolio standard from 20 percent to 25 percent by 2020. The bill also sets aside $10 million to assist small businesses in retooling so they may participate in the supply chain. As part of the state's 2013 Offshore Wind Energy Act, Maryland offers developers 20-year offshore renewable-energy credits that are worth about $130 per megawatt hour generated, to incentivize as much as 400 megawatts of offshore wind.

The credits gave the state leverage in extracting job benefits. The Maryland Public Service Commission requires developers of the two offshore wind projects—Orsted (which bought original developer Deepwater Wind) and U.S. Wind—to invest in building a manufacturing supply chain to support their wind farms 17 miles out from Ocean City as a condition of receiving ratepayer credits. In 2017, the companies agreed to invest a combined $115 million in manufacturing facilities, including a steel fabrication plant. The funds will also be used for improvements to Tradepoint Atlantic, a 3,100-acre shipyard east of Baltimore, which can support the cranes needed to load turbine towers, blades, and nacelles for the turbines onto ships. The companies also committed to using ports in Baltimore (for marshaling) and Ocean City (for operations and maintenance). Finally, each developer is contributing $6 million to the Maryland Offshore Wind Business Development Fund. The state estimates that the two projects will create between 7,000 and 9,700 new direct and indirect jobs, and contribute $74 million in state tax revenues over 20 years.[32]

But extracting these commitments comes with a price: Maryland offered 13 cents per kilowatt hour to the developers, considerably less than the 24 cents Rhode Island paid for a 2016 pilot off Block Island, but still expensive. When developer commitments are extracted as part of procurement, the cost goes into the price of the energy. Massachusetts governor Charlie Baker focused on price in developing the Commonwealth's first 1,600 megawatts in 2016. He knew that European offshore prices were about six cents per kilowatt hour[33] and bet that European offshore developers would find the long-term fixed price contract for developing 1,600 megawatts for Massachusetts attractive. One official told me that by not adding jobs or investment requirements, bidders felt confident that with the investment tax credit and economies of scale, combined with freedom to import some European content, the project could produce electricity at 6.5 cents a kilowatt hour. They bet that with site control as well (the lease for water in which the turbine is placed), developers could develop a business model that would attract financing. "Now that we have price locked in," one state official told me, "we can use other policy levers to incentivize local content."

To capture economic development benefits, the Massachusetts Clean Energy Center (MassCEC) published a report in October 2017 that identifies the potential manufacturing supply chain and which of the state's ports would best serve the industry. MassCEC also produced an online directory that identifies

320 businesses with specializations related to offshore turbine construction, including engineering, electrical, and marine services; welding; concrete and steel fabrication and supply; underwater construction; and heavy-lift crane operations. Massachusetts invested in configuring New Bedford's Marine Commerce Terminal, which is operated by the Massachusetts Clean Energy Center, to build, assemble, and deploy offshore wind farms. In 2016, Massachusetts signed an agreement to lease the facility to Ørsted (formerly DONG Energy), Deepwater Wind, and OffshoreMW. The port is committed to Vineyard Wind for staging its turbines for 18 months starting December 2020. It is likely to be occupied fully for years to come as the existing contracts go into effect.

New York lies somewhere between Maryland and Massachusetts in its approach to planning for offshore wind. Its bids are evaluated 70 percent on price, 20 percent on economic development potential, and 10 percent on the economic viability of the bidder (project experience, management qualifications, and ability to obtain financing). Among all three states the economic development considerations are both expectations of direct jobs and contingent commitments in which the state agrees to invest in, say, port development, and the bidder also agrees to specified levels of investment.

So what kind of economic development is likely to come from these three northeastern state projects? The 2017 Roadmap Project for Multi-State Cooperation on Offshore Wind estimated that if eight gigawatts were to come online in these states by 2030 (which commitments have already surpassed), about 320,000 baseline full-time equivalent (FTE) job years will be created. FTE jobs would peak in 2028 and then go down if no new projects were in the pipeline after 2030, and hold steady if more projects are developed. This sanguine scenario assumes that blades, towers, foundations, and array cables would be produced domestically.[34] Liz Burdock, president and CEO of the Business Network for Offshore Wind, estimates a lower figure of 96,000 jobs by 2030. By her reckoning, most of the permanent jobs will be in project development and management, supply and installation of electrical substations and underwater cable, and operations and maintenance. Depending on how the supply chain plays out, she estimates that as many as 36,000 FTE manufacturing jobs could be created between 2026 and 2028.

Several people I talked to, including wind developers, state officials, and consultants, thought the most likely scenario is that the turbines would be supplied by a European offshore manufacturer that would build a facility somewhere on the eastern seaboard. And manufacturers of other major wind component suppliers already in the United States could move or build new plants along the

East Coast as well. The Block Island turbines were designed and fabricated domestically by two Louisiana companies, Keystone Engineering and Gulf Island Fabrication, respectively. The companies had experience in designing and building offshore technology for the oil industry in the Gulf of Mexico. According to Stephanie McClellan, director of the Special Initiative on Offshore Wind at the University of Maryland, these companies will likely supply the turbines for the new offshore projects through 2030 (as well as for Lake Erie). Most of the specialized heavy-lift vessels used to install offshore foundations are built in Asia. Officials in Massachusetts, New York, and elsewhere are in conversations with original equipment manufacturers, and all are no doubt hopeful that they will land a turbine production facility, which would have very specific location requirements—it needs to be near water for movement to site and have access to a harbor with no bridges or overhead obstructions.

A key need will be specialized port facilities that can handle the huge vessels needed to get the 100-meter turbines to the wind farms. Already, Connecticut has invested $25 million in upgrading port facilities in New London. Proximity will be essential, as developers attempt to build 50–100 units each season. New England weather will impede full-year installations, so everyday efficiencies are imperative. New Jersey has invested $100 million to transform its vacant Paulsboro port to build wind energy converter platforms in preparation for the German company EnBW Energie-Baden-Württemberg's development of the state's first offshore wind farm. It has a key advantage the industry needs: a 130- to 150-mile coastal land zone without bridges or power lines that interfere with the movement of large vessels. Virginia and Delaware are also seeking to develop ports that can the serve the needs of offshore wind.

Wind energy will create good jobs. Among the unions representing wind energy workers are the Utility Workers Union of America, the International Brotherhood of Electrical Workers, the United Association of Plumbers, the Pipefitters and Steamfitters, the Laborers' International Union of North America, and the International Union of Operating Engineers.[35] To prepare new workers for the industry, New York is launching a training academy as part of the New York State Energy Research and Development Authority master plan, which is investing $10 million in workforce development for wind-related occupations between 2018 and 2025.

For both land-based and offshore wind, continued growth in the US market will require grid improvements. The US Department of Energy notes that the cost of integrating wind energy into the grid varies from below $5 per megawatt hour to almost $20 per megawatt hour if wind is to support at least 40 percent of the system's peak load where wind power is delivered.[36]

Los Angeles: Linking the Development of Electric Buses and Subway Expansion to Good Jobs

In principle, the conversion of America's transit buses from the current mix of 65 percent conventional fuel, 35 percent hybrid, and less than 1 percent electric to an all-electric fleet could blend environmental and economic goals, especially if the new electric buses are made in America. But the story to date, though it includes some hopeful signs, is a series of cautionary tales. And once again, as in solar and to a lesser extent wind, at the center of the story is China, whose state-connected company, Build Your Dreams (BYD), has had a massive head start in US electric bus manufacturing.

This is not surprising, since more than 95 percent of global electric bus sales are in China, via a domestic market created by government incentives and subsidies and fuel-efficiency standards. Its market leadership positioned China to take a leading role in bus manufacturing worldwide. But with US cities spending about $5 billion annually to purchase buses and railcars, they too could channel contracts to domestic producers, creating about 30,000 well-paying manufacturing jobs.[37] A natural place to start is California, where state policies mandate a rapid conversion to electric buses.

In 2017, the California Air Resources Board approved a $208 million budget for transitioning all the state's bus and truck fleets to electric by 2040. A year later, the board mandated that the state's transit agencies begin purchasing an increasing percentage of electric or hydrogen fuel cell buses. Starting in 2029, they can *only* purchase electric or hydrogen buses. In addition, California has provided about $100 million in subsidies to school districts for replacing conventional school buses with low- or zero-emissions ones.

A diverse coalition spent three years lobbying the Air Resources Board to mandate and partially fund the transition to electric buses, including the Sierra Club, Earthjustice, the Union of Concerned Scientists, the American Lung Association, the BlueGreen Alliance, the Coalition for Clean Air, Los Angeles for a New Economy, Jobs to Move America, the United Steelworkers, the Communication Workers of America, and the International Brotherhood of Electrical Workers. Several of these organizations would become key players in making sure transit agency contracts required local production and job creation, as would state and local elected officials.

A key target was Chinese company BYD, which was launched in 1995 as a battery manufacturer to compete with Japanese imports. It grew into a powerhouse with massive subsidies from the Chinese government. By early in this century, BYD had become a world-class manufacturer of electric vehicles, batteries, and solar panels.[38] Warren Buffet invested heavily in the company, which in 2010 Bloomberg Businessweek ranked the eighth most innovative company in the world.[39] Seeing the potential for electric car production in California, BYD began courting state, county, and city officials in 2008 as Governor Arnold Schwarzenegger, Los Angeles mayor Antonio Villaraigosa, and other elected officials were courting Chinese green technology companies to invest in California, activity that continued with Governor Jerry Brown and Los Angeles mayors Gavin Newsom and Eric Garcetti. As a result, BYD is currently the only electric bus producer that does all its manufacturing in California. And it is the only one that is unionized and paying living wages. But it's a messy story.

Buy American, Build Your Dreams

US transit agencies purchase about 6,000 buses a year, which has always led to some jobs because of the Buy America Act. Passed in 1933 and adapted since then, it requires the federal government to give preference to domestic suppliers in its contracting. The Federal Transit Administration today requires that final assembly of buses and railcars occur domestically and that 65 percent of the total cost of components be supplied domestically in FY 2018–19, and 70 percent after FY 2020.[40]

Community-labor coalitions have long argued that cities and states should strengthen Buy America by requiring that more of the manufacturing supply chain be domestically produced and that wages be family supporting. One of these "jobs and justice" organizations, Los Angeles Alliance for a New Economy (LAANE), led the campaign for the city's living-wage amendment and has negotiated community benefits agreements with employers moving to Los Angeles County. LAANE began a project, Jobs to Move America (JMA), to target train and bus production when Los Angeles began piloting electric buses. LAANE and JMA would be key to the negotiations with BYD.

In 2009, the nonprofit Los Angeles County Economic Development Corporation pitched BYD on the benefits of locating in the county and offered subsidies to help it do so.[41] By January 2010, BYD announced that it would begin electric car production in California in August and committed to locating its US headquarters in downtown Los Angeles. The city used federal Community Development Block Grant funds to provide BYD with a $1.6 million grant to refurbish a downtown building. For its end of the bargain, BYD agreed to create 58 full-time jobs at its headquarters by August 2015, with 51 percent of the hires being Los Angeles residents. BYD also claimed it would create as many as 150 green-collar jobs in engineering, management, and research and development of EVs in Los Angeles.

But it soon became clear to BYD officials that the company would have difficulty selling its electric cars to US consumers. The public was not sold on electric vehicles and didn't trust Chinese brands. So BYD decided that transit buses would be a stronger market and began searching for a place to build a production facility. By March 2013, BYD had a $12 million order from Long Beach, just south of Los Angeles, to produce 15 buses. All it needed was a place to assemble them.

Enter Rex Parris, then mayor of Lancaster, about 70 miles east of Los Angeles, who also had been courting Chinese investors to create jobs. He, along with state and Los Angeles elected officials, wooed and were wooed by BYD and reached an agreement to retrofit an old RV-manufacturing facility for electric bus production in April 2013. Lancaster committed to lowering electricity rates for the company and to spending $1.4 million to expand its production facility on 12 additional acres of land. In exchange, BYD would meet hiring milestones. In addition, the Governor's Office of Business and Economic Development provided a $3 million tax credit in 2014 for the expansion, with BYD promising to increase employment by at least 500 jobs by 2018.

Meanwhile, as part of a $30 million clean-emissions project, LA Metro signed a $20.7 million contract with BYD in June 2013 to purchase up to 25 zero-emission buses. The contract, negotiated with the city, LAANE, and JMA, called for purchasing five buses as a pilot, with an option to purchase up to 20 more contingent on performance and a BYD commitment to create local jobs that pay the living wage. Although JMA offered to work with the company to recruit, hire, and train workers, a task with which it had experience, BYD officials declined, saying that JMA's process would hinder the company's ability to grow quickly.

All seemed to be in place to fulfill the order, but trouble soon emerged on several fronts. BYD didn't create the promised jobs at the Lancaster plant, and complaints of labor violations prompted a California Labor Commission inspection of the plant in October 2013. The commission issued almost $100,000 in fines for violations of laws on minimum wages, rest breaks, and workers' compensation. Further, the company brought in Chinese workers who were allegedly paid just $1.50 an hour.[42] Although the fine was later reduced to $38,000 when BYD produced documentation that the Chinese workers were temporary technicians paid at a higher scale, critics accused the company of doctoring the pay documents. Worse, it turns out that after the BYD contract was signed, LA Metro agreed to another deal that allowed BYD to produce buses at its Changsha, China factory. Finally, when the Federal Transit Administration discovered that BYD was not adequately contracting with minorities and women, it blocked the company's contract with Long Beach Transit.

JMA observed that fewer jobs than promised were delivered at headquarters as well. Although most jobs were primarily administrative, clerical, and management, there were openings for test drivers and other more entry-level positions. JMA reported to the city's Bureau of Contract Administration that BYD hadn't turned over payment records to determine if it was paying the living minimum wage of $12.42 per hour (without health insurance) for these jobs. BYD officials responded that the city's Community Development Department exempted it from the living wage law after the contract was signed because it was refurbishing a vacant downtown building. Madeline Janis of JMA argued that the city should claw back the headquarters subsidy unless BYD agreed to pay the agreed-upon wages. BYD shot back that she was unfairly targeting the company to gain leverage in JMA's unionization campaign.[43]

In response, JMA led a very public campaign exposing BYD's violations of its hiring and pay agreements. By the end of 2016, BYD officials knew public opinion was moving against them. Further, they were aware that the *Los Angeles Times* was conducting a deep investigation of their business and had filed requests for public records, including emails between BYD staff and elected officials. BYD officials maintained that the investigation would absolve them of wrongdoing but expressed concern that asking customers to turn over emails and other material would result in lost contracts. Just as BYD realized that having JMA as a partner might be beneficial to both the production process and public relations, the story broke.

And then there were problems with the buses. In spring 2015, BYD delivered its first five buses to LA Metro, which were sent back after a little over four months because of quality and reliability problems. BYD took a few months to fix the buses, but when they went into regular service, the problems continued. Four months later, BYD agreed to take the buses back. To date, the city has not taken possession of any of the 65 buses it ordered from BYD.

Los Angeles wasn't the only city having problems with BYD buses. Other cities, including Albuquerque, Anaheim, Denver, and Columbia, Missouri, returned buses that had major mechanical and structural problems and weren't holding the promised battery charges.[44] A *Los Angeles Times* investigation revealed that state and local elected officials continued to support BYD despite these problems, arguing that with new technologies there will be glitches until the production process is perfected. But the investigation suggested that this didn't justify the no-bid contracts the city was awarding BYD, against the recommendations of Metro staff.[45]

Losing support on several fronts, BYD invited JMA to assist with hiring and training workers to help with quality control. In March 2017, after three years of fighting the union, BYD accepted its workers' vote to join the International Association of Sheet Metal, Air, Rail and Transportation Workers union (SMART). In addition to the union contract, BYD signed a legally enforceable community benefits agreement with JMA and the union to hire 40 percent of its workforce from groups with barriers to employment such as veterans, the formerly incarcerated, racial minorities, and women and to provide these workers the training and support, such as English classes and transportation, needed to succeed on the job.

JMA staffer Erika Thi-Patterson notes that since BYD unionized, shop floor systems have been improved, injuries have decreased due to increased safety training, and the time frame for producing buses has improved. Thi-Patterson also notes that BYD has increased the domestic content of its supply chains to about 77 percent, among the highest of any bus producer in the United States.

Taking its work to a national scale, JMA, along with academic and industry experts, co-developed the US Employment Plan, which provides contract language that state and local government agencies can include in their requests for proposals that give preference to bidders who commit to hiring locally, providing living wages with benefits, and hiring low-income workers. To date, nine transit agencies, including those in Los Angeles, Chicago, and New York, use the US Employment Plan tool. LA Metro was the first to adopt it for all bids above a certain dollar level, while the others use it on a contract-by-contract basis. In Los Angeles, JMA negotiates the specific expectations for a community benefits agreement with the company. Unionization and the community benefits agreement would prove essential to LA Metro's July 2017 decision to contract with BYD for sixty 40-foot all-electric buses.

So BYD, which now employs about 750 workers in the Lancaster bargaining unit, seems to be on solid ground—at least with respect to US orders. But the company is not out of the water yet. With demand rising, competition among EV producers is heating up. And in 2017, China reduced subsidies for electric cars and buses that it had been providing since 2010, and will completely phase them out by 2020. The move led to an almost 20 percent drop in BYD's net profit in 2017. In August 2018 net profits declined by 72 percent even though revenue was growing.[46] But with Tesla's decline, BYD profits soared in 2019. It's a volatile sector.

Other electric bus manufacturers have located in California, thanks to its hardwon experience developing an e-bus cluster and generous state climate subsidies. Silicon Valley–based Proterra is the only one that produces electric vehicles exclusively, but it has experienced several fits and starts since it was founded in 2010. Proterra opened its first manufacturing facility in 2011 in Greenville, South

Carolina, and is now the nation's largest electric-bus producer. The company will be bidding on future contracts with Los Angeles, where it is expected to open another production site, and sell in other western cities.

LA's commitment to piloting and producing new technologies clearly carries risks. As noted by Austin Beutner, deputy mayor at the time of the 2010 BYD agreement, "Things like this are about planting seeds. Some grow fast, some grow slow, but you've got to plant them."[47] Negotiations moved faster with a contract for subway expansion. As a condition of winning the $890 million contract, Japanese railcar manufacturer Kinkisharyo agreed to expand its light-rail assembly and testing facility in Palmdale, a community in Los Angeles County, and to create about 235 jobs averaging about $21 an hour plus benefits. The deal almost fell apart because it required the company to accept the union, but Mayor Garcetti helped to negotiate a deal with the company, JMA, and the International Brotherhood of Electrical Workers. And LA Metro's $647 million March 2017 contract with China's CRRC Corp to build 64 subway cars required the company to build a new factory in the Los Angeles area and to exceed the Buy America obligation to make 60 percent of its components domestically.

Chicago also used the US Employment Plan in structuring a deal with CRRC to manufacture 846 railcars. It built a new factory in Southeast Chicago in 2018 that will create a minimum of 170 new unionized manufacturing jobs. The company's community benefits agreement commits it to hiring local residents with barriers to employment and supporting pre-apprenticeship and workforce training programs. CRRC also landed a $567 million contract with Boston's Massachusetts Bay Transportation Authority to build 402 subway cars and a facility in Springfield to produce them, which started operations in late 2017.

The Connection between Energy Efficiency and Employment

Since Amory Lovins coined the term *negawatt*—a unit of energy not used—in 1989, there has been widespread agreement that energy efficiency must be the first priority of climate action. Yet many of the programs that offer residential and commercial building owners free energy audits and discounts on systems and appliances to reduce their energy consumption have not done as well as expected. It seems like such a no-brainer—guaranteed savings on utility bills. Why wouldn't people be lining up?

Most programs' participation rates are typically less than 10 percent. The public is not clamoring for the free energy audits, and those who have them don't often follow through with the recommended investments, even with deep discounts and a list of recommended providers. A key reason, one energy official from Boston told me, is that "the new TV or the granite countertop will always win out over insulation or a new furnace." For the middle class, utility payments are not a big enough expense to justify an outlay that would mean forgoing another purchase. Low-cost financing hasn't proved to be a draw. Take the UK's Green New Deal energy-efficiency program that provided households $16,500 in financing toward weatherization, eliminating the upfront costs that are considered a barrier. The problem, as one energy-efficiency expert noted: "It's different to finance projects people are already doing versus using financing to motivate someone to do something they wouldn't do on their own."[48] With few takers, the UK program was shut down after three months. For the poor, who pay a larger percentage of their income on utilities (what is referred to as energy poverty), they either don't own their homes or can't afford to consider even deeply subsidized improvements.

Still, energy efficiency is one of the fastest-growing job sectors in the nation, and it has even more potential to create living-wage jobs than electric vehicle manufacturing. Almost 1.3 million people are employed in construction and repairs related to energy efficiency, and another 450,000 are in professional services related to energy efficiency.[49] Most are employed in occupations such as heating, ventilation, and air conditioning (HVAC) in both manufacturing and installation/repair; energy-efficient lighting; construction; and manufacturing green building materials, where employers report that an increasing amount of their time and products are focused on energy-efficient technologies. The electricians, HVAC installers, and insulation workers retrofitting the nation's buildings have respective median hourly wages of about $26, $23, and $19.[50] And about 14 percent of the energy-efficiency workforce is unionized.[51]

Philadelphia: A Surprise Leader in Energy-Efficiency Installation Jobs

Energy-efficiency programs can achieve significant energy savings and create good jobs for residents of low-income communities who need to reduce their utility outlays. Philadelphia has taken an approach to meeting these needs that other cities could replicate.

Although Philadelphia has not been considered a leading city with respect to climate action, that may be changing. In October 2018, it was one of 20 cities to win a Bloomberg American Cities Climate Challenge award. And as we'll see, Philadelphia has been more successful than many cities in increasing the efficiency of existing buildings, particularly in low-income neighborhoods, and job-training programs are helping residents of these communities get on career ladders in the construction industry. This twin focus emerged from the bottom up through various advocacy groups working in these neighborhoods.

The city had established the foundations of today's accomplishments in 1984 with the creation of the Philadelphia Energy Coordinating Agency (ECA), which helps residents having trouble paying their utility bills to access federal low-income weatherization assistance programs. Key to ECA's success in attracting residents to take advantage of these programs are the agency's 15 "one stop" Neighborhood Energy Centers, located in neighborhoods throughout the city, in which trained specialists work directly with residents. Further, the ECA's Heater Hotline repairs or replaces heating systems at no cost to income-eligible households. Funded by the city's Division of Housing and Community Development, the Heater Hotline does about 5,000 repairs or replacements per year.

ECA originally certified energy assessors and auditors, and eventually provided training for hands-on technical field work. The training program came about when the city began receiving federal funds for weatherization under the American Recovery and Reinvestment Act, which required specific credentials for those doing weatherization work. Then-executive director Liz Robinson saw an opportunity and successfully applied to be one of seven agencies in the state approved to offer the certification training.

In 2009, ECA opened the Knight Green Jobs Training Center to offer un- and underemployed residents certification in various environment-related occupations. They range from Environmental Protection Agency certification programs in removing and containing lead-based paint to ECA Building Performance Institute certification programs for the energy performance sectors. ECA's director of training, Walter Yakabosky, estimates that most of ECA's energy-efficiency graduates go into entry-level jobs paying $15–$18 per hour. Since 2009, ECA has trained more than 5,700 workers, 4,000 of which are new entrants to the field (the remainder were already employed in the field but lacked certification). During the ARRA-funded period, all workers were placed, and the current placement rate is about 88 percent.

New training programs are added to meet new needs. One was for building operations managers. Yakabosky explains that as more buildings adopt sophisticated digital energy-management systems, more highly skilled operations managers must be trained. ECA also partners with Philadelphia's Energy Authority and school district in offering solar installation training. Another program offered by ECA, launched in April 2019, is the Johnson Controls, Inc. Commercial HVAC Pathways Vocational Lab. The first phase offers a 600-hour HVAC-maintenance program that prepares students for jobs paying from $35,000 to $45,000 a year. The second and third phases, also 600 hours each, are offered to graduates while they are working. Phase two training is in HVAC installation and trouble-shooting, and phase three is in HVAC automation and controls. The

Community College of Philadelphia is considering linking the curriculum to advanced-placement technical degrees in fields such as building science.

In addition, Philadelphia is one of a few US cities with an agency dedicated to energy efficiency: the Philadelphia Energy Authority (PEA). As energy deregulation came into play in 2010, Philadelphia City Council president Darrell Clarke and then-mayor Michael Nutter had been seeking ways to address high levels of energy poverty in the city. They developed an ordinance to create the authority, which would counter potentially higher energy prices caused by deregulation by increasing energy efficiency, thus reducing energy demand. PEA describes its mission as driving and supporting the development of long-term energy projects, policy, and education programs in Philadelphia. While some cities' efficiency initiatives focus on the largest emitters, the downtown area, or all residents, PEA primarily targets low-income housing and public buildings. The need is evident: Philadelphia mirrors national statistics showing that average households pay about 5 percent of their monthly income on utilities, while those in subsidized housing pay about 20 percent.[52]

Meanwhile, Clark continued his focus on linking energy efficiency, renewable energy, and job creation for residents. To make it happen, he conceived of the Philadelphia Energy Campaign as a key initiative of PEA, which was launched in 2016. The $1 billion campaign is installing solar energy and providing energy-efficiency retrofits in four types of buildings: municipal, public schools, low- and moderate-income housing, and small buildings. The campaign will retrofit 25,000 residential units and 2,500 small businesses, and spend hundreds of millions of dollars on projects in schools and city-owned buildings, creating 10,000 jobs over 10 years. True to its mission, the language PEA uses to describe the campaign emphasizes social equity and the disproportionate needs of low-income neighborhoods.

Clarke found the perfect person to run the campaign in Emily Schapira. Her extensive experience in managing large energy-efficiency programs in the private and public sectors while advocating for low-income energy assistance would allow her to bring together the partners needed to fund the work. Schapira's unique strength lay in figuring out how to bring energy service companies to the table for jobs and leveraging both public and private funds, depending on the type of project.

The campaign's first project was the city's highest energy emitter, the Philadelphia Museum of Art. The city floated bonds to pay for the energy retrofit. At the school district, a pilot retrofitted three high schools using tax-exempt financing and produced a 20 percent savings in energy costs in each. It also used these energy savings to finance major capital improvements, such as new boilers and windows, for which the district otherwise did not have capital funds. Building on this success, the project has scheduled another 20 schools for retrofitting.

Retrofits of multifamily buildings have been financed with utility energy-efficiency subsidies and rebates. With multifamily affordable housing, each unit is too small to attract energy-efficiency service companies and other vendors that need to get paid upfront. Schapira aggregates these projects so she can attract bigger companies that can float the money for them. To date, she's done one round of affordable multifamily retrofitting of six buildings with different owners, totaling 200 units. They have achieved between 15 and 30 percent energy savings at little cost to the owners. A second group of affordable housing complexes is being assembled for retrofits now.

Moving efficiency measures into low-income housing required Schapira to do a couple of years of relationship building. "We thought everyone in the nonprofit housing community would be excited about the efficiency resources we were bringing to the table," she notes.[53] But as a newcomer to an area where housing groups had been working for decades, PEA was met with skepticism. Schapira relates that in Philadelphia, as in most cities, the community development, housing, and public health organizations historically operated in silos and seldom talked to each other, let alone collaborated. After much discussion involving group convenings and meetings, a few key partners decided to buy in, and many more organizations are on board with the energy justice agenda. In addition to working with housing groups and energy service companies, PEA has developed partnerships with utilities, lenders, property owners, and city programs to bring each pilot to fruition. Gradually, a lot of players came to see the benefits PEA brings to the table: in contrast with the city's lengthy RFP and approval process, its contracting is more streamlined, and it is designed to support public-private partnerships.[54]

Another project integrated into the Philadelphia Energy Campaign is Solarize Philly, initially seed-funded by the US DOE's Solar in Your Community Challenge. As the largest solarizing initiative in the country, the program installed solar on over 360 households. While Philadelphia's solar market is now booming (it's the fourth fastest growing in country), the first two rounds of Solarize Philly did not reach as many low- and moderate-income homes as PEA had hoped. To ensure that solar is equitably deployed across the city, PEA developed a pilot program to test a subsidized financing model for installing solar PV on low- and moderate-income housing. The first pilot of 30 low- and moderate-income households had solar PV installed in June 2019. The financing mechanism involves PEA partnering with a tax equity partner and low-interest lenders to purchase the solar panels and lease them to homeowners over the 15-year payment period, after which they own them. PEA's goal is for the monthly lease to be 20 percent less than the homeowner's current utility bill. This model for democratizing renewable energy is replicable if it proves effective. An evaluation of the program started in the spring of 2019. Next the Energy Campaign will install solar panels on schools.

Solar installation is turning into the best job creator of any investment PEA makes, which came as a surprise to staff. In two years, three companies working with Solarize Philadelphia have added 52 employees—half of them women and minorities. ECA is developing a solar installation training program to support the demand. One solar installation program operates at the high school level. In October 2018, PEA received a $1.25 million US DOE award to develop the nation's first clean-energy curriculum for vocational high school students, Bright Solar Futures. The three-year curriculum will prepare students for careers as solar installers and technicians, a fast-growing occupation in the Philadelphia area. PEA is partnering with YouthBuild Philly to develop a parallel program track in solar training for Opportunity Youth, young people aged 18–24 who are out of school or out of work. Another program was started in 2018 for un- and underemployed adults.

PEA's strategy has been to understand market barriers to efficiency projects and then to create ways of structuring projects that can be financed. But there are still obstacles to overcome in funding energy retrofits in low-income housing and in rental housing generally. The main one is the split-incentive problem—if tenants pay utilities, building owners are not motivated to invest in energy efficiency. As Schapira reports, that's why PEA's energy-efficiency work to date has primarily been with buildings in which owners pay utilities. For buildings in which resident homeowners pay utilities, the federal Department of Housing and Urban Development readjusts the utility allowance to reflect the savings, making it hard for owners to get returns on their efficiency investments. HUD is considering changing the rules, but until it does so, efficiency won't be a priority.

The Potential of a Green New Deal

In this chapter, we've explored several realms of energy and climate policy that also have economic development potential, and the leading role cities can play in bringing them about. These include solar, wind, electric bus, and energy-efficiency strategies with employment payoffs. There are of course several other policy realms with huge economic development potential, such as upgrading the electricity grid, producing rolling stock for subways and light rail, planning high-speed rail, devising microgrid technology, and developing infrastructure to protect against sea-level rise, to name a few. These measures, however, require national planning and public investments that are beyond cities' capacity—even though cities are on the front lines of their implementation. To a large extent, they are all infrastructure projects. A major national infrastructure initiative—a Green New Deal—and a green infrastructure bank to finance it are essential.

But climate action needs to be market driven as well. We see in these examples that markets are moving in the direction of renewable energy, electric vehicles, and energy efficiency, as these technologies become more cost-effective. In each case, businesses are profiting from reducing emissions. That is the economic development of the future; government's job is to facilitate it. With guidance from city government, nonprofits, and unions, we can be assured that economic development strategies will also produce payoffs in the form of well-paying and stable jobs.

THE ELEMENTS OF GREENOVATION

AS WE'VE SEEN, STATE and federal policies affect what cities can do on the climate front. Cities have limited fiscal resources and to differing degrees are creatures of state and national policies. In the current bitter red-blue division in the United States, some states facilitate, some obstruct. The limited progress President Obama could make with an obstructionist Congress has been largely reversed under Trump. Yet cities are on the front lines of this struggle. The key question for urban climate action is the same one noted by Campbell and Fainstein for urban planning overall: "what kind of role planning can play in developing the city and region within the constraints of a capitalist economy and a democratic system"[1]— a question I examine here.

A second key question is how environmental justice and social equity are incorporated into climate action, when the forces creating increasing inequality are more national and global than local. Yet environmental hazards are disproportionately borne by residents of low-income neighborhoods. The movement for climate-just cities seeks to reverse this pattern, remediate the damage done, and ensure that the benefits of urban climate action—green buildings, renewable energy, public transit, electric vehicles and charging stations, and green jobs and the training needed for them—are provided in these neighborhoods and that residents are involved in the prioritizing process.

A third core question asks what are the effective local policies and planning practices/approaches that cities can employ to reduce greenhouse gas emissions. I examine these questions in this final chapter.

National Politics and Urban Climate Action

As we have seen throughout the book, urban climate action in leading European cities starts with mandates from the European Union, national policies, and municipal planning. In several cities we examined, we saw that northern European cities in particular have powers that cities in the United States do not. Funding for climate initiatives is available through the EU and national governments. In the United States, by contrast, states can attempt to provide leadership and support, but in the context of a federal administration that seeks to ridicule the idea of climate change and dismantle environmental regulation. It plays out differently among cities.

Conflict over policies sometimes emerges because a blue/green city is in a red state, as when Georgia's Republican-majority, largely rural legislature rescinded EV subsidies that benefited Atlanta, but there's often more complicated local politics at play. In Nashville's failed attempts at BRT and light rail, Republican legislature and interference from the Koch-funded Americans for Prosperity were far from the whole story. Race played a major role, with historic distrust from the black community over displacement and the city government's commitment to providing decent bus service, let alone doing so with major investments in BRT and rail. In Nashville, the coalition of community, labor, and transit advocates, the People's Alliance for Transit, Housing and Employment, had to fight both local and state interests in attempting to link transit with affordable housing.

State and national policies also affect the ability of cities to connect climate action with economic development. Wind development was going strong in Ohio until the Republican legislature put a three-year freeze on the state's renewable portfolio standard. Several projects were stopped, and it cast doubt on the viability of Cleveland's offshore wind project. When the legislature sought to make the freeze permanent, Governor Kasich, a Republican, vetoed the bill, citing the job-creation capacity of both offshore and onshore wind. But that doesn't mean the answer is necessarily in projects like Cuomo's Buffalo Billion solar factory. Panasonic is producing panels there, but the gigawatt production promised by Tesla is nowhere in sight. Critics of a Green New Deal will pounce on this failure as proof that government can't pick winners.

Current national trade policy is not working in favor of a key Green New Deal goal—bringing back solar manufacturing. We learned in chapter 8 how China's flooding the market with cheap solar panels killed most of the solar manufacturing in the United States and Germany. President Trump was right that China's trade practices, which have led to China becoming the dominant player in solar production, were unfair. But solar manufacturing is not likely to come back. To get an idea of the investment a Green New Deal would have to take to re-establish leadership, China invested at least $18 billion in low-interest loans over a period of about six years to solar manufacturers while local governments provided cheap land for factories.[2] Imposing tariffs is not the answer. Tariffs would have to be linked to a comprehensive domestic industrial policy. Solar tariffs have not boosted US solar PV production. But China's retaliation by placing tariffs on the American polysilicon used to make the panels has reduced the competitiveness of this strong US industry as Chinese producers seek other sources.

It's the same story with electric vehicles. China accounts for about 60 percent of the world market, according to Bloomberg New Energy Finance, and has made significant investment to get there. But unlike solar, China is going beyond subsidies and free or low-cost land to attract firms that can catalyze technological innovation. By requiring fewer commitments from companies, China has been able to attract innovators like Tesla, which broke ground on a factory to build its Model 3 and a crossover vehicle in January 2019. As the trade war escalates, we could see the United States ceding this important industry to China as well. The story of Chinese dominance continues with batteries for electric vehicles; China has about 60 percent of global manufacturing capacity and is poised for rapid growth. And China leads in grid-connected battery storage as well.[3]

Against this backdrop, mayors and community organizations have to be strong advocates for the state and federal policies that support their work on climate change. That hasn't happened consistently. In July 2019, hundreds of mayors passed resolutions at the US Conference of Mayors convention calling for a carbon tax and holding fossil fuel companies accountable for the pollution they create, maintaining existing vehicle emissions standards, and supporting the Green New Deal, among others. But these resolutions have no legal force. At least nine cities and counties have filed lawsuits against fossil fuel companies for the pollution created in their cities. It remains to be seen whether these political statements are the beginning of an era of cities leading the charge for national policy.

Climate-Just Cities

A climate-just city achieves aggressive mitigation and adaptation goals that create job opportunities in the green economy and protects all residents from climate impacts.[4] As defined earlier, that means reversing past harms and making sure that the goods of urban climate action—affordable green buildings, renewable energy, public transit, electric vehicles and charging stations, and so forth—are prioritized in low-income neighborhoods and that residents are involved in the prioritizing process. Achieving the climate-just city, then, requires integrating environmental and economic justice into all city functions—housing, transportation, parks, and so on. Although studies on urban governance discuss the need for integration across departments, we know how hard it is to achieve in practice. Even approaches designed with integration in mind, such as transit-oriented development, seldom achieve transit and affordable housing goals. Planners have long grappled with the delicate balance of development leading to gentrification, and climate planning is no exception. Some cities are attempting to achieve these goals against all odds.

In this book, Los Angeles and Malmö stand out for having a combination of committed mayors and city councils committed to climate justice. In the case of Los Angeles, city government works in lockstep with environmental justice and community organizations to advance an agenda of climate justice, economic, and community development.

Environmental and economic justice is at the core of climate action in Los Angeles. It's not random, but integrated into many aspects of climate action. Bottom-up organizing connects to progressive city government to create a safe environment and economic opportunity for low-income residents. Blue LA has taken a step toward making EVs available to residents of low-income communities by putting the cars and their charging stations there, charging lower fees, and waiving membership fees to residents whose income qualifies them. A stringent Green Retrofits Ordinance in 2009 was the work of the Los Angeles Apollo Alliance working with the mayor's office. It committed the city to upgrading the energy efficiency on city-owned buildings larger than 7,500 square feet, with priority given to low-income neighborhoods. Residents had access to construction training programs so residents could get jobs in retrofitting that would have advancement potential. Likewise, greening the port involved environmental justice and community development groups working together as the Coalition for Clean and Safe Ports; and a progressive mayor, Antonio Villaraigosa, appointing board members sympathetic to the environmental justice goals and working with unions to ensure that the labor conditions of the deregulated trucking industry were linked in one agenda.

The Los Angeles Alliance for a New Economy has been working with city government to ensure that new developments benefit low-income residents. Its spinoff organization, Jobs to Move America, has been a key player in connecting transit development to local manufacturing jobs to produce the transit vehicles—both buses and subway cars. The mayor, the city council, planners, and grassroots organizations are working in lockstep to achieve environmental and economic justice.

While Malmö gets a lot of attention for the showcase Western Harbour, the city has put sustainability at the center of its efforts to better integrate poor immigrant communities. We saw in Augustenborg that attention to improving building energy efficiency and addressing stormwater management transformed the appearance of the area into a parklike setting. Input from residents added solar panels, community gardens, and programs in schools. Likewise in Rosengård—an even tougher neighborhood in terms of unemployment and isolation from the rest of the city and Swedish culture generally. Planners engaged residents and school students to create a comprehensive plan that includes transit links, densification, affordable housing, community gardens, education programs, and attractive community gathering spaces. A unique strategy employed by Malmo planners is creating a reason for people who don't live in these isolated communities to visit them. Augustenborg's Scandinavian Green Roof Institute, for example, hosts thousands of international visitors. In Rosengård, the Climate-SMART food center and ecologically restored ice rinks are attractions for people throughout the city.

Of course we can't expect that inequality has been eliminated in either Los Angeles or Malmö—that's why the chapter starts with the dilemma of planning in a capitalist economy in which income and wealth polarization is widening. What city planners can do is make all neighborhoods green with access to transit and affordable housing.

The Elements of Effective Urban Climate Action

In this scan of cities seeking to greenovate, a list of common practices emerges. While these elements of greenovation play out differently among different cities, they define effective practice in planning and policymaking. This isn't to say that there aren't controversies and backsliding in implementation—it's all part of the process.

Bold Plans

Daniel Burnham, considered the father of urban planning in the United States, is quoted as saying: "Make no little plans; they have no magic to stir men's blood and probably themselves will not be realized. Make big plans; aim high in hope and work." Boldness isn't about platitudes—"We're going to be the greenest city in the nation"—nor does it mean setting aggressive targets such as "We'll reduce GHG emissions by 80 percent by 2030" without a clear plan for achieving them and measuring progress along the way. If San Diego fails to make progress on its goal of being powered 100 percent by renewables by 2025, environmental groups and the state attorney general can sue elected officials to force them to comply with their own plan. Cambridge, Massachusetts, is making net-zero construction and renovation standard practice. In each case, a solid plan for achieving the goal was put in place, and city staff at all levels were charged with taking it seriously.

A city can't develop a bold plan, however, without the political support of the people. Even in a progressive city like Seattle, we saw pushback when people were inconvenienced by the reduction in parking or the expense and prioritization of bike lanes. As supportive as the business and university communities were of Cambridge adopting ZNE, it took some convincing of owners of lab buildings that they wouldn't be singled out as energy hogs.

Most importantly, bold plans have interim goals and public accountability for achieving them. Leading cities post progress updates on their websites and offer specific road maps for how goals will be met.

Leadership

Strong leaders are usually behind bold plans. Leadership comes from many quarters. The obvious starting point is mayors—such as former Los Angeles mayor Antonio Villaraigosa linking climate action to economic development and environmental justice, or Jaime Lerner in Curitiba developing bus rapid transit as a less expensive version of metros.

Leadership can also be driven by city planners. Wulf Daseking in Freiburg conceived and developed the eco-district of Vauban, powered 100 percent by renewable energy. It took 25 years from conception to planning to final construction—and he led for the duration.

Leadership also comes from outside the city. Frustrated by the minimal impact LEED certification had on building energy efficiency, Ed Mazria of Architecture 2030 created the 2030 Challenge, which committed mayors who signed on to new buildings, developments, and major renovations to be carbon neutral by 2030. But being voluntary, it was easily ignored. Then Mazria came up with the idea of 2030 Districts, which would solicit the support of property owners and developers for the bold standards. Seattle was the first to sign on, and there are now cities that engage building owners to commit to major reductions in energy and water use as well as reducing the transportation footprint of the occupants of their buildings. These initiatives have ramped up climate goals in most of the cities in which they operate.

In addition to his leadership on climate action while mayor of New York City, Michael Bloomberg's role in accelerating urban climate action as the United Nations Special Envoy for Cities and Climate Change has been transformative.

His philanthropy's American Cities Climate Challenge is providing millions of dollars to at least 25 cities. As cochair the Global Covenant of Mayors for Climate and Energy, he has advanced a vision that, beginning in New York, has created what is arguably the most important international coalition of mayors committed to addressing climate change.

Yet another type of urban leader is Madeline Janis, cofounder and former executive director of the Los Angeles Alliance for a New Economy (LAANE), which strives to link environmental justice and green jobs. Seeing a need to make the connection between public transit and jobs more forcefully in cities throughout the nation, she now leads LAANE's Jobs to Move America program as a national project working in other cities. Similar organizations exist in many cities and either work with or apply pressure to elected officials to keep economic justice at the core of climate action.

Experimentation and Organizational Learning

Cities didn't explicitly address climate change until very recently, so it will take some trial and error to figure out the most effective policies and strategies. Mistakes will be made. Course corrections are needed.

Experimentation became a mantra for planners addressing climate change in Malmö, Sweden. As former deputy mayor Anders Rubin told me years ago, "We don't allow anyone not to innovate, and we don't say we haven't done this before. Experimentation is essential to our progress." He credits hiring innovative thinkers and promoting knowledge sharing among all city departments as critical to the city's ability to achieve its aggressive goals. The planning strategy was to test policies and technologies such as solar or small-scale wind turbines in different areas of the city, assess results, and either take it citywide or correct course and try again.[5] It has worked. Malmö is one of a handful of cities that has reduced vehicle miles traveled and is on track for achieving its 100 percent renewable goals.

Experimentation is not an end in itself, but a strategy for learning what works. It's a deliberate process of experimentation, reevaluation, and adaptation of practices.[6] Argyris and Schön refer to this process as double-loop learning, which includes an ongoing modification of organizational values, policies, and norms to incorporate new practices.[7] Malmö planners and elected officials formalized a process for double-loop learning. While less intentional, ongoing reflection and course changes were also prevalent among Seattle planners in various departments as programs were evaluated. Oslo planners also adapted practices that were producing unintended effects (recall that allowing electric vehicles in bus lanes slowed buses down).

District-scale strategies lend themselves to far-reaching experimentation. Fort Collins, Colorado, approaches zero net energy at the district level in FortZED, which includes a business and residential area of the downtown and the Colorado State University campus. The eco-innovation districts of Stockholm—Hammarby Sjöstad and the Royal Seaport—are test beds for linking elements of climate action and for developing green technologies that can be exported. Vancouver's Southeast False Creek and Malmö's Western Harbour show that mistakes and course corrections are a part of the process.

Public Participation and Engagement

Since Sherry Arnstein's 1969 classic "ladders of participation," meaningful citizen input has been a concern of urban planning. If it is more than the cynical lip service that concerned Arnstein, citizen participation serves many functions, from taking advantage of their knowledge, to empowering residents, testing alternatives, and resolving conflicts.[8] While citizen input into climate action plans is important, having a process for input as policies and programs are implemented is equally essential. Many elements of climate action are disruptive—recall how upset some residents were when Seattle reduced street parking and made room for more bikes. Even in Oslo, with overwhelming public support on EVs and carbon reduction, creating a car-free zone was controversial. Cities need to have a process in place for residents to express their concerns and create mutually agreeable solutions.

Nashville offers a negative example. With a history of using roads to isolate the black community, distrust ran high with initiatives to create BRT in another part of the city when the community was poorly served by existing bus service. Distrust was even higher that light rail would benefit the black community. Rich white residents were concerned about "riffraff" having access to their neighborhoods. Had city officials engaged residents about their transit needs and employed Salt Lake City's line that even if you don't use transportation, you need it, the ballot initiatives to support transit might have passed.

In Stockholm's Hammarby Sjöstad we see that residents have taken it upon themselves to advance the Hammarby model, particularly on electric vehicles. Engagement built in from the beginning makes strong community partners in future problem-solving.

Business Community and Developer Engagement

We've seen how owning most of the land gives northern European cities quite a bit of leverage in demanding developers build to high energy-efficiency standards and incorporate solar energy in their buildings. Malmö's leverage motivated developers to participate in the Building/Living Dialogue, from which they gained expertise on green building techniques. American cities have to get builders and property owners involved by pointing out their self-interest. In Charlotte, building efficiency became a competition among businesses and building owners. The 2030 Districts instill a sense of mutual problem-solving among building and property owners to make their buildings more energy and water efficient and to reduce the transportation footprint of building users. Fort Collins's FortZED district involved six technology companies, the university, and the Colorado Clean Energy Center to figure out how to reduce peak energy demand with load management. Amsterdam works with delivery companies to speed adoption of EVs. Boston's Green Ribbon Commission engages key sectors of Boston's economy, which are now leading in their independent climate agendas. In these examples, the private sector becomes an advocate for city climate action policies.

Carrots and Sticks

All students of planning learn about balancing carrots and sticks. Building energy efficiency employs both to motivate developers and building owners to invest in efficiency. Expedited permitting is a carrot long used to defray additional costs of more efficient construction. The path to ZNE in Cambridge, Massachusetts, offers a guide on how to get the balance right. A first step to ZNE is building energy reporting, seen as a cost and nuisance by many building owners. But because of a participatory planning process and explaining why it was important, builders were on board. So the first step was getting builder and property owners to want to be part of the solution. Then the actual first step—reporting—seemed less of a stick, particularly when they were given all the assistance needed in submitting their reports.

Despite widespread agreement that street parking has to be more expensive and less plentiful as a step toward more transit-, biking-, and pedestrian-friendly streets, doing so creates conflicts. Free or cheap parking has for so long been perceived as a right, that the public reacts strongly, as we saw in Seattle. Similarly, Stockholm residents opposed congestion pricing before it was put in place, but once its benefits in terms of less traffic and pollution were observed, public support was overwhelming. It hasn't been an easy case to make in the United States, as we see in New York City's attempts to institute it.

Conclusion

As this book has suggested, cities are limited by state and national policy mandates and restrictions for good or for bad, as well as by their own fiscal limits. Yet cities are on the front lines of both the impact of climate change and the effort to devise creative responses. They are closer to the citizenry than higher levels of government. And when a crisis occurs, people look to their local officials to help. Cities are also the places where injustice is visible, palpable, and remediable given the political will.

To a surprising degree, cities have been innovators, instigators, and channels for public engagement in addressing the climate crisis. This book only begins to document the success and the promise of cities in the struggle to maintain and improve a habitable earth.

To review city efforts in the race to contain and manage climate change is to appreciate a broad range of frustration and ingenuity in the face of challenges that sometimes seem insurmountable. These efforts inspire hope as well as foreboding. In fact, there are technical solutions to all of the factors creating the impending catastrophe. The question is whether our politics will allow us to carry them out in time.

NOTES

Chapter 1

1. See Liu et al. 2014.
2. IPCC 2018; Walsh et al. 2017.
3. United Nations Environment Programme 2018.
4. Yanarella and Levine 2011.
5. Kennedy, Demoullin, and Mohareb 2012; Corfee-Morlot et al. 2009.
6. Brooks 2017.
7. See McCormick et al. 2013; Slavin 2011; Fitzgerald 2010; Wheeler and Beatley 2009; Birch and Wachter 2008; Beatley 2000.
8. See Bulkeley and Kern 2006.
9. Daigneau 2017.
10. Graham 2017.
11. Climate Mayors 2017.
12. Bloomberg Philanthropies, 2018.
13. Agyeman, Bullard, and Evans 2002, 2003.
14. Boston University Initiative on Cities 2017.
15. Schrock, Bassett, and Green 2015.
16. Bulkeley and Castán Broto 2013.
17. Steele et al. 2012.
18. Burke and Stephens 2017.
19. Labor Network for Sustainability, n.d.
20. In the United States, buildings consume 74 percent of electricity and 40 percent of total energy used. In Europe, on average, buildings consume 40 percent of all energy used. See International Energy Agency 2017.
21. Farrell et al. 2008.
22. About 87 percent of primary energy is produced from fossil fuels. See BP Statistical Review 2016.
23. Grauthoff, Janssen, and Fernandes 2012.
24. European Environment Agency 2016.
25. Hull 2016.
26. Copenhagen and Amsterdam: O'Sullivan 2017a; Freiburg: EcoMobility 2015.

Chapter 2

1. Energy Information Administration 2018; European Commission 2018. According to the US Energy Information Administration, buildings in the United States consume 75 percent of electricity and 47.6 percent of total energy used, and account for 40 percent of carbon dioxide emissions. In Europe, the European Commission estimates that buildings consume 40 percent of all energy and produce 36 percent of carbon emissions.

2. Farrell and Remes 2009.

3. Lucon et al. 2014.

4. Layke et al. 2016.

5. Fulton et al. 2012.

6. International Energy Agency 2015.

7. Layke et al. 2016.

8. International Passive House Association, n.d.

9. Even though I define ZNE and passive house as the "gold standard," there are other paths to building efficiency. One higher standard growing in use is the Living Building Challenge, valued for its wholistic approach to building and community development.

10. Gilleo et al. 2015.

11. American Council for an Energy-Efficient Economy 2019.

12. Hermelink et al. 2013.

13. Institute for Market Transformation 2017.

14. Energy Star, n.d.

15. City of New York, n.d.

16. New York City Mayor's Office of Sustainability, n.d.

17. Zaleski et al. 2015.

18. City of New York, n.d.a.

19. City of New York, n.d.b.

20. Halfnight 2016.

21. City of New York 2016.

22. Personal interview, December 8, 2017.

23. Seattle, Cleveland, Pittsburgh, Los Angeles, Denver, San Francisco, Stamford, Dallas, Toronto, Albuquerque, San Antonio, and Grand Rapids. 2030 Districts 2017.

24. In addition to cities, towns, and counties, tribal nations are eligible for the program, which had funded 50 pilots as of mid-2016.

25. The Living Building Challenge (LBC), launched in 2006 and currently the world's most stringent green-building certification program, is based on seven core performance areas (called petals): site, water, energy, health, materials, equity, and beauty. A key difference with LEED is that LBC certification is earned by demonstrating performance over 12 months of occupancy rather than immediately after construction.

26. Cited in Silver 2014.

27. Enlow 2016.

28. Personal interview, February 21, 2017.

29. Fitzgerald and Lenhart 2016.

30. Smedby and Neij 2013.

31. Metzger and Olsson 2013.

32. Dastur 2005.

33. Beatley 2012, 2007; Fitzgerald 2010.

34. For a detailed timeline of sustainability initiatives and policies see FWTM Freiburg Wirtschaft Touristikund Messe GmbH & Co. KG, n.d.

35. Thorpe 2014.

36. Architecture 2030, 2016.

37. Part of the American Recovery and Reinvestment Act of 2009, the DOE Renewable and Distributed Systems Integration Program funded 191 projects. US Department of Energy, n.d.

38. The project demonstrated peak load reductions at the distribution feeder level. Fort Collins is a retail distribution utility, providing no power generation or transmission. Power is distributed from seven feeders; the pilot demonstrated peak load reduction on two of them.

39. Duggan 2017.

40. Personal interview, February 22, 2017.

41. Personal interview, March 2, 2018.

42. Personal interview, March 2, 2018.

43. City of Cambridge 2018.

44. A Better Cambridge, n.d.

45. Energy efficiency in existing and new buildings is anticipated to achieve a 48 percent reduction in GHG emissions, with renewable energy contributing an additional 22 percent, for a total of 70 percent.

46. Personal interview, October 18, 2016.

47. Personal interview October 18, 2016.

48. Karolides and Ravanesi 2005.

49. City of Boston 2017.

50. Health Care Without Harm 2017.

51. Personal interview, September 20, 2017.

52. Personal interview, September 26, 2017.

53. The two facilities were the legacy of a merger between Boston City and Boston University hospitals in 1996.

54. Chandler 2016.

55. For BMC the green commitment goes beyond building efficiency and clean energy. A 7,000-square-foot rooftop of BMC's power plant has been turned into a garden that produces as much as 15,000 pounds of produce each season, which goes to patients, employees, and neighborhood residents. The "farm" was designed and installed by Recover Green Roofs and is managed by Higher Ground Farm. Its crops supply BMC's food pantry, which serves 7,000 meals a month. Hospital kitchens compost their food waste in compliance with state law. To reduce its carbon footprint from food, the hospital has instituted a meatless day and serves sustainably sourced fish.

56. This section draws on Fitzgerald and Lenhart 2016. For a discussion of environmental gentrification in several cities, see Dooling 2008; Shaw 2008; Quastel 2009; Checker 2011; Sandberg 2014; and Baeten 2012.

57. Personal interview, February 9, 2017.

58. In addition, five greenfield sites within the urban ring will be developed in accordance with the city's master plan goals to increase density and make public transportation more accessible. While greenfield development is discouraged, some has to occur to accommodate rapid population growth.

59. Personal interview, February 9, 2017.

60. Personal interview, February 9, 2017.

61. Thermal-bridge-free means that the building is free of elements that bridge between the inside and outside (e.g., a concrete balcony in which the concrete floor of the apartment is unbroken with the concrete floor of the balcony). The bridge is "thermal" because heat is lost through that bridge. The air-tightness standard for passive-house construction is .6

ACH50—the number of air changes per hour at a pressure difference of 50 Pascals—compared with the typical 7 ACH50 in most code-built construction.

62. Personal interview, January 24, 2017.
63. State of California 2015.
64. Tayor, 2017.
65. New Buildings Institute, 2018.
66. Cited in Mooney 2015.
67. Personal interview, September 23, 2017.
68. Personal interview, January 20, 2017.

Chapter 3

1. Rao et al. 2017.
2. Woodford 2018. A heat exchanger is a device that transfers heat from a fluid in a tube or pipe to a second fluid without their coming into direct contact. In other words, the heat, not the fluid, is transferred. For cooling, heat exchangers remove heat from a tube or pipe and pump it away.
3. Baker 2009.
4. Lund et al. 2014.
5. Stanisteanu 2017.
6. International District Energy Association, n.d.
7. Robb 2009.
8. International Energy Agency 2017.
9. Lund et al. 2014.
10. Heat Roadmap Europe, n.d.
11. Tredinnick 2013.
12. Chittum and Kelly 2016.
13. Official Journal of the European Union 2012.
14. European Commission 2016.
15. European Association for the Promotion of Cogeneration 2016.
16. Euro Heat and Power 2015.
17. United Nations Environmental Program and ICLEI 2015.
18. Tredinnick, 2013.
19. Danish Energy Agency 2017; Parajuli 2012.
20. Sovacool 2013.
21. Patronen, Kauna, and Torvestad 2017.
22. Chittum and Østergaard 2014.
23. Chittum and Østergaard 2014.
24. Chittum and Østergaard 2014.
25. Think Denmark 2016.
26. C40 Cities 2011a.
27. State of Green 2018.
28. State of Green 2018.
29. Galindo Fernandez et al. 2016.
30. Galindo Fernandez et al. 2016.
31. Climate Change Adaptation 2009.
32. Burrows 2010.
33. British Columbia Climate Action Toolkit, n.d.
34. Personal communication, December 11, 2017.
35. Personal interview, April 28, 2017.

36. Personal interview, July 26, 2017.
37. Department of Energy and Climate Change 2013.
38. Department of Energy and Climate Change 2013.
39. UK Government 2017.
40. Mayor of London, n.d.
41. Argent St George, London and Continental Railways, and Exel 2004.
42. For a detailed case study of the planning and development process, see Urban Land Institute 2014.
43. King's Cross, n.d.
44. King's Cross, n.d.
45. Camden 2016.
46. Mottola 2007.
47. The system would use heat exchangers, described previously.
48. Personal interview, Paul Robbins, March 13, 2017.
49. Personal Interview, March 31, 2017.
50. Personal interview, March 3, 2017.
51. United Nations Environment Programme 2015.
52. C40 Cities 2011.
53. City of Toronto 2007.
54. The Suzuki Foundation named Toronto the North American leader in combating climate change, and the London-based Climate Group listed Toronto as one of the five low-carbon leaders.
55. Enwave owns and operates 11 district energy systems in North America.
56. Official Journal of the European Union 2012.
57. British Columbia, n.d.

Chapter 4

1. http://content.sierraclub.org/press-releases/2017/06/us-conference-mayors-passes-landmark-resolution-supporting-100-clean.
2. Ram et al. 2017.
3. See https://thesolutionsproject.org.
4. See Clack et al. 2017.
5. Roberts 2018, 3.
6. Efstathiou 2019.
7. http://www.utilityconnection.com/page2e.asp#muni_util.
8. Kishimoto and Olivier 2017.
9. Kishimoto and Olivier 2017.
10. Utilities argue that solar customers don't pay their fair share of grid maintenance, shifting this cost to nonsolar customers. Supporters argue that cost shifting would only happen at very high rates of renewable penetration. See Andorka and Roselund 2017.
11. The Solutions Project estimates that the 100 percent renewable composition for the United States with respect to solar and wind would be 14.5 percent rooftop solar, 19.5 percent utility-scale, 11.5 percent concentrating solar, 21.3 percent onshore wind, and 17.1 percent offshore wind.
12. National Renewable Energy Laboratory 2013. See https://thesolutionsproject.org/why-clean-energy/#/map/countries/location/USA.
13. Ritchie 2017; Roberts 2016a, 2016b.
14. BloombergNEF 2019.
15. Hockenos 2019.

16. Robbins 2018b.
17. Plas 2017.
18. Burger 2018.
19. National Renewable Energy Lab 2012.
20. Part of the American Recovery and Reinvestment Act of 2009, the DOE Renewable and Distributed Systems Integration Program funded 191 projects. US Department of Energy, n.d.
21. The project demonstrated peak load reductions at the distribution feeder level. Fort Collins is a retail distribution utility, providing no power generation or transmission. Power is distributed from seven feeders; the pilot demonstrated peak load reduction on two of them.
22. Meister Consultants Group 2017.
23. For a discussion of bundling of RECs, for example, see Hagedorn 2011.
24. Meister Consultants Group 2017.
25. St. John 2018.
26. Seven states have enacted CCA legislation: California, Illinois, Massachusetts, New Jersey, New York, Ohio, and Rhode Island.
27. Zahn 2017.
28. Zahn 2017.
29. Gattaciecca, DeShazo, and Trumbull 2018.
30. Personal interview, May 13, 2019.
31. Meisen and Black 2010.
32. Personal communication, Chenin Dow, assistant to the city manager, May 24, 2019.
33. Mead 2015.
34. League of California Cities 2012.
35. Personal interview, October 13, 2017; personal communication, June 17, 2019.
36. City of San Diego 2014.
37. Personal interview. October 13, 2018.
38. Willdan Financial Services and EnerNex 2017.
39. California Public Utilities Commission 2018.
40. For new single-family construction this means the main electrical service panel has to have sufficient capacity and space for future solar PV and EV charging systems; conduit and electrical junction boxes must enable easier and less invasive future installation of wiring and equipment for solar PV and EV charging systems; and that south-facing rooftops are reserved for a future solar PV solar water-heating systems. San Diego County Planning and Development Services, April e-blast. https://www.sandiegocounty.gov/content/dam/sdc/pds/docs/PDS_Newsletter/eBlast_April2015.pdf.
41. Bradford et al. 2017.
42. Personal interview, June 19, 2019.
43. Personal communication, June 24, 2019.
44. Personal interview, June 19, 2019.
45. Personal interview, June 16, 2019.
46. Gattaciecca, DeShazo, and Trumbull 2018.
47. See Massachusetts Climate Action Network 2019.
48. Shemkus 2019.
49. Solar Foundation 2013.
50. Fitzgerald 2010.
51. Hicks 2018.
52. Personal interview, June 26, 2019.
53. Texas Vox 2017.

54. Fitzgerald 2010.
55. Robbins 2018a.
56. Meyer 2015; personal communication with Hamburg energy secretary Jens Kerstan, September 28, 2018.
57. Rüdinger 2017.
58. World Future Council 2016.
59. Becker 2017, 124–25.
60. Rudinger 2017.
61. Richter 2019.
62. Simcock, Willis, and Capener 2016.
63. Becker 2017, 122.
64. Deuschland.de 2017.
65. Wettengel 2019.
66. European Committee of the Regions 2018.
67. Dubb 2018.
68. Kettles 2008.
69. Sovocool et al. 2017.
70. Sovocool and Dworkin 2014.
71. Burke and Stephens 2017; Farrell 2016; Speth 2015; Weinrub and Giancatarino 2015; Kunze 2014; Kunze and Becker 2014.
72. Hess 2018.
73. Trade Unions for Energy Democracy 2015.

Chapter 5

1. Allen and You 2002.
2. International Energy Agency 2015.
3. Broder 2009.
4. Office of the Press Secretary 2015.
5. Office of the Press Secretary 2016.
6. It should be noted, however, that the tax credit can only be applied to vehicles manufactured by companies that have not hit the 200,000 mark in electric vehicle sales. This will hurt the two leading US producers, GM and Tesla, while advantaging foreign companies yet to penetrate the American market.
7. European Commission Climate Action, n.d.
8. European Commission, n.d.
9. Lee 2018.
10. Jain, n.d.
11. Barton and Schütte 2016; Lutsey 2015; Zhang et al. 2014.
12. Holland et al. 2016.
13. See Holland et al. 2016 on EV subsidies and coal, and Worth 2016 on lifetime analysis of EV emissions reduction.
14. Quoted in Georgiadou, n.d.
15. Schaal 2017.
16. Dawid 2016.
17. Holtsmark and Skonhoft 2014.
18. Material related in personal communication, August 21, 2017, with Marianne Mølmen, Oslo's former head of EV infrastructure.
19. City of Oslo, n.d.
20. Stranden 2014.

21. A conversation with Darlene Steward, a senior engineer at NREL, clarified several aspects of V2G for me. She says there are three V2G services that EVs could provide with respect to the grid. The first is bulk energy storage, which is charging EV batteries when generation exceeds demand (such as midday solar output) and selling it back to the grid later. This service works for EV owners who typically make one round trip per day and buy power at a low price and sell it back at a higher price. Steward notes that the difference between the high and low prices, while seemingly attractive, isn't large, nor is an individual car battery. Many vehicles would be needed to supply enough energy to make this a viable option for grid operators. Steward points out that electric school buses may be a better option for V2G since they are parked all day in one place and have much bigger batteries.

Using EVs for frequency regulation is more promising. Throughout the day demand for electricity fluctuates, but power generators run at a steady level. To keep the grid stable when there is fluctuation, utilities buy small amounts of power from providers that can deliver it quickly to balance fluctuations. EVs could potentially be such a source. A third approach to V2G integration is to use EVs to provide power for a utility's operating reserve. Utilities are required to maintain an operating reserve (referred to as a spinning reserve) so if a main generator cuts out, a reserve is available. Operating reserve power is relatively expensive. It could be provided by EVs, but it would require a lot of them. Such a system would require an aggregator, who would offer to guarantee an amount of power in a specified time period, to bid into markets. Aggregators are paid just to guarantee the power is available, but are rarely called on to provide it, according to Steward.

Though it is exciting in principle, the National Renewable Energy Lab identifies several barriers to implementing V2G technology. First, the existing residential and commercial circuit infrastructure has a capacity of 10 and 25 kilowatts, respectively, while most EVs have a power capacity of 100 kilowatts. So the grid would have to be upgraded to accommodate the higher capacity. Steward analogizes the grid as a tree. The trunk is the big power line coming into a city, while the service to an individual household or business is a tiny little branch. If you are trying to feed power from an EV to the grid, the connection is very narrow, so only a small amount of electricity can pass through. If the electricity were needed for frequency control, it could be provided quickly, but only about 5–10 kilowatts from a single vehicle, which is why lots of vehicles are needed. In theory, an individual residence or business could increase the size of the twig to provide more current flow when needed and make money on providing power. But as Steward points out, most people buy a vehicle to drive, not to earn income from the battery. So even though some studies have shown it is a worthwhile investment, people may feel it is inconvenient to be bound to a schedule of when they would have to have the EV plugged in and possibly how many hours a day they could drive. People are more likely to be willing to sell power to the grid if they don't have to schedule around it. And many people might find such management of their driving an invasion of privacy. So the most likely scenario is an EV parked at a workplace all day long at a managed charging point and earning a few thousand dollars a year for providing frequency control. Individual customers would have to weigh the benefits and drawbacks before committing to participating in V2G. Implementation would require communication technologies that determine when vehicles should be adding or drawing electricity from the grid, locate available vehicles to do either, and track the energy provided so owners can be paid. In addition, battery management software that converts a vehicle's DC power to AC hasn't yet been perfected (Steward 2017, 3; Mullan et al. 2012).

22. Personal interview, August 27, 2018.

23. Courtney 2017.

24. Jolly 2015.

25. Doyle and Adomaitis 2013.

26. Haugneland et al. 2016.

27. There is some movement to shift the economy. Innovation Norway, a national industrial development agency that supports innovation, is investing in new growth sectors. For example, Ocean Sun seeks to create floating solar farms on the ocean. And Statoil is a partner in a Baltic Sea wind farm.

28. Stockholm Environmental Institute, cited in Sengupta 2017.

29. Transport for London 2016.

30. Boffey 2018.

31. Walton et al. 2015.

32. Green et al. 2016; Leape 2006. The extent to which the congestion charge versus less-polluting vehicles is the cause of emissions reductions is not clear.

33. The charges are based on EU emissions standards. For more detailed description of charges by vehicle type and penalties, see Transport for London, n.d.

34. Transport for London 2016.

35. Mayor of London and Transport for London 2015.

36. Hull 2016. The other awardees were Bristol (£7 million), Milton Keynes (£9 million), Nottinghamshire (£6 million), and Derby (£6 million).

37. Go Ultra Low, n.d.

38. Mayor of London 2016.

39. Interview with Rhona Munck, senior strategy and planning manager, Transport for London, June 1, 2017; Transport for London 2016.

40. Mayor of London and Transport for London 2015.

41. Since the European Commission has strict rules on providing public funds to private companies, only £2.9 million will be invested in this project.

42. Mayor of London & Transport for London, 2015.

43. Smith 2017.

44. Mayor of London 2017.

45. Zero-emission capable means that the vehicle can operate in zero-emission mode for a range of 30 miles.

46. *Op.cit.* n. 11.

47. Personal interview, May 21, 2017.

48. In 2015, VDL's 2015 annual statement reported the company delivered 72 fully electric-powered buses and charging systems to Dutch public transport operators.

49. Netherlands Enterprise Agency 2016.

50. Van Rooj 2017.

51. If permission is granted, a plan is posted online for six weeks to allow public comment. After conducting a soil test, the grid operator creates the connection, and the charge point contractor connects the unit.

52. Personal interview, September 7, 2017.

53. Personal interview, August 25, 2018.

54. Vertelman and Bardok 2016.

55. New Editor 2015.

56. Netherlands Enterprise Agency 2016.

57. California Public Utilities Commission, n.d. Transportation accounts for 37 percent of state GHG emissions, 83 percent of nitrous oxide emissions, and 95 percent of diesel emissions.

58. Lutsey 2015.

59. Brown and Edmund 2016.

60. O'Dell 2017.

61. California Air Resources Board 2017.

62. California Clean Vehicle Rebate Project, n.d.

63. Rubin and St-Louis 2016.

64. St. John 2016.

65. St. John 2017.

66. Melaina and Helwig 2014.

67. Office of Governor Edmund G. Brown 2018.

68. National Renewable Energy Laboratory 2017.

69. Edison International, n.d.

70. California Public Utilities Commission, n.d.

71. Personal interview, February 28, 2018.

72. Office of Los Angeles Mayor 2016.

73. Lambert 2017.

74. Edelstein 2017.

75. Ryan 2017.

76. Vock 2018.

77. Lambert 2017.

78. Nelson 2017.

79. Nelson and Reyes 2017.

80. Personal interview, February 19, 2018.

81. It serves Echo Park, Boyle Heights, Koreatown, West Lake, Pico-Union, Downtown, and Chinatown.

82. See BlueLA, n.d.

83. This history draws on Fitzgerald 2010.

84. Port of Los Angeles 2015a.

85. Port of Los Angeles 2015b.

86. Personal interview, March 7, 2018.

87. Lopez, n.d.

88. United States Securities and Exchange Commission 2010.

89. Personal interview, February 22, 2018.

90. Joyner 2017.

91. National Alternative Fuels Hotline 1998.

92. Personal interview, January 25, 2018.

93. Union of Concerned Scientists 2015.

94. Caputo 2016.

95. The Tesla Superchargers are free for Tesla Model S and Model X owners. The level 2 charging stations are priced at $1 per hour for the first two hours and $5 an hour thereafter. The DC fast chargers installed for the vehicles other than Tesla are priced at $4.95 for a 30-minute session; after the initial 30 minutes the price is $0.20 per minute. The 10 level 1 charging stations located under one of the office buildings on Seventeenth Street are free.

96. Personal interview, February 8, 2018.

97. Personal interview, February 12, 2018.

98. Personal interview, February 15, 2018,

99. Of the total, $800 million is earmarked for California, the world's largest EV market, and the remaining $1.2 billion in the rest of the country.

100. Georgia Government Department of Revenue, n.d.

101. Personal interview, February 8, 2018.

102. Plug In America 2017.

Chapter 6

1. Manaugh, Badami, and El-Geneidy 2015.
2. https://www.visitflorence.com/tourist-info/driving-in-florence-ztl-zone.html.
3. https://www.livablecities.org/articles/freiburg-city-vision.
4. Shoup 2011; McCahill et al. 2016.
5. Center for Neighborhood Technology 2016; Chester et al. 2015.
6. Weinberger and Karlin-Resnick 2014; Cervero, Adkins, and Sullivan 2010.
7. See http://www.citylab.com/cityfixer/2015/09/an-unusual-objection-to-less-parking-it-will-make-our-city-too-nice/406096/.
8. Eckerson 2014.
9. Skero and Coy 2017.
10. Phand and Toh 2009.
11. Palliyani and Lee 2017.
12. Transport for London 2004.
13. Börjesson et al. 2012.
14. Albalate and Bel 2009; Phang and Toh 2004.
15. Provonsha and Sifuentes 2017, 16.
16. Eliasson 2009.
17. Naparstek 2007; Hugosson and Eliasson 2006.
18. Institute for Transportation and Development Policy et al. 2013.
19. Levinson et al. 2003; Currie and Delbosc 2011; Deng and Nelson 2011.
20. Cervero 2013.
21. Maseo-González and Pérez-Cerón 2014.
22. See review in Wirasinghe et al. 2013.
23. Perk 2016; Nelson et al. 2013.
24. Gustafsson and Kelly 2012.
25. C40 Cities 2014.
26. Lindau, Hidalgo, and Facchini 2010, 25.
27. Ellis 2015.
28. Mejìa-Dugand et al. 2012.
29. Mason, Fulton, and McDonald 2015.
30. Copenhagen and Amsterdam: http://blog.publicbikes.com/2016/05/bike-work-style-commute-european/; Freiburg: Beatley 2012.
31. Personal communication, July 23, 2018.
32. Mekuria, Furth, and Nixon 2012.
33. Gregg and Hess 2018: 414.
34. Smart Growth American and National Complete Streets Coalition 2017.
35. Golub 2015; Hoffman 2015; Miller and Lubitow 2015.
36. Muller 2017.
37. Cervero 2009, 2001.
38. Rattner and Goetz 2013.
39. Zhang, Wang, and Barchers 2018; Duncan 2011; Hess 2007.
40. Chapple 2014.
41. Rattner and Goetz 2013.
42. Soursourian 2010.
43. Clewlow and Mishra 2017.
44. Hill 2018.
45. Cited in Badger 2018.
46. Personal communications, August 11 and 17, 2017, March 7, 2018.

47. Naess, Naess, and Strand 2009.

48. Urban Transit Group 2016.

49. https://www.google.com/search?ei=9yGpWsH1E4jaswWf6o3QBQ&q=10+billion+n orwegian+kroner+to+dollar&oq=10+billion+norwegian+kroner+to+dollar&gs_l=psy-ab.3. ..4910.8819.0.12564.15.13.2.0.0.0.125.1288.6j7.13.0....0...1c.1.64.psy-ab..1.5.449...0i67k1j0i7i1 0i30k1j0i10k1j0i7i30k1j0i5i30k1j0i5i10i30k1j0i8i30k1j0i8i10i30k1j0i8i7i30k1j0i8i7i10i30k1. 0.yciS_YBpG-0.

50. Peters, 2019.

51. Erickson, Down, and Broekhoff 2016.

52. Seattle is the tenth densest city in the nation.

53. An electric trolley ran from downtown to a ferry dock at Fauntleroy from 1906 through 1941, when it was taken down to make room for cars. In 1982, the trolley was brought back, running 1.6 miles on the waterfront. It could have been extended, but instead was dismantled in 2005.

54. https://grist.org/cities/seattles-smart-plan-to-remake-its-streets/.

55. Commute Seattle is supported by a partnership of the Seattle Department of Transportation, King County Metro, Sound Transit, and the Downtown Seattle Association.

56. Hopkins explains that the public-private partnership was created by the Downtown Seattle Association, Seattle, King County Metro Transit, and Sound Transit in 2004 to assist employers in meeting the demands of state policy and to promote transit more broadly.

57. Personal interview, April 15, 2018.

58. The tax varies for cities and towns in the Sound Transit taxing district, which includes the most populated areas of King, Pierce, and Snohomish Counties. ORCA Lift—subsidized passes at up to a 50 percent discount for low-income residents— have been available since 2015.

59. Federal Transit Administration 2017.

60. Courtney 2017.

61. See editorial "Put Brakes on Seattle Streetcar Until These Four Questions Can Be Answered," *Seattle Times*, April 3, 2018. See Malott and Broesamle 2017 for arguments for building the connector.

62. All figures provided by Commute Seattle, a partnership of the city of Seattle, the Downtown Seattle Association, King County, and Sound Transit. Data provided by Jonathan Hopkins, executive director, April 15, 2018.

63. Oldham 2006.

64. About the Commute Trip Reduction Law, King County, 2017, https://www. kingcounty.gov/depts/transportation/commute-solutions/About.aspx.

65. http://sdotblog.seattle.gov/2018/01/03/a-closer-look-at-seattles-rising-transit-ridership/.

66. Seattle Department of Transportation 2014.

67. Personal interview, May 26, 2018.

68. Personal interview, April 15, 2018.

69. Personal communication, July 12, 2018.

70. City of Seattle 2012, 1–3.

71. London and Williams-Derry 2013.

72. Sisolak 2018.

73. Jones 2018; Gruener and Radke 2017.

74. Stephens 2015.

75. http://lawfilesext.leg.wa.gov/biennium/2017-18/Pdf/Bills/House%20Passed%20 Legislature/2382-S3.PL.pdf.

76. Gutman 2018.

77. Personal interview, March 23, 2018.

78. This section draws on Fitzgerald 2018.

79. Quoted in Cherry 2015.

80. Enclave 2014.

81. Cited in Woods 2012.

82. https://publications.tnsosfiles.com/acts/108/pub/pc0998.pdf.

83. Personal interview, June 21, 2018.

84. The tax increases included raising an existing local sales tax from 2.25 to 2.75 percent immediately and to 3.25 in 2023; an immediate 0.25 percent surcharge on a hotel/motel tax, going to 0.375 percent in 2023; adding a 20 percent surcharge to the city's rental car tax; and a 20 percent surcharge to the city's business and excise tax to generate between $7 and $8 million annually.

85. Personal interview, June 11, 2018.

86. Tennessean Editorial Board 2018.

87. Garner 2018.

88. Tabuchi 2018.

89. Entman 2018.

90. Personal interview, June 21, 2018.

91. Santasieri 2014.

92. Personal interview, June 27, 2018.

93. Personal interview June 30, 2018.

94. Personal interview, June 29, 2018.

95. Houston 2012.

96. Hale 2018.

97. Cited in Reicher 2017.

98. https://publications.tnsosfiles.com/acts/110/pub/pc0685.pdf.

99. Cavendish 2018.

Chapter 7

1. From Fitzgerald and Lenhart 2016.

2. See Fitzgerald and Lenhart 2016.

3. Foletta and Field 2011; Harguindeguy and Arias 2002.

4. Holden, Li, and Molina 2015.

5. Fitzgerald, Tumber, and Corley 2013.

6. Rutherford 2008.

7. Sussman 2012.

8. See Dooling 2008; Checker 2011.

9. Quastel 2009.

10. Rutherford 2008.

11. Sandberg 2014; Baeten 2012.

12. Weber and Reardon 2015.

13. Argyris and Schön 1996.

14. Fitzgerald and Lenhart 2015, 14.

15. Fortum 2017.

16. Stockholms Stad 2016.

17. US Department of Transportation 2017; https://international.fhwa.dot.gov/travelinfo/stockholm.cfm.

18. Berger 2017.

19. O'Sullivan 2017.

20. Cited in O'Sullivan 2017.

21. See Nykvist and Nilsson 2015 on Stockholm not leading.

22. Callahan 2017.

23. Sisson 2016.

24. Eliasson 2009.

25. Berger 2017.

26. C40 Cities 2018.

27. Personal communication, Alm Brandt, head of stormwater, lakes, and streams, Sweco Environment AB, January 28, 2016.

28. Svane 2006.

29. Fränne 2007, cited in Mahzouni 2015.

30. The model can be viewed at http://image.slidesharecdn.com/drive4s-130822001730-phpapp01/95/d-ri-ve4s-4-638.jpg?cb=1377130725.

31. Invest Stockholm 2016.

32. Iverot and Brandt 2011.

33. Danielski and Kunze 2008, 54; Iveroth and Brandt 2009, 32, 43.

34. Marcus, Balfors, and Haas 2013; Iveroth and Brandt 2011.

35. See also Bylund 2006.

36. Institute for Transportation and Development Policy 2011.

37. Foletta and Field 2011.

38. Personal communication, August 29, 2018.

39. Personal communication, Allan Larsson, June 19, 2019.

40. Arman et al. 2012; City of Stockholm 2010.

41. Holmstedt and Karl-Hendrik 2017.

42. Stockholms Stad 2014.

43. City of Stockholm 2010.

44. See Shahrokni et al. 2015 for operational details.

45. Metzger and Olsson 2013.

46. Dastur 2005.

47. Dastur 2005.

48. Between 1997 and 2003, the Local Investment Program (LIP) for Ecological Sustainability provided €812 million to cities for building efficiency, infrastructure, and energy systems (Kern and Alber 2009; Granberg and Elander 2007). LIP was replaced by the Climate Investment Program (KLIMP) in 2003 to more specifically target GHG reductions. Between 2003 and 2008, 126 KLIMP projects representing an investment of €214.9 million achieved an estimated 631,000 tons of CO_2 reduction per year (11 million tons of CO_2 reduction over the lifetime of the measures) and 2.2 tWh reduction in fossil-fuel usage per year (Poblocka 2014).

49. Bylund 2006.

50. Conway 2010.

Chapter 8

1. Carlan 2018.

2. International Trade Union Confederation 2012.

3. Jordan 2017.

4. Lang and Lang 2015. Germany became one of the first European countries to promote renewable energy through the 1991 Stromeinspeisungsgesetz, also known as the

Grid Feed-In Law. This law obliged utility companies to connect renewable power plants to the grid and pay renewable-energy producers a guaranteed feed-in tariff.

5. Pentland 2013.
6. Simon 2018.
7. Energy Information Administration 2019.
8. Fialka 2016.
9. Colville 2019.
10. Wehrmann 2018.
11. US Energy Information Administration 2017.
12. US Energy Information Administration 2016.
13. Personal communication, October 16, 2016.
14. MIT Energy Initiative 2015.
15. Hull and Martin 2016.
16. Carr and Eckhouse 2018.
17. Alvarez 2018.
18. Solar Foundation 2018.
19. Conrad 2018.
20. Girouard 2018.
21. Gilman et al. 2016.
22. Musial et al. 2017.
23. International Renewable Energy Agency 2018.
24. American Wind Energy Association 2018.
25. Wiser and Bolinger 2017.
26. Bureau of Labor Statistics 2017.
27. McCarty 2018.
28. Personal communication, June 14, 2017.
29. Hess 2012.
30. US Department of Energy 2018.
31. Orsted 2017.
32. Milligan 2019.
33. Trabish 2018.
34. BVG Associates Limited 2017.
35. Gold and Cresswell 2017.
36. US Department of Energy 2018, ix–x.
37. Jobs to Move America, n.d.
38. Clifford 2016; Masiero et al. 2016.
39. Einhorn 2010.
40. https://www.transit.dot.gov/buyamerica.
41. St. John 2018.
42. Medina 2013.
43. Reyes 2015.
44. St. John 2018.
45. St. John 2018.
46. Huang 2018.
47. Quoted in Yang 2012.
48. Chris Kramer, senior consultant with Energy Futures Group, cited in Tweed 2015.
49. E2, E4TheFuture, and Environmental Entrepreneurs 2018.
50. US Department of Energy 2018.
51. Sen 2019.
52. US Department of Housing and Urban Development 2004.

53. Personal interview, February 14, 2019.

54. Lauer 2018.

Chapter 9

1. Campbell and Fainstein 2005, 2.

2. Bradsher 2017.

3. Wood Mackenzie 2019.

4. This definition draws on three conceptions of justice: Steele et al.'s (2012) definition of a climate-just city as one that is committed to equitable protection from climate impacts, proactive inclusion of all residents in climate action planning processes (generally and in their neighborhoods), and providing information and education on climate action (both adaptation and mitigation) that reaches all residents; Agyeman's (2005) conception of just sustainability as ensuring a better quality of life for residents, now and in the future, in a just and equitable manner, while living within the limits of supporting ecosystems; and Fainstein's (2011) definition of a just city as one in which equity, democracy, and diversity are important considerations.

5. Cited in Fitzgerald and Lenhart 2016.

6. Lenhart et al. 2014; Bulkeley and Castán Broto 2012; Shaw and Theobald 2011; Storbjörk 2010; Holden 2008.

7. Argyris and Schön 1996.

8. See Glucker et al. 2013.

BIBLIOGRAPHY

Agyeman, Julian. 2005. *Sustainable Communities and the Challenge of Environmental Justice.* New York: New York University Press.

Agyeman, Julian, Robert D. Bullard, and Bob Evans. 2002. "Exploring the Nexus: Bringing Together Sustainability, Environmental Justice and Equity." *Space and Polity* 6 (1): 77–90.

Agyeman, Julian, Robert D. Bullard, and Bob Evans. 2003. *Just Sustainabilities: Development in an Unequal World.* Cambridge, MA: MIT Press.

Allen, Adriana, and Nicholas You. 2002. *Sustainable Urbanisation: Bridging the Green and Brown Agendas.* London: Development Planning Unit, University College London.

Alvarez, Simon. 2018. "Tesla Solar Factory in NY Caught in the Crossfire of Buffalo Billion Corruption Case." *Bloomberg*, July 18.

American Council for an Energy-Efficient Economy. 2019. "Buildings Summary." American Council for an Energy-Efficient Economy State and Local Policy Database. Available from http://database.aceee.org/state/buildings-summary.

American Wind Energy Association. 2018. "Wind Energy Facts at a Glance." Available from https://www.awea.org/wind-101/basics-of-wind-energy/wind-facts-at-a-glance.

Andorka, Frank, and Christian Roselund. 2017. "Net Metering Is Dead. Long Live Net Metering." *PV Magazine*, July 12.

Architecture 2030. 2016. "Zero Net Carbon (ZNC): A New Definition." *Architecture 2030*, July.

Argent St George, London and Continental Railways, and Exel. 2004. *King's Cross Central: Environmental Sustainability Strategy.* King's Cross Central.

Argyris, Chris, and Donald Schon. 1996. *Organizational Learning II: Theory, Method and Practice.* Reading, MA: Addison-Wesley.

Arnstein, Sherry R. 1969. "A Ladder of Citizen Participation." *Journal of the American Planning Association* 35 (4): 216–24.

Austin Energy and Clean Power Research. 2012. *Designing Austin Energy's Solar Tariff Using a Distributed PV Value Calculator.* Austin: Austin Energy and Clean Power Research.

Baeten, Guy. 2012. "Normalising Neoliberal Planning: The Case of Malmö, Sweden." In *Contradictions of Neoliberal Planning*, edited by Guy Baeten and Tuna Tasan-Kok, 21–42. New York: Springer.

Baker, Linda. 2009. "Heating the 'Hood." American Planning Association. Available from http://www.seattlesteam.com/documents/HeatingtheHood-Dec09PlanningMag.pdf.

Barton, Barry, and Peter Schütte. 2016. "Electric Vehicle Law and Policy: A Comparative Analysis." *Journal of Energy and Natural Resources Law* 35 (2): 147–70. doi: https://doi.org/10.1080/02646811.2017.1262087.

Beatley, Timothy. 1999. *Green Urbanism: Learning from European Cities*. Washington, DC: Island Press.

Beatley, Timothy. 2000. "Preserving Biodiversity: Challenges for Planners." *Journal of the American Planning Association* 66 (1): 5–20.

Beatley, Timothy. 2007. "Envisioning Solar Cities: Urban Futures Powered by Sustainable Energy." *Journal of Urban Technology* 14 (2): 31–46.

Beatley, Timothy, ed. 2012. *Green Cities of Europe*. Washington, DC: Island Press.

Becker, S., R. Beverage, and M. Naumann. 2015. "Remunicipalization in German Cities: Contesting Neoliberalism and Reimagining Urban Governance?" *Space and Polity* 19 (1): 76–90. doi: 10.1080/13562576.2014.991119.

Berg, Weston, Seth Nowak, Meegan Kelly, Shruti Vaidyanathan, Mary Shoemaker, Anna Chittum, Marianne DiMascio, and Heather DeLucia. 2017. *The 2017 State Energy Efficiency Scorecard*. Research Report U1710. American Council for an Energy-Efficient Economy.

Berger, John J. 2017. "Stockholm Pursues Climate Holy Grail—a Fossil Fuel-Free Future—Part 4: Transforming Transportation." *HuffPost*, May 30.

A Better Cambridge. 2016. "Cambridge Planning Board: Vote NO on Connolly Net Zero Zoning Petition." Change.org. Available from https://www.change.org/p/cambridge-planning-board-vote-no-on-connolly-net-zero-zoning-petition

Birch, Eugenie, and Susan Wachter. 2008. *Growing Greener Cities: Urban Sustainability in the Twenty-First Century*. Philadelphia: University of Pennsylvania Press.

Bloomberg Philanthropies. 2017. *America's Pledge Phase 1 Report: States, Cities, and Businesses in the United States Are Stepping Up on Climate Action*. New York.

BloombergNEF. 2018. "Cumulative Global EV Sales Hit 4 Million." Available from https://about.bnef.com/blog/cumulative-global-ev-sales-hit-4-million/.

BlueLA. 2018. "Welcome to BlueLA.com." Available from https://www.bluela.com.

Boffey, Daniel. 2018. "UK Drives into E-Vehicle Fast Lane with 11 Percent Sales Rise." *The Guardian*, April 19.

Boston Medical Center. 2017. *Boston Medical Center Grows First Hospital-Based Rooftop Farm in Massachusetts*. Boston Medical Center.

Boston University Initiative on Cities. 2017. *Menino Survey of Mayors: 2017 Results*. Boston: Boston University.

BP Statistical Review. 2016. BP Statistical Review of World Energy.

Bradford, Abi, Gideon Weissman, Rob Sargent, and Brett Fanshaw. 2017. *Shining Cities 2017: How Smart Local Policies Are Expanding Solar Power in America*. Los Angeles: Environment America Research and Policy Center.

British Columbia. 2017. "Carbon Tax." Available from https://www2.gov.bc.ca/gov/content/environment/climate-change/planning-and-action/carbon-tax.

British Columbia Climate Action Toolkit. 2016. "Southeast False Creek Neighbourhood Energy Utility." Available from http://www.toolkit.bc.ca/success-story/southeast-false-creek-neighbourhood-energy-utility-neu.

British Columbia Utilities Commission. 2010. *Ontario Power Authority District Energy Management Briefing Note*. Available from https://www.bcuc.com/Documents/Proceedings/2011/DOC_28532_A2-6-Ontario-Power-Authority-District-Energy-Research-Report-Briefing-Notes_Submission.pdf.

Broder, John M. 2009. "Obama to Announce New Mileage and Emissions Standards." *New York Times*, May 18.

Brooks, Sam. 2017. *No, Cities Are Not Actually Leading on Climate: Enough with the Mindless Cheerleading*. Greentech Media.

Brown, Edmund G., Jr. 2016. *2016 ZEV Action Plan: An Updated Roadmap toward 1.5 Million Zero-Emission Vehicles in California Roadways by 2025*. Office of Governor Edmund G. Brown Jr., Governor's Interagency Working Group on Zero-Emission Vehicles.

Bulkeley, Harriet. 2006. "Urban Sustainability: Learning from Best Practice?" *Environment and Planning A: Economy and Space* 38 (6): 1029–44. doi: https://doi.org/10.1068/a37300.

Bulkeley, Harriet, and Vanesa Castán Broto. 2013. "Government by experiment? Global cities and the governing of climate change." *Transactions of the Institute of British Geographers* 38(3): 361-375.

Bulkeley, Harriet, and Kristine Kern. 2006. "Local Government and the Governing of Climate Change in Germany and the UK." *Urban Studies* 43 (12): 2237–59. doi: https://doi.org/10.1080/00420980600936491.

Bureau of Labor Statistics. 2017. *Occupational Outlook Handbook: Fastest Growing Occupations*. Available from https://www.bls.gov/ooh/fastest-growing.htm.

Burger, Andrew. 2018. *DC Microgrids: Can They Win Acceptance in an AC World?* Microgrid Knowledge. Available from https://microgridknowledge.com/dc-microgrids/.

Burke, Matthew J., and Jennie C. Stephens. 2017. "Energy Democracy: Goals and Policy Instruments for Sociotechnical Transitions." *Energy Research and Social Science* 33: 35–48. doi: https://doi.org/10.1016/j.erss.2017.09.024.

Burr, Judee, Lindsey Hallock, and Rob Sargent. 2014. *Star Power: The Growing Role of Solar Energy in America*. Boston: Environment America Research and Policy Center.

Burr, Judee, Lindsey Hallock, and Rob Sargent. 2015. *Shining Cities: Harnessing the Benefits of Solar Energy in America*. Frontier Group and Environment America Research and Policy Center.

Burrows, Matthew. 2010. "Olympic Village District Heating System Should Be Replicated across Canada, Mayor Says." Georgia Straight. Available from https://www.straight.com/article-281089/vancouver/neighbourhood-energy-utility-opens-olympic-village.

BVG Associates Limited. 2017. U.S. Job Creation in Offshore Wind. Webinar, Northeast Wind Center.

Bylund, Jonas R. 2006. *Planning, Projects, Practice: A Human Geography of the Stockholm Local Investment Programme in Hammarby Sjöstad*. Stockholm: Kulturgeografiska institutionen.

California Air Resources Board. 2017. Proposed Fiscal Year 2017–18 Funding Plan for Clean Transportation Incentives.

California Public Utilities Commission. 2018. Resolution E-4907: Registration Process for Community Choice Aggregators.

California Public Utilities Commission. N.d. "Zero-Emission Vehicles." Available from http://cpuc.ca.gov/zev/#Infrastructure.

Callahan, David. 2017. "With New Tool, Cities Can Plan Electric Bus Routes, and Calculate the Benefits." KTH Research News.

Camden Newsroom. 2016. "KX Recruit." Available from https://news.camden.gov.uk/kx-recruit/.

Campbell, Scott. 1996. "Green Cities, Growing Cities, Just Cities? Urban Planning and the Contradictions of Sustainable Development." *Journal of the American Planning Association* 62 (3): 296–312. doi: 10.1080/01944369608975696.

Capitol Hill Housing. 2012. *Capitol Hill EcoDistrict: A Proposal for District-Scale Sustainability*. Seattle.

Capitol Hill Housing. 2015. Capitol Hill EcoDistrict.

Caputo, Michael. 2016. "Georgia EV Sales Sputter without Tax Credit." Kbia.org. Available from https://www.kbia.org/post/georgia-ev-sales-sputter-without-tax-credit#stream/0.

Carlock, G., and E. Mangan. 2018. *A Progressive Vision for Environmental Sustainability and Economic Stability.* Washington, DC: Data for Progress.

Cavendish, S. 2018. "Unpacking the Transit Referendum's Spectacular Failure." *Nashville Scene*, May 8. https://www.nashvillescene.com/news/features/article/21004093/unpacking-the-transit-referendums-spectacular-failure.

Cervero, Robert. 2013. *Bus Rapid Transit (BRT): An Efficient and Competitive Mode of Public Transport.* Berkeley: Institute of Urban and Regional Development, University of California, Berkeley.

Cervero, Robert, and Cathleen Sullivan. 2010. *Toward Green TODs.* Institute for Transportation Studies, University of California, Berkeley.

C40 Cities. 2011. *Case Study: 98 percent of Copenhagen City Heating Supplied by Waste Heat.* Copenhagen: C40 Cities.

C40 Cities. 2017. *Case Study: Toronto's Atmospheric Fund Makes Sustainability Affordable.* C40 Cities.

C40 Cities. 2018. "City Membership Profile." Available from https://www.c40.org/cities/stockholm.

Chandler, David L. 2016. "MIT to Neutralize 17 Percent of Carbon Emissions through Purchase of Solar Energy." *MIT News*, October 19. Available from http://news.mit.edu/2016/mit-neutralize-17-percent-carbon-emissions-through-purchase-solar-energy-1019.

Checker, Melissa. 2011. "Wiped Out by the 'Greenwave': Environmental Gentrification and the Paradoxical Politics of Urban Sustainability." *City and Society.* 2: 210-29.

Chittum, Anna, and Meegan Kelly. 2016. "Uncovering the Emissions Benefits of Combined Heat and Power." *Magazine for Environmental Managers*, March.

Chittum, Anna, and Poul Alberg Østergaard. 2014. "How Danish Communal Heat Planning Empowers Municipalities and Benefits Individual Consumers." *Energy Policy* 74: 465–74. doi: https://doi.org/10.1016/j.enpol.2014.08.001.

City and County of San Francisco. N.d. "Production, Distribution, and Repaid (PDR)." Available from https://oewd.org/Industrial.

City of Boston. 2017. Building Energy Reporting and Disclosure Ordinance.

City of Cambridge. 2018. "Cambridge's Dr. Martin Luther King Jr. School Project Achieves LEED Platinum Certification."

City of New York. 2016. "NYC Sustainability 2016." Available from http://www1.nyc.gov/site/sustainability/index.page.

City of New York. N.d.a. "LL87: Energy Audits & Retro-Commissioning." Available from http://www.nyc.gov/html/gbee/html/plan/ll87.shtml.

City of New York. N.d.b. "LL88: Lighting Upgrades and Sub-metering." Available from http://www.nyc.gov/html/gbee/html/plan/ll88.shtml.

City of Oslo. N.d. "The Electric Vehicle Capital of the World." Oslo Kommune. Available from https://www.oslo.kommune.no/politics-and-administration/city-development/car-free-city/#gref.

City of Seattle. 2012. Comprehensive Plan: Toward a Sustainable Seattle.

City of Stockholm. 2010. *Stockholm Royal Seaport: Vision 2030.* Available from https://international.stockholm.se/globalassets/ovriga-bilder-och-filer/visionsrs2030_medium.pdf.

City of Stockholm. 2015. *General Sustainability Program for Sustainable Urban Development in the Stockholm Royal Seaport.* Stockholm.

City of Toronto. 2007. "Toronto's Exhibition Place Unveils the First Municipally-Owned Trigeneration System in Canada."

Clack, Christopher, Staffan Qvist, Jay Apt, Morgan Bazilian, Adam Brandt, Ken Caldeira, Steven Davis, et al. 2017. "Evaluation of a Proposal for Reliable Low-Cost Grid Power with 100 Percent Wind, Water, and Solar." *Proceedings of the National Academy of Sciences of the United States of America* 114 (26). doi: 10.1073/pnas.1610381114.

Clifford, Mark L. 2016. "Chinese Government Subsidies Play Major Part in Electric Car Maker BYD's Rise." *Forbes*, July 26.

Climate Change Adaptation. 2009. "Seawater Keeps Copenhagen Buildings Cool." Ministry of the Environment and Food of Denmark. Available from http://en.klimatilpasning.dk/cases/items/seawaterkeepscopenhagenbuildingscool.aspx.

Climate Mayors. 2017. "388 #ClimateMayors Adopt, Honor and Uphold Paris Climate Agreement Goals." Medium.com.

Conrad, Roger. 2018. "Wind and Solar: The Adopters Win." *Forbes*, June 26.

Conway, Isabel. 2010. "A Brave New World." *Irish Times*, December 17.

Corfee-Morlot, Jan, Lamia Kamal-Chaoui, Michael G. Donovan, Ian Cochran, Alexis Robert, and Pierre-Jonathan Teasdale. 2009. "Cities, Climate Change and Multilevel Governance." OECD Environmental Working Papers No. 14. Paris: OECD Publishing.

Coughlin, Jason, Jennifer Grove, Linda Irvine, Janet F. Jacobs, Sarah Johnson Phillips, Leslie Moynihan, and Joseph Wiedman. 2010. *A Guide to Community Solar: Utility, Private, and Non-profit Project Development.* National Renewable Energy Laboratory.

Courtney, R. 2017. "Seattle Streetcar Ridership Takes Big Hit." King 5 News, June 29. https://www.king5.com/article/news/local/seattle/seattle-streetcar-ridership-takes-big-hit/453123767.

Courtney, Will Sabel. 2017. "Norway Doubles Down on Plans to Make Gas Cars Obsolete by 2025." The Drive.com. Available from http://www.thedrive.com/news/7917/norway-doubles-down-on-plans-to-make-gas-cars-obsolete-by-2025.

Currie, G., and A. Delbosc. 2011. "Understanding Bus Rapid Transit Route Ridership Drivers: An Empirical Study of Australian BRT Systems." *Transport Policy* 18: 755–64.

Daigneau, Elizabeth. 2017. "Will States Stop Cities from Combating Climate Change?" Governing.com.

Danielski, Itai, and Jonas Kunze. 2008. *Large Variation in Utilized Energy with New Buildings in Stockholm.* Stockholm: Royal Institute of Technology.

Danish Energy Agency. 2017. *Regulation and Planning of District Energy in Denmark.* Danish Energy Agency.

Dastur, Arish. 2005. "How Should Planning Engage the Issue of Sustainable Development? The Case of Hammarby Sjöstad, Stockholm." Columbia University.

Dawid, Irvin. 2016. "Who Killed the Electric Car (in Georgia)?" Planetizen. Available from https://www.planetizen.com/node/83394/who-killed-electric-car-georgia.

Deng, T., and J. Nelson. 2011. "Recent Developments in Bus Rapid Transit: A Review of the Literature." *Transport Reviews* 31: 69–96.

Department of Energy and Climate Change. 2012. *The Future of Heating: A Strategic Framework for Low Carbon Heat in the UK.* London: Department of Energy and Climate Change.

Department of Energy and Climate Change. 2013. *The Future of Heating: Meeting the Challenge.* British Government.

Deutschland.de. 2017. "Strong Support for the Energy Transition." Available from https://www.deutschland.de/en/topic/environment/strong-support-for-the-energy-transition.

Dooling, Sarah. 2008. "Ecological Gentrification: Re-negotiating Justice in the City." *Critical Planning* 15: 40–57.

Doyle, Alister, and Nerijus Adomaitis. 2013. "Norway Shows the Way with Electric Cars, but at What Cost?" *Reuters*, March 13.

Dubb, Steve. 2018. "In Europe, Nonprofit and Local Public Utilities Are Seen as Key to Green Future." *NPQ: Nonprofit Quarterly*, May 9. Available from https://nonprofitquarterly.org/europe-nonprofit-local-public-utilities-seen-key-green-future/.

Duggan, Kevin. 2017. "Fort Collins Zero-Energy District Powers Down." *Coloradoan*, September 10.

EcoMobility. 2015. "Freiburg, Germany City Summary." Available from https://ecomobility.org/wp-content/uploads/2017/10/REPORT-2017_Final_web_.pdf

Edelstein, Stephen. 2017. "Four Large West Coast Cities Unite to Buy 24,000 Electric Cars." Green Car Reports.

Efstathiou, Jim, Jr. 2019. "The Race to Build the World's Largest Solar-Storage Plant Is On." *Bloomberg*. (March 28)Available from https://www.bloomberg.com/news/articles/2019-03-28/the-race-to-build-the-world-s-largest-solar-storage-plant-is-on.

Einhorn, Bruce. 2010. "The 50 Most Innovative Companies." *Bloomberg Businessweek*, April 15.

Eliasson, Jonas. 2009. "A Cost-Benefit Analysis of the Stockholm Congestion Charging System." *Transportation Research Part A: Policy and Practice* 43 (4): 468–80.

Ellis, Graham. 2015. "Bus Rapid Transit in Europe." Intelligent Transport.

News Editor. 2017. "Car2go—Amsterdam's Innovative Electric Car-Sharing Scheme (Netherlands)." Eltis.

Emerald Cities Seattle. 2015. *Energy Efficiency Policies to Achieve Seattle's Climate Reduction Goals.*

Energy Information Administration. 2018. *Annual Energy Outlook 2018*. Washington, DC.

Energy Star. N.d. "What Is Energy Use Intensity (EUI)?" Available from https://www.energystar.gov/buildings/facility-owners-and-managers/existing-buildings/use-portfolio-manager/understand-metrics/what-energy.

Enlow, Clair. 2016. "Design Perspectives—District Energy: Lots of Talk, but Still Little Action." *IDEA Industry News.* (June 8).

Entman, L. 2018. "Vanderbilt Poll: Nashville Wants Transit Overhaul; Unsure about Mayor's Plan." March 4. https://news.vanderbilt.edu/2018/03/04/vanderbilt-poll-nashville-2018/.

Envision America. 2017. *Envision: America.* Available from http://www.envisionamerica.org/.

E2, E4TheFuture, and Environmental Entrepreneurs. 2018. *Energy Efficiency Jobs in America.* Washington, DC.

Euro Heat and Power. 2015. *Country by Country 2015.*

European Association for the Promotion of Cogeneration. 2016. *CHP in Europe: Today and Tomorrow.*

European Commission. 2016. Communication from the Commission to the European Parliament, the Council, the European Economic and Social Committee and the Committee of the Regions: An EU Strategy on Heating and Cooling. Brussels: European Commission.

European Commission. 2018. EU Building Stock Observatory.

European Commission. N.d. Clean Vehicles Directive. Available from https://ec.europa.eu/transport/themes/urban/vehicles/directive_en.

European Commission Climate Action. 2017. *Reducing CO_2 Emissions from Passenger Cars.* European Commission. Available from https://ec.europa.eu/clima/policies/transport/vehicles/cars_en.

European Environment Agency. 2016. *Greenhouse Gas Emissions from Transport.* Available from https://www.eea.europa.eu/data-and-maps/indicators/transport-emissions-of-greenhouse-gases/transport-emissions-of-greenhouse-gases-10.

European Federation of Public Service Unions. 2014. *Public and Private Sector Efficiency*. Brussels.

Fainsetin, Susan. 2010. *The Just City*. Ithaca, NY: Cornell University Press.

Farrell, Diana, and Jaana Remes. 2009. "Promoting Energy Efficiency in the Developing World." *McKinsey Quarterly*, February.

Farrell, Diana, Jaana Remes, Florian Bressand, Mark Laabs, and Anjan Sundaram. 2008. *The Case for Investing in Energy Productivity*. Washington, DC: McKinsey Global Institute.

Federal Transit Administration. 2017. *Annual Report on Funding Recommendations, 2017*. https://www.transit.dot.gov/sites/fta.dot.gov/files/docs/FY17_Annual_Report.pdf.

Ferguson, David. 2015. "How Hospitals Can Blaze a Trail on Climate Change." Fierce Healthcare.com.

Fitzgerald, Joan. 2010. *Emerald Cities: Urban Sustainability and Economic Development*. New York: Oxford University Press.

Fitzgerald, Joan, and Jennifer Lenhart. 2016. "Eco-districts: Can They Accelerate Urban Climate Planning?" *Environment and Planning C: Government and Policy* 34 (2): 364–80.

Fleet News. 2017. "Greater fleet take-up will help car clubs reach million member mark." Fleet Industry News. Available from https://www.fleetnews.co.uk/news/fleet-industry-news/2017/08/08/greater-fleet-take-up-will-help-car-clubs-reach-million-member-mark.

Foletta, Nicole, and Simon Field. 2011. "Europe's Vibrant New Low-Carbon Communities." Transport Matters. Available from https://www.itdp.org/2011/09/22/europes-vibrant-new-low-carbon-communities/.

Fortum. 2017. "Vartaverket CHP Plant." Available from https://www.fortum.com/about-us/our-company/our-energy-production/our-power-plants/vartaverket-chp-plant.

Fowlie, Meredith, Michael Greenstone, and Catherine Wolfram. 2018. "Do Energy Efficiency Investments Deliver? Evidence from the Weatherization Assistance Program." *Quarterly Journal of Economics* 133 (3): 1597–1644.

Fränne, L. 2007. *Miljöprogram för Hammarby Sjöstad! inriktningsmål 2008–10* [Environmental program for Hammarby Sjöstad: operational targets, 2008–10]. Land Development Office, City of Stockholm.

Froese, Michelle. 2018. "US Wind Selects Two Maryland Firms for Offshore Wind Development." Wind Power Engineering.

Fulton, Mark, Jake Baker, Margot Brandenburg, Ron Herbst, John Cleveland, Joel Rogers, Chinwe Onyeagoro, and Heather Grady 2012. *United States Building Energy Efficiency Retrofits: Market Sizing and Financing Models*. Rockefeller Foundation DB Climate Change Advisors.

Galindo Fernandez, Maria, Cyril Roger-Lacan, Uwe Gahrs, and Vincent Aumaitre. 2016. *Efficient District Heating and Cooling Systems in the EU*. European Commission.

Gattaciecca, Julien, J. R. DeShazo, and Kelly Trumbull. 2018. *The Growth in Community Choice Aggregation*. Los Angeles: Luskin Center for Innovation.

Georgia Government Department of Revenue. "Annual Alternative Fuel Vehicle Fees—Frequently Asked Questions." Georgia Government Department of Revenue. Available from https://dor.georgia.gov/annual-alternative-fuel-vehicle-fees-faq#field_related_links-486-0.

Georgiadou, V. *Removing the Last Hurdle to EV's Integration: Policies and Regulations Overdue Make-Over*. Amsterdam: Green It, European Union European Regional Development Fund, EV Energy.

Gilleo, Annie, Seth Nowak, Meegan Kelly, Shruti Vaidyanathan, Mary Shoemaker, Anna Chittum, and Tyler Bailey. 2015. "The 2015 State Energy Efficiency Scorecard." American Council for an Energy-Efficient Economy.

Gilman, Patrick, Ben Maurer, Luke Feinburg, Alana Duerr, Lauren Peterson, Walt Musial, Philipp Beiter, et al. 2016. *National Offshore Wind Strategy*. Washington, DC: US Department of Energy and US Department of Interior.

Girouard, Coley. 2018. "The Numbers Are in and Renewables Are Winning on Price Alone." Advanced Energy Perspectives.com.

Gitlin, Jonathan M. 2018. "Tesla Sold 200,000 Cars in the US, So the $7,500 Tax Credit Is Going Away." *ARS Technica*.

Go Ultra Low. N.d. "About Us." Available from https://www.goultralow.com/about/.

Goldberg, Keith. 2016. "Austin Council OKs Plan to Add 600MW of Solar by 2019." Law360. Available from https://www.law360.com/articles/715195/austin-council-oks-plan-to-add-600mw-of-solar-by-2019.

Graham, David A. 2017. "Red State, Blue City." *The Atlantic*, March 15.

Grauthoff, Manfred, Ulrike Janssen, and Joana Fernandes. 2012. *Identification and Mobilisation of Solar Potentials via Local Strategies*. Polis and Intelligent Energy Europe.

Green, Colin P., John S. Heywood, and Maria Navarro. 2016. "Traffic Accidents and the London Congestion Charge." *Journal of Public Economics* 133: 11–22.

Greenovate City of Boston. 2017. "Greenovate." Available from http://greenovateboston.org.

Gregg, Kelly, and Paul Hess. 2018. "Complete streets at the municipal level: A review of American municipal Complete Streets Policy. *International Journal of Sustainable Transportation* 13(6): 407-418.

Gruener, P., and B. Radke. 2017. "Seattle Is in the Eye of the Housing Affordability Storm." KUOW, September 20. http://kuow.org/post/seattle-eye-housing-affordability-storm.

Gustafsson, R., and E. Kelly. 2012. *Urban Innovations in Curitiba: A Case Study*. New Haven: Eugene & Carol Ludwig Center for Community and Economic Development, Yale University.

Gutman, D. 2018. "King County Moves to Allow Affordable Housing at Future Northgate Light-Rail Station." *Seattle Times*, June 10. https://www.seattletimes.com/seattle-news/transportation/king-county-moves-to-allow-affordable-housing-at-future-northgate-light-rail-station/.

Hagedorn, L. 2011. "All RECs Are Not Equal: Bundling and Geographic Sourcing." *Energy Law Insider*, March 7.

Hale, S. 2018. "History Repeats Itself in Nashville." Nashville Scene, June 7. https://www.nashvillescene.com/news/cover-story/article/21007855/history-repeats-itself-in-north-nashville.

Halfnight, Christopher. 2016. "Greener, Greater Mid-Size Buildings in NYC." *Urban Green Council*, October 13.

Hand, M. M., S. Baldwin, E. DeMeo, J. M. Reilly, T. Mai, D. Arent, G. Porro, M. Meshek, and D. Sandor. 2012. *Renewable Electricity Futures Study*. Golden, CO: National Renewable Energy Laboratory.

Harguindeguy, Jean-Baptiste, and Sergio Argul Arias. 2002. *All That Glitters Is Not Gold: Urban Sustainability and Ecodistricts in Spain*. Madrid: Center of Political and Constitutional Studies, National University.

Haugneland, Petter, Christina Bu, and Espen Hague. 2016. *The Norwegian EV Success Continues*. Montreal.

Health Care Without Harm. 2017. *Metropolitan Boston Health Care Energy and Greenhouse Gas Profile: 2011 through 2015, and 2020 Projection*.

Heat Roadmap Europe. 2016. *A Low-Carbon Heating and Cooling Strategy for Europe*. Stratego.

Hermelink, Andreas, Sven Schimschar, Thomas Boermans, Lorenzo Pagliano, Paolo Zangheri, Roberto Armani, Karsten Voss, Eike Musall. 2013. *Towards Nearly Zero-Energy Buildings: Definition of Common Principles under the EPBD*. Ecofys.

Hernandez, Diana. 2015. "Sacrifice along the Energy Continuum: A Call for Energy Justice." *Environmental Justice* 8 (4): 151–56. doi: 10.1089/env.2015.0015.

Hess, David. 2012. *Good Green Jobs in a Global Economy*. Cambridge, MA: MIT Press.

Hess, David. 2018. "Energy Democracy and Social Movements: A Multi-coalition Perspective on the Politics of Sustainability Transitions." *Energy Research and Social Science* 40: 177–89. doi: https://doi.org/10.1016/j.erss.2018.01.003.

Hicks, Nolan. 2018. In "Windswept West Texas, Austin Energy's Future Is Powered by the Sun." *Statesman*, December 15. Available from https://www.statesman.com/news/20171215/in-windswept-west-texas-austin-energys-future-is-powered-by-the-sun.

Holden, Meg, Charling Li, and Ana Molina. 2015. "The Emergence and Spread of Ecourban Neighbourhoods around the World." *Sustainability* 7 (9): 11418–37.

Holland, Stephen P., Erin T. Mansur, Nicholas Z. Muller, and Andrew J. Yates. 2016. "Are There Environmental Benefits from Driving Electric Vehicles? The Importance of Local Factors." *American Economic Review* 106 (12): 3700–729. doi: 10.1257/aer.20150897.

Holmstedt, Louise, Nils Brandt, and Robert Karl-Henrik. 2017. "Can Stockholm Royal Seaport Be Part of the Puzzle towards Global Sustainability? From Local to Global Sustainability Using the Same Set of Criteria." *Journal of Cleaner Production* 140: 72–80.

Holtsmark, Bjart, and Anders Skonhoft. 2014. "The Norwegian Support and Subsidy Policy of Electric Cars: Should It Be adopted by Other Countries?" *Environmental Science and Policy* 42: 160–68.

Houston, B. 2012. *The Nashville Way: Racial Etiquette and the Struggle for Social Justice in a Southern City*. Athens: University of Georgia Press.

Huang, Echo. 2018. "The Worst Is Not Yet Over for BYD, China's Biggest EV Maker." Quartz, August 29. Available from https://qz.com/1368687/the-worst-is-not-yet-over-for-byds-earnings/.

Hull, Dana, and Chris Martin. 2016. "Tesla Seals $2 Billion SolarCity Deal." *Bloomberg*, Available from https://www.bloomberg.com/news/articles/2016-11-17/tesla-seals-2-billion-solarcity-deal-set-to-test-musk-s-vision.

Hull, Rob. 2016. "Lamp Posts with Charging Points and Free Parking for Green Cars: Four Cities Get £40m Pot to Improve Electric Car Infrastructure." This is Money.com. Available from http://www.thisismoney.co.uk/money/cars/article-3415350/Four-cities-40m-pot-improve-electric-car-infrastructure.html.

Institute for Transportation and Development Policy. 2011. *Hammarby Sjöstad Site Facts*. New York: Institute for Transportation and Development Policy.

Institute for Transportation and Development Policy, ClimateWorks Foundation, Deutsche Gesellschaft für Internationale Zusammenarbeit, International Council on Clean Transportation, and Rockefeller Foundation. 2013. *The BRT Standard 2013*. New York: ITDP.

Intergovernmental Panel on Climate Change (IPCC). 2018. "Summary for Policymakers." In *Global Warming of 1.5°C: An IPCC Special Report on the Impacts of Global Warming of 1.5°C above Pre-industrial Levels*. Geneva.

International District Energy Association. N.d. *What Is District Energy?* Westborough, MA.

International Energy Agency. 2015. *Energy and Climate Change*. Paris: International Energy Agency.

International Energy Agency. 2017. *Energy Technology Perspectives 2017*. Paris.

International Trade Union Confederation. 2012. *Growing Green and Decent Jobs*. Brussels.

Invest Stockholm. 2016. "Leading the Way in Clean Energy Innovation." *The Local*.

Invest Stockholm and The Local. 2016. "Why Stockholm Is Leading the Way in Clean Energy Innovation." Stockholm: The Capital of Scandinavia.

Iverot, Sofie P., and Nils Brandt. 2011. "The Development of a Sustainable Urban District in Hammarby Sjöstad, Stockholm, Sweden." *Environment Development and Sustainability* 13 (6): 1043–64.

Iveroth, Sofie P., Stefan Johansson, and Nils Brandt. 2013. "The Potential of the Infrastructural System of Hammarby Sjöstad in Stockholm, Sweden." *Energy Policy* 59: 716–26.

Jacobson, Mark, and Mark Delucchi. 2009. "A Path to Sustainable Energy to 2030." *Scientific American*, 65: 58–65.

Jaffe, Eric. 2016. "An Unusual Objection to Less Parking: It Will Make Our City Too Nice." CityLab 2015. Available from https://www.citylab.com/solutions/2015/09/an-unusual-objection-to-less-parking-it-will-make-our-city-too-nice/406096/.

Jain, Anil Kumar. N.d. *Investment "Lock-ins" and Technological Advancements in the Energy Sector.* India Energy.

Johansson, Rolf, and Örjan Svane. 2002. "Environmental Management in Large-Scale Building Projects: Learning from Hammarby Sjöstad." *Corporate Social Responsibility and Environmental Management* 9 (4): 206–14.

Johnson, Nathanael. 2018. "Lessons from Boulder's Bad Breakup." Grist, January 19. Available from https://grist.org/article/lessons-from-boulders-bad-breakup/.

Jolly, David. 2015. "Norway Is a Model for Encouraging Electric Car Sales." *New York Times*, October 16.

Jones, D. 2018. "Concern for Seattle's Housing Crisis Is Rising." *Seattle Magazine*, April 5. http://www.seattlemag.com/news-and-features/concern-seattles-housing-crisis-rising.

Jordan, Heather. 2017. "Suniva Owes Saginaw Township Money If Closure Is Permanent." Mlive. Available from https://www.mlive.com.

Joyner, Chris. 2017. "Here's Why Electric Car Sales Are Plummeting in Georgia." AJC Watchdog.

Karolides, Alexis, and Bill Ravanesi. 2005. "Design for Health: Summit for Massachusetts Health Care Decision Makers." Health Care Without Harm.

Kennedy, Christopher, Stephanie Demoullin, and Eugene Mohareb. 2012. "Cities Reducing Their Greenhouse Gas Emissions." *Energy Policy* 49: 774–77.

Kettles, Colleen. 2008. *A Comprehensive Review of Solar Access Law in the United States.* Orlando: Florida Solar Energy Research and Education Foundation.

KG, FWTM Freiburg Wirtschaft Touristikund Messe GmbH & Co. N.d. "Green City Freiburg." Approaches to Sustainability.

King's Cross. 2017. "Power It Up! The Energy Centre and CHP Plant at King's Cross." Available from https://www.kingscross.co.uk/energy-centre.

Kunze, Conrad. 2014. "What Is Energy Democracy?" Available from https://www.researchgate.net/publication/282336742_Energy_Democracy_in_Europe_A_Survey_and_Outlook

Kunze, Conrad, and Soren Becker. 2014. *Energy Democracy in Europe: A Survey and Outlook.* Brussels.

Labor Network for Sustainability. N.d. *"Just Transition"—Just What Is It?"* Takoma Park, MD: Labor Network for Sustainability; Berkeley, CA: Strategic Practice.

Lambert, Fred. 2017. "U.S. Cities' Massive Electric Vehicle Order Increases to 114,000 Vehicles, ~40 Companies Competing." Electrek. Available from https://electrek.co/2017/03/15/electric-vehicle-order-114000-vehicles-40-companies-competing/.

Lancaster County Planning Commission. 2014. *Annual Report 2014.* https://lancastercountyplanning.org/DocumentCenter/View/472/2014-LCPC-Annual-Report?bidId=

Lauer, Caroline. 2018. *A Pathway to Preservation? Planning Processes at the Intersection of Climate Change and Affordable Housing in Philadelphia, Pennsylvania.* Cambridge, MA: Harvard Joint Center for Housing Studies.

Layke, Jennifer, Eric Mackres, Sifan Liu, Nate Aden, Renilde Becqué, Peter Graham, Katrina Managan, Clay Nesler, Ksenia Petrichenko, and Susan Mazur-Stommen. 2016. *Accelerating Building Efficiency: Eight Actions for Urban Leaders.* World Resources Institute. Available from http://www.wri.org/publication/accelerating-building-efficiency-actions-city-leaders.

Lazar, Jim. 2016. *Teaching the "Duck" to Fly.* Montpelier, VT: Regulatory Assistance Project.

League of California Cities. 2012. "Creation of the Lancaster Power Authority." Available from https://www.cacities.org/Top/Partners/California-City-Solutions/2012/Creation-of-the-Lancaster-Power-Authority.

Leape, Jonathan. 2006. "The London Congestion Charge." *Journal of Economic Perspectives* 20 (4): 156–76. doi: 10.1257/jep.20.4.157.

Lee, Amanda. 2018. "China's Electric Car Market Is Growing Twice as Fast as the US. Here's Why." *South China Morning Post*, April 27.

Lee, Joyce. 2015. *2030 Districts as a Movement.* Green Building Information Gateway. Available from http://insight.gbig.org/2030-districts-as-a-movement/.

Levinson, H., S. Zimmerman, J. Clinger, S. Rutherford, R. Smith, J. Cracknell, and R. Soberman. 2003. *Bus Rapid Transit: Case Studies in Bus Rapid Transit.* Transit Cooperative Research Program Report 90, vol. 1. Washington, DC: Transportation Research Board.

Li, Xianting. 2016. *District Cooling/Heating Systems in China: Challenges and Opportunities.* Tsinghua University.

Liu, Z., C. He, Y. Zhou, and J. Wu. 2014. "How much of the world's land has been urbanized, really? A hierarchial framework for avoiding confusion." *Landscape Ecology* 29(5): 763-771.

Lindau, L. A., D. Hidalgo, and D. Facchini. 2010. "Bus Rapid Transit in Curitiba, Brazil: A Look at the Outcome after 35 Years of Bus-Oriented Development." *Transportation Research Record: Journal of the Transportation Research Board* 2193: 17–27.

London, J., and C. Williams-Derry. 2013. *Who Pays for Parking: How the Oversupply of Parking Undermines Housing Affordability.* Seattle: Sightline Institute.

Lopez, Theresa Adams. *Electric Truck Demonstration Project Fact Sheet.* Port of Los Angeles.

Lucon, O., D. Ürge-Vorsatz, A. Zain Ahmed, H. Akbari, P. Bertoldi, L. F. Cabeza, N. Eyre, et al. 2014. "Buildings." In *Mitigation of Climate Change: Contribution of Working Group III to the Fifth Assessment Report of the Intergovernmental Panel on Climate Change*, 671–738.

Lund, Henrik, Sven Werner, Robin Wiltshire, Svend Svendsen, Jan Eric Thorsen, Frede Hvelplund, and Brian Vad Mathiesen. 2014. "4th Generation District Heating (4GDH): Integrating Smart Thermal Grids into Future Sustainable Energy Systems." *Energy* 68: 1–11.

Lutsey, Nic. 2015. *Global Climate Change Mitigation Potential from a Transition to Electric Vehicles.* International Council on Clean Transportation.

Lutsey, Nic, Stephanie Searle, Sarah Chambliss, and Anup Bandivadekar. 2015. *Assessment of Leading Electric Vehicle Promotion Activities in United States Cities.* Washington, DC: International Council on Clean Transportation.

MacCallum, Diana, Jason Byrne, and Wendy Steele. 2014. "Whither Justice? An Analysis of Local Climate Change Responses from South East Queensland, Australia." *Environment and Planning C* 32 (1): 70–92.

Mahzouni, Arian. 2015. "The 'Policy Mix' for Sustainable Urban Transition: The City District of Hammarby Sjöstad in Stockholm." *Environmental Policy and Governance* 25 (4): 288–302. doi: https://doi.org/10.1002/eet.1688.

Marcus, Lars, Berit Balfors, and Tigran Haas. 2013. "A Sustainable Urban Fabric: The Development and Application of Analytical Urban Design Theory." In *Sustainable Stockholm: Exploring Sustainability in Europe's Greenest City*, edited by Jonathan Metzger and Amy Rader Olsson, 71–101. New York: Routledge.

Masiero, Gilmar, Mario H. Ogasavara, Ailton C. Jussani, and Marcelo L. Risso. 2016. "Electric Vehicles in China: BYD Strategies and Government." *RAI: Revista de Administracao e Inovacao* 13 (1): 3–11. doi: https://doi.org/10.1016/j.rai.2016.01.001.

Mason, J., L. Fulton, and Z. McDonald. 2015. *The Potential for Dramatically Increasing Bicycle and E-Bike Use in Cities around the World, with Estimated Energy, CO2 and Cost Impacts*. New York: Institute for Transportation and Development Policy and the University of California, Davis.

Massachusetts Climate Action Network. 2019. *What's the Score: A Comparative Analysis of Massachusetts Municipal Light Plants' Clean Energy and Climate Action Performance*.

Mayor of London. 2018. "Mayor Launches New Taskforce to Expand Electric Vehicle Infrastrfucture. Available from https://www.london.gov.uk/press-releases/mayoral/taskforce-will-work-on-shared-delivery-plan.

Mayor of London. 2016. "Mayor Welcomes £13m of Ultra-low Emission Funding for London." Available from https://www.london.gov.uk/press-releases/mayoral/mayor-welcomes-13m-of-ultra-low-emission-funding.

Mayor of London. 2017. "New Funding Announced to Improve Air Quality across London."

Mayor of London. N.d. "London Heat Map."

Mayor of London and Transport for London. 2015. *An Ultra Low Emission Vehicle Delivery Plan for London: Cleaner Vehicles for a Cleaner City*. London: Transport for London.

Mazria, Edward. 2015. *Achieving 80 X 50: Transforming New York City's Building Stock*. Santa Fe.

McCahill, Christopher T., Norman Garrick, Carol Atkinson-Palombo, and Adam Polinski. 2015. "Effects of Parking Provision on Automobile Use in Cities: Inferring Causality." *Journal of the Transportation Research Board* 2543. doi: https://doi.org/10.3141/2543-19.

McCormick, Kes, Stefan Anderberg, Lars Coenen, and Lena Neij. 2013. "Advancing Sustainable Urban Transformation." *Journal of Cleaner Production* 50: 1–11.

Mead, Peter. 2015. "Lancaster, Calif's Net-Zero Energy Goals Are Expanding the Community's Future." *Government Technology*, July 14. Available from https://www.govtech.com/fs/Lancaster-Califs-Net-Zero-Energy-Goals-Are-Expanding-The-Communitys-Future.html.

Medina, Jennifer. 2013. "Chinese Company Falling Short of Goal for California Jobs." *New York Times*, October 25.

Meisen, Peter, and Jeremy Black. 2010. *San Diego Regional Plan for 100 Percent Renewable Energy*. San Diego: Global Energy Network Institute.

Meister Consultants Group. 2017. Pathways to 100: An Energy Supply Transformation Primer for U.S. Cities. Boston: author.

Mejía-Dugand, S., O. Hjelm, L. Baas, and R. Alberto Ríos. 2012. "Lessons from the Spread of Bus Rapid Transit in Latin America." *Journal of Cleaner Production* 50: 82–90.

Melaina, Marc, and Michael Helwig. 2014. *California Statewide Plug-In Electric Vehicle Infrastructure Assessment*. National Renewable Energy Laboratory.

Metzger, Jonathan, and Amy Rader Olsson, eds. 2013. *Sustainable Stockholm: Exploring Urban Sustainability in Europe's Greenest City*. New York: Routledge.

Milligan, Carley. 2019. "Maryland Offshore Wind Developers Look to Partner with Local Business." *Baltimore Business Journal*, January 23.

Mock, Peter, and Zifei Yang. 2014. *Driving Electrification: A Global Comparison of Fiscal Policy for Electric Vehicles*. Washington, DC: International Council on Clean Transportation.

Mooney, Chris. 2015. "Obama Just Released the Biggest Energy Efficiency Rule in U.S. History." *Washington Post*, December 17.

Mortensen, Bent Ole Gram. 2014. "Legal Framework as a Core Element of District Cooling Success: The Case of Denmark." *Journal of Power and Energy Engineering* 2: 41–48.

Mottola, Daniel. 2007. "Downtown Coolin' Plant Chillin' Like Paul Robbins." *Austin Chronicle*, July 27.

Mullan, Jonathan, David Harries, Thomas Bräunl, and Stephen Whitely. 2012. "The Technical, Economic and Commercial Viability of the Vehicle-to-Grid Concept." *Energy Policy* 48: 394–406.

Musial, Walt, Donna Heimiller, Philipp Beiter, George Scott, and Caroline Draxl. 2017. *2016 Offshore Wind Energy Resource Assessment for the United States*. Golden, CO: National Renewable Energy Laboratory.

National Alternative Fuels Hotline. 1998. *The Clean Fuel Fleet Program as Part of the Clean Air Act Amendments (CAAA)*. National Alternative Fuels Hotline.

National Renewable Energy Laboratory. 2013. *Concentrating Solar Power Projects by Country*. US Department of Energy. Available from https://solarpaces.nrel.gov/by-country.

National Renewable Energy Laboratory. 2017. *Connecting Electric Vehicles to the Grid for Greater Infrastructure Resilience*. National Renewable Energy Laboratory.

Nelson, Arthur, Bruce Appleyard, Shyam Kannan, Reid Ewing, Matt Miller, and Dejan Eskic. 2013. "Bus Rapid Transit and Economic Development: Case Study of the Eugene-Springfield BRT System." *Journal of Public Transportation* 16 (3): 41–57.

Nelson, Laura J. 2017. "L.A. Metro Wants to Spend $138 Million on Electric Buses. The Goal: An Emission-Free Fleet by 2030." *Los Angeles Times*, July 21.

Nelson, Laura J., and Emily Alpert Reyes. 2017. "Metro Agrees to Buy 95 Electric Buses, in the First Step toward an Emissions-Free Fleet." *Los Angeles Times*, July 27.

Netherlands Enterprise Agency. 2016. *Electric Transport in the Netherlands: 2016 Highlights*.

New York City Mayor's Office of Sustainability. N.d. "NYC Benchmarking Law." Available from http://www.nyc.gov/html/gbee/html/plan/ll84.shtml.

O'Dell, John. 2017. "California Readies $398-Million Green Truck Incentive Package." Trucks.com. Available from https://www.trucks.com/2017/12/11/california-green-truck-incentive-package/.

Office of Energy Delivery and Energy Reliability. 2016. *Grid Modernization and the Smart Grid*. Available from http://energy.gov/oe/services/technology-development/smart-grid.

Office of Governor Edmund G. Brown 2018. "Governor Brown Takes Action to Increase Zero-Emission Vehicles, Fund New Climate Investments."

Office of Los Angeles Mayor. 2016. "Mayor Garcetti Announces That City of Los Angeles Is Now Home to Largest Electric Vehicle Fleet in the U.S."

Official Journal of the European Union. 2012. "Legislation." *Official Journal of the European Union* 55. doi: http://dx.doi.org/10.3000/19770677.L_2012.315.eng.

O'Shaughnessy, Eric, Jenny Heeter, Julien Gattaciecca, Jenny Sauer, Kelly Trumbull, and Emily Chen. 2019. *Community Choice Aggregation: Challenges, Opportunities, and Impacts on Renewable Energy Markets*. Golden, CO: National Renewable Energy Laboratory.

O'Sullivan, Feargus. 2017a. "The Many Ways Europe's City-Dwellers Get to Work." CityLab, October 18.

O'Sullivan, Feargus. 2017b. "Stockholm Is Coming for Oslo's Car-Free Crown." CityLab, May 12.

Oldham, K. 2006. "Washington Legislature Enact Growth Management Act on April 1, 1990." History Link.org. http://www.historylink.org/File/7759.

Orsted. 2017. "Deepwater Wind Proposing World's Largest Offshore Wind, Energy Storage Combination." New Bedford, MA.

Parajuli, Ranjan. 2012. "Looking into the Danish Energy System: Lesson to Be Learned by Other Communities." *Renewable and Sustainable Energy Reviews* 16 (4): 2129–99.

Patronen, Jenni, Eeva Kaura, and Cathrine Torvestad. 2017. *Nordic Heating and Cooling: Nordic Approach to EU's Heating and Cooling Strategy.* Copenhagen: Nordic Council of Ministers.

Perk, Victoria. 2016. *Assessing Property Value Impacts of Access to Bus Rapid Transit (BRT): Case Study of the Cleveland HealthLine.* University of South Florida.

Peters, A. 2019. "What happened when Oslo decided to make its downtown basically car-free?" *Fast Company*, Jan 24.

Phang, Sock-Yong, and Rex S. Toh. 2004. "Road Congestion Pricing in Singapore: 1975–2003." *Transportation Journal* 43: 16–25.

Plas, Patrick. 2017. "Expediting a Renewable Energy Future with High-Voltage DC Transmission." Greentech Media. Available from https://www.greentechmedia.com/articles/read/expediting-a-renewable-energy-future-with-high-voltage-dc-transmission#gs.m3ryn3.

Plug In America. 2017. *The Economic Opportunities of Electric Vehicles in Georgia.*

Poblocka, A. 2014. Assessment of Climate Change Policies in the Context of the European Semester. Country Report: Sweden. Berlin: Ecologic Institute.

Port of Los Angeles. 2015a. "2005–2014 Air Quality Report Card."

Port of Los Angeles. 2015b. *Zero Emission White Paper.* Los Angeles: Port of Los Angeles.

Quastel, Noah. 2009. "Political Ecologies of Gentrification." *Urban Geography* 30 (7): 694–725.

Ram, Manish, Dmitrii Bogdanov, Arman Aghahosseini, Solomon Oyewo, Ashish Gulagi, Michael Child, and Christian Breyer. 2017. *Global Energy System Based on 100 Percent Renewable Energy Power Sector.* Berlin.

Rao, Laxmi, Anna Chittum, Michael King, and Taeyoon Yoon. 2017. *Governance Models and Strategic Decision-Making Processes for Deploying Thermal Grids.* International Energy Agency.

Reardon, Patrick. 1992. "Burnham Quote: Well, It May Be." *Chicago Tribune*, January 1.

Reicher, M. 2017. "Black Share of Population Plummets in Some Nashville Neighborhoods." *Tennessean*, December 27.

Renner, Michael, Celia Garcia-Banos, Divyam Nagpal, and Arslan Khalid. 2018. *Renewable Energy and Jobs: Annual Review 2018.* Abu Dhabi: International Renewable Energy Agency.

Reyes, Emily Alpert. 2015. "Electric Vehicle Firm BYD Accused of Violating L.A. Wage Rules." *Los Angeles Times,* December 1.

Richter, Alexander. 2019. "The City of Hamburg Bets on Geothermal for District Heating Plans." Think Geoenergy.com.

Ritchie, Earl. 2017. "The Cost of Wind and Solar Intermittency." *Forbes*, January 24.

Robb, Drew. 2009. "District Energy for Helsinki: A Highly Efficient Heating and Cooling Model." Power Engineering International.

Robbins, Paul. 2018a. "Austin Should Lead the Way for Next Wave of Renewable Energy." *Statesman*, May 11. Available from https://www.statesman.com/news/20180511/robbins-austin-should-lead-the-way-for-next-wave-of-renewable-energy.

Robbins, Paul. 2018b. "Austin's Energy Goals Laudable but Counter to Laws of Physics." *Statesman*, September 4. Available from https://www.statesman.com/news/20140904/

robbins-austins-energy-goals-laudable-but-counter-to-laws-of-physics?_ga=2.220514008.
1586382919.1558804956-1632245412.1558804956.

Roberts, David. 2016a. "California Has Too Much Solar Power: It Needs Another Grid to Share With." Vox. Available from https://www.vox.com/2016/4/8/11376196/california-grid-expansion.

Roberts, David. 2016b. "Flattening the 'Duck Curve' to Get More Renewable Energy on the Grid." Vox, April 8. Available from https://www.vox.com/2016/2/12/10970858/flattening-duck-curve-renewable-energy.

Roberts, David. 2018. "The Green New Deal Explained." Vox, December 21. Available from https://www.vox.com/energy-and-environment/2018/12/21/18144138/green-new-deal-alexandria-ocasio-cortez.

Rocky Mountain Power. 2017. *Clean Energy Implementation Plan*. Salt Lake City.

Roselund, Christian. 2018. "Xcel Gets In Front Of the 100 Percent Renewable Energy Movement." *PV Magazine*, December 5.

Rubin, Dana, and Evelyne St-Louis. 2016. "Evaluating the Economic and Social Implications of Participation in Clean Vehicle Rebate Programs: Who's in, Who's Out?" *Transportation Research Record: Journal of the Transportation Research Board*. 2598: 67-74.

Rüdinger, Andreas. 2017. *Local Energy Ownership in Europe*. Paris: Institute for Sustainable Development and International Relations.

Rutherford, Jonathan. 2008. "Unbundling Stockholm: The Networks, Planning and Social Welfare Nexus beyond the Unitary City." *Geoforum* 39: 1871–83.

Ryan, Joe. 2017. "Cities, Defying Trump, Seek to Dangle $10 Billion Order for EVs." *Automotive News*, March 14. Available from http://www.autonews.com/article/20170314/OEM/303149926/cities-defying-trump-seek-to-dangle-10-billion-order-for-evs.

Salt Lake City Mayor's Office. 2016. "Salt Lake City and Rocky Mountain Power Reach Agreement on Ambitious Clean Energy Goals for City." SLC.gov. Available from https://www.slc.gov/mayor/2016/09/19/salt-lake-city-and-rocky-mountain-power-reach-agreement-on-ambitious-clean-energy-goals-for-city/.

Sandberg, Anders. 2014. *Environmental Gentrification in a Post-industrial Landscape: The Case of the Limhamn Quarry*. Malmö: Local Environment.

Santasieri, C. 2014. *Planning for Transit-Supported Development: A Practitioner's Guide*. Report No. 0056. Washington, DC: Federal Transit Administration.

Schaal, Eric. 2017. "10 Cities Where People Buy the Most Electric Vehicles." Autos CheatSheet. Available from https://www.cheatsheet.com/automobiles/10-cities-where-people-buy-the-most-electric-vehicles.html/?a=viewall.

Schrock, Greg, Ellen M. Bassett, and Jamaal Green. 2015. "Pursuing Equity and Justice in a Changing Climate: Assessing Equity in Local Climate and Sustainability Plans in U.S. Cities." *Journal of Planning Education and Research* 35: 282-295.

Seattle Department of Transportation. 2014. *Seattle Bike Master Plan*. Seattle: author.

Sengupta, Somini. 2017. "Both Climate Leader and Oil Giant? A Norwegian Paradox." *New York Times*, June 17.

Shaw, Kate. 2008. "A Response to 'The Eviction of Critical Perspective from Gentrification Research.'" *International Journal of Urban and Regional Research*. 32: 192-194.

Shemkus, Sarah. 2019. "Mass. Climate Group Says Municipal Utilities Moving Too Slow on Clean Power." Energy News. https://energynews.us/2019/02/27/northeast/mass-climate-group-says-municipal-utilities-moving-too-slow-on-clean-power/.

Shoup, Donald. 2011. *The High Cost of Free Parking*. Routledge: Taylor & Francis.

Silver, Jon. 2014. "Clise, McKinstry Form Eco District to Build Energy System for Amazon." *Seattle Daily Journal of Commerce*, September 24.

Simon, Frederic. 2018. "Solar Industry Promises 'Jobs Bonanza' If EU Lifts China Duties." Euractiv.com. https://www.euractiv.com/section/energy/news/solar-industry-promises-jobs-bonanza-if-eu-lifts-china-duties/.

Sisolak, J. 2018. "It's Time to Make the ORCA Passport Word for All." *Seattle Transit Blog*, June 18. https://seattletransitblog.com/2018/06/15/time-make-orca-passport-program-work/.

Sivaram, Varun. 2015. "Why Concentration of the Solar Industry in China Will Hurt Technology Innovation." Greentech Media. Available from https://www.greentechmedia.com/articles/read/why-concentration-of-the-solar-industry-in-china-will-stunt-innovation.

Slavin, Matthew I. 2011. "The Rise of the Urban Sustainability Movement in America." In *Sustainability in America's Cities: Creating the Green Metropolis*, edited by Matthew I. Slavin, 1–19. New York: Springer.

Smedby, Nora, and Lena Neij. 2013. "Experiences in Urban Governance for Sustainability: The Constructive Dialogue in Swedish Municipalities." *Journal of Cleaner Production* 50: 148–58.

Smith, Rebecca. 2017. "Mayor Launches £1.4bn Neighbourhoods of the Future Scheme to Tackle London's Air Quality Crisis at a Local Level." *City A.M.*, June 20.

Sovacool, Benjamin. 2013. "Energy Policymaking in Denmark: Implications for Global Energy Security and Sustainability." *Energy Policy* 61: 829–39. doi: https://doi.org/10.1016/j.enpol.2013.06.106.

Sovacool, Benjamin. 2015. "Fuel Poverty, Affordability, and Energy Justice in England: Policy Insights from the Warm Front Program." *Energy* 93: 361–71. doi: https://doi.org/10.1016/j.energy.2015.09.016.

Sovacool, Benjamin, Matthew Burke, Lucy Baker, Kumar Kotikalapudi, and Holle Wlokas. 2017. "New Frontiers and Conceptual Frameworks for Energy Justice." *Energy Policy* 105: 677–91. doi: https://doi.org/10.1016/j.enpol.2017.03.005.

Sovacool, Benjamin, and Michael Dworkin. 2014. *Global Energy Justice: Problems, Principles, and Practices*. Cambridge: Cambridge University Press.

Speth, Gus. 2015. *Getting to the Next System: Guideposts on the Way to a New Political Economy*. Next System Project.

St. John, Jeff. 2016. "Southern California Utilities to Deploy 5,000 EV Chargers in First-of-Their-Kind Pilots." Greentech Media. Available from https://www.greentechmedia.com/articles/read/southern-california-utilities-to-deploy-5000-ev-chargers-in-first-of-a-kind#gs.vrm03h.

St. John, Jeff. 2017. "California Utilities Seek $1B to Build Out Electric Vehicle Infrastructure." Greentech Media. Available from https://www.greentechmedia.com/articles/read/california-utilities-seek-1b-to-build-out-electric-vehicle-infrastructure#gs.47cCRSg.

St. John, Jeff. 2018. "California Sets New Rules for Community Choices Aggregators." Greentech Media. Available https://www.greentechmedia.com/articles/read/california-rules-community-choice-aggregators#gs.f9lymy.

St. John, Paige. 2018. "Stalls, Stops and Breakdowns: Problems Plague Push for Electric Buses." *Los Angeles Times*, May 20.

Stanisteanu, Cristina. 2017. "Smart Thermal Grids—a Review." *Scientific Bulletin of Electrical Engineering Faculty* 17 (1): 1–7.

State of California. 2015. "California's Existing Buildings Energy Efficiency Action Plan." Energy.ca.gov.

State of Green. 2018. *District Energy: Energy Efficiency for Urban Areas*. Copenhagen: State of Green.

Steele, Wendy, Diana Maccallum, Jason Byrne, and Donna Houston. 2012. "Planning the Climate-Just City." *International Planning Studies* 17 (1): 67–83.

Steward, Darlene. 2017. *Critical Elements of Vehicle-to-Grid (V2G) Economics*. Golden, CO: National Renewable Energy Laboratory.

Stranden, Anne Lise. 2017. "EU Cites Norway for Air Poor Quality." ScienceNordic. Available from http://sciencenordic.com/eu-cites-norway-air-poor-quality.

Stockholms Stad. 2014. *Eco-Cycle Model 2.0 for Stockholm Royal Seaport City District*. Stockholm.

Stockholms Stad. 2016. *Stockholm Environmental Programme 2016–2019*. Stockholm.

Sweeney, Sean. 2012. *Resist, Reclaim, Restructure: Unions and the Struggle for Energy Democracy*. New York: Unions for Energy Democracy.

Tabuchi, H. 2018. "How the Koch Brothers Are Killing Public Transit Projects across the Country." *New York Times*, June 18.

Tennessean Editorial Board. 2018. "Nashville transit plan a bold step forward." *Tennessean*, April 20.

Texas Vox. "Archive for the 'Austin Energy' Category." Available from http://www.texasvox.org/category/utilities/austin-energy/.

Think Denmark. 2016. *District Energy: Energy Efficiency for Urban Areas*.

Thorpe, David. 2014. "The World's Most Successful Model for Sustainable Urban Development?" Smart Cities Dive.

Trabish, Herman. 2018. "Getting to 'Head-Spinning' Low Prices for U.S. Offshore Wind." Utility Dive, January 23.

Trade Unions for Energy Democracy. 2015. "Our History." Available from http://unionsforenergydemocracy.org/about/our-history/.

Transport Analysis. 2017. *Forecasts of the Swedish Vehicle Fleet*. Summary Report 2017:8. Stockholm.

Transport for London. 2016. *Plug-in Electric Vehicle Uptake and Infrastructure Impacts Study*. London.

Transport for London. N.d. "Ultra-low Emission Zone." Mayor of London. Available from https://tfl.gov.uk/modes/driving/ultra-low-emission-zone#on-this-page-5.

Tredinnick, Steve. 2013. "Why Is District Energy Not More Prevalent in the U.S.?" HPAC Engineering. Available from https://www.hpac.com/heating/why-district-energy-not-more-prevalent-us.

Tweed, Katherine. 2015. "The Failure of the UK's Green Deal Offers Lessons for US Efficiency Programs." Greentech Media. Available from https://www.greentechmedia.com/articles/read/the-failure-of-uk-green-deal-offers-us-lessons#gs.vrmljl.

2030 Districts. 2016. "2030 Districts." Available from http://www.2030districts.org/.

UK Government. 2017. "Heat Networks Delivery Unit." Available from https://www.gov.uk/guidance/heat-networks-delivery-unit.

United Nations Environment Program. 2015. *District Energy in Cities*.

United Nations Environment Program. 2018. *Emissions Gap Report 2018*. New York.

United Nations Environmental Program and ICLEI. 2015. *District Energy in Cities*. New York.

Union of Concerned Scientists. 2015. "Electric Vehicles and Georgia Fact Sheet."

Urban Land Institute. 2014. *King's Cross*. ULI Case Studies.

US Department of Energy. 2016. "Project Information." Available from https://www.smartgrid.gov/recovery_act/project_information.html?pff=r.

US Department of Energy. 2018. *U.S. Energy and Employment Report Card*. Washington, DC.

US Department of Housing and Urban Development. 2004. *Public Housing Energy Conservation Clearinghouse News*, March–April.

US Department of Transportation. 2017. *City Summaries, Stockholm, Sweden*. Available from https://international.fhwa.dot.gov/travelinfo/stockholm.cfm.

US Energy Information Administration. 2016. *Washington—State Energy Profile Overview*.

US Energy Information Administration. 2018. *What Is U.S. Electricity Generation by Energy*.

US Energy Information Administration. 2019. *Levelized Cost and Levelized Avoided Cost of New Generation Resources in the Annual Energy Outlook 2019*. Washington, DC.

US Environmental Protection Agency. 2017a. *Commercial and Residential Sector Emissions*. Available from https://www.epa.gov/ghgemissions/sources-greenhouse-gas-emissions#commercial-and-residential.

US Environmental Protection Agency. 2017b. *Electricity Sector Emissions*. Available from https://www.epa.gov/ghgemissions/sources-greenhouse-gas-emissions#electricity.

US Securities and Exchange Commission. 2010. Balqon Corporation Annual Report on Form 10K.

van Rooj, Rogier. 2017. "Dutch Grocery Webstore to Buy 2,000 Electric Delivery Vans in Coming Years." Clean Technica. Available from https://cleantechnica.com/2017/03/29/dutch-grocery-webstore-buy-2000-electric-delivery-vans-coming-years/.

Vertelman, Bart, and Doede Bardok. 2016. *Amsterdam's Demand-Driven Charging Infrastructure*. City of Amsterdam / Beakers Scholma.

Vock, Daniel C. 2018. "On Eve of Global Climate Summit, 19 U.S. Cities Launch Electric Car Effort." *Governing the States and Localities*, September 11.

Walker, Gordon, and Rosie Day. 2012. "Fuel Poverty as Injustice: Integrating Distribution, Recognition and Procedure in the Struggle for Affordable Warmth." *Energy Policy* 49: 69–75. doi: https://doi.org/10.1016/j.enpol.2012.01.044.

Walsh, Brian, Philippe Ciais, Ivan A. Janssens, Josep Peñuelas, Keywan Riahi, Felicjan Rydzak, Detlef P. van Vuuren, and Michael Obersteiner. 2017. "Pathways for Balancing CO_2 Emissions and Sinks." *Nature Communications* 8. doi: 10.1038/ncomms14856.

Walton, Heather, David Dajnak, Sean Beevers, Martin Williams, Paul Watkiss, and Alistair Hunt. 2015. *Understanding the Health Impacts of Air Pollution in London*. London: School of Biomedical Sciences, King's College London.

Weber, Ryan, and Mitchell Reardon. 2015. "Do Eco-districts Support the Regional Growth of Cleantech Firms? Notes from Stockholm." *Cities* 49: 113–20.

Wehrmann, Benjamin. 2018. "Germany Needs Plan to Unleash Solar Power Again—Researcher." Clean Energy Wire. Available from https://www.cleanenergywire.org/news/germany-needs-plan-unleash-solar-power-again-researcher.

Weinrub, Al, and Anthony Giancatarino. 2015. "Toward a Climate Justice Energy Platform: Democratizing Our Energy Future." Local Clean Energy.com.

Wettengel, Julian. 2018. "Citizens' participation in the Energiewende." Clean Energy Wire. https://www.cleanenergywire.org/factsheets/citizens-participation-energiewende.

Wettengel, Julian. 2019. "German Coal Power Generation Drops by One Fifth in First Quarter of 2019." Clean Energy Wire. https://www.cleanenergywire.org/news/german-coal-power-generation-drops-one-fifth-first-quarter-2019.

Wheeler, Stephen M., and Timothy Beatley, eds. 2009. *The Sustainable Urban Development Reader*. 2nd ed. London: Routledge.

Wheeler, Stephen M., and Timothy Beatley, eds. 2014. *The Sustainable Urban Development Reader*. 3rd ed. New York: Routledge.

White House, Office of the Press Secretary. 2015. "Fact Sheet: President Obama to Announce Historic Carbon Pollution Standards for Power Plants."

White House, Office of the Press Secretary. 2016. "Fact Sheet: Obama Administration Announces Federal and Private Sector Actions to Accelerate Electric Vehicle Adoption in the United States."

Willdan Financial Services and EnerNex. 2017. *Feasibility Study for a Community Choice Aggregate.* City of San Diego.

Wirasinghe, C., L. Kattan, M. M. Rahman, J. Hubbell, R. Thilakaratne, and S. Anowar. 2013. "Bus Rapid Transit—a Review." *International Journal of Urban Sciences* 17: 1–31.

Wiser, Ryan, and Mark Bolinger. 2017. *2016 Wind Technologies Market Report: Summary.* Washington, DC.

Wood Mackenzie. 2019. "China to become largest energy storage market in Asia Pacific by 2024." Available from https://www.woodmac.com/press-releases/china-to-become-largest-energy-storage-market-in-asia-pacific-by-2024/.

Woodford, Chris. 2018. "How Do Heat Exchangers Work?" Explain that Stuff.com.

World Future Council. 2016. "Energy Remunicipalisation: How Hamburg Is Buying Back Energy Grids." World Future Council. Available from https://www.worldfuturecouncil.org/energy-remunicipalisation-hamburg-buys-back-energy-grids/.

Worth, Pamela. 2016. "Electric Vehicles: Just How Green Are They?" Union of Concerned Scientists. Available from https://www.ucsusa.org/publications/catalyst/winter16-electric-vehicles-just-how-green-are-they#.WvJMT2VFXp4.

Yanarella, Ernest, and Richard Levine. 2011. "Don't Pick the Low-Hanging Fruit!" *Sustainability* 1 (4): 256–61.

Yang, Zhao. 2012. "Can BYD Build Its American Dream in Los Angeles?" 4EverRiders.org. Available from http://www.4evriders.org/2012/03/usa-can-byd-build-its-american-dream-in-los-angeles/.

Zahn, Peter. 2017. "Power of Choice—Cheaper, Cleaner Renewables a Win." *San Diego Tribune*, August 25. http://www.sandiegouniontribune.com/opinion/commentary/sd-utbg-energy-renewables-choice-20170825-story.html.

Zaleski, Sarah, Cody Taylor, Ken Seiden, Jay Luboff, Dan Chwastyk, Emily Merchant, Robert Russell, Sonrisa Cooper, Adam Szlachetka, and Maria Rode. 2015. *New York City Benchmarking and Transparency Policy Impact Evaluation Report.* US Department of Energy.

Zhang, Xingping, Jian Xie, Rao Rao, and Yanni Liang. 2014. "Policy Incentives for the Adoption of Electric Vehicles across Countries" *Sustainability* 6: 8056–78. doi: 10.3390/su6118056.

Zhou, Shan, and Douglas Noonan. 2019. "Justice Implications of Clean Energy Policies and Programs in the United States: A Theoretical and Empirical Exploration." *Sustainability* 11 (3). doi: https://doi.org/10.3390/su11030807.

INDEX